DISSENT FROM THE HOMELAND

EDITED BY STANLEY HAUERWAS

AND FRANK LENTRICCHIA

DISSENT FROM THE HOMELAND

essays after September 11

DUKE UNIVERSITY PRESS • DURHAM & LONDON • 2003

© 2003 Duke University Press

All rights reserved

Printed in the United States of America

on acid-free paper ⊗

Designed by C. H. Westmoreland

Typeset in Cycles and Scala Sans by

Tseng Information Systems, Inc.

Library of Congress Cataloging-in-

Publication Data appear on the last

printed page of this book.

The text of this book originally was

published in 2002 as volume 101,

number 2 of the *South Atlantic Quarterly*,

in slightly different form and with the

exception of the following: the first

introductory note, the essays by David

James Duncan and Srinivas Aravamudan,

the postscript by Stanley Hauerwas, the

afterword by Donald E. Pease, and

the index.

FOR TAMMI BROOKS,

WHO GAVE US THE IDEA

Contents

DISSENT FROM THE HOMELAND

Introductory

Notes from the Editors

FRANK LENTRICCHIA

The enemy of the moment always represented absolute evil,
and it followed that any past or future agreement with him was
impossible.—George Orwell, *1984*

Intolerance of political dissent in the United States at the present time
makes it necessary to say, before we exercise our right to work against
the grain, that we, also, abominate the slaughter of the innocent, even
as we find it unacceptably childish that Americans refuse to take any
responsibility for September 11; unacceptably childish because the
Americans in question are not (presumably) children.

Two weeks after the events of September 11, 2001, *The New Yorker* published a series of brief responses, including one by Susan Sontag, which
began this way:

> The disconnect between last Tuesday's monstrous dose of reality and the
> self-righteous drivel and outrageous deceptions being peddled by pub-
> lic figures and TV commentators is startling, depressing. The voices li-
> censed to follow the event seem to have joined together in a campaign
> to infantilize the public. Where is the acknowledgment that this was not
> a "cowardly" attack on "civilization" or "liberty" or "humanity" or "the
> free world" but an attack on the world's self-proclaimed superpower,
> undertaken as a consequence of specific American alliances and actions?

Sontag went on to suggest that it requires no "courage" to kill with missiles and bombs from high in the sky, beyond the reach of the pathetic
air defenses of the Taliban; that, in any case, "courage" is a morally neutral term, one that might reasonably be applied to the intrepid mass
murderers of September 11.

It did not matter that Sontag said what most Americans have long believed: that politicians and media commentators speak drivel and lies, because that is their natural mode; that politicians and media commentators routinely infantilize us; that the United States is the world's one superpower—a truth we hold to be self-evident, so why do we proclaim it? No matter—Sontag said the unsayable when she wrote that the attacks were the result of specific American alliances and actions. So what kind of person is Susan Sontag, really, if she can say, in one breath, that the attackers did a monstrous thing and that the American government has done, and does, monstrous things too? She's a clear-eyed adult who rejects the widely held belief in this country that we represent Good, that God is on our side.

In so many words, Sontag said that the United States had, in the pursuit of its happiness, given unspeakable pain. For this she could not be forgiven. Vilification swiftly followed. The stalwart New York intellectual was savaged, especially in New York, and not by a few intellectuals—in New York, where so many seem to believe that their city had become the most grievous victim in modern history.

Now, more than two years later, Bush has cleverly turned the American public's attention to that supposed menace to American life, Saddam Hussein, when it is clearer than ever that a war on terrorism cannot be won and that whenever it is the will of Al Qaeda to do terror its will likely will be done. Unlike Al Qaeda, Iraq can be invaded and overwhelmed, and Saddam decapitated. But where is the evidence that Saddam is connected with bin Laden and that he—like Kim Jong Il of North Korea—had the means to deliver and detonate weapons of mass destruction in the United States? Bush's claims to have had evidence are empty because he has no evidence. The ability to deliver weapons of mass destruction anywhere on this globe at any time our so-called interests are threatened belongs to the United States, Great Britain, and Israel, and the United States and Israel have announced policies of preemption. If you are not an Israeli, a Brit, or an American—that is to say, if you are among the majority billions of this planet—you may well think that the United States, Great Britain, and Israel represent the axis of evil. Thanks to the lies of Bush and his lap dogs in the media, who were hot for war, the great majority of Americans now believe the double absurdity that Iraq was involved with September 11 and that Iraq represented a threat to the U.S. mainland.

A German political official was forced to resign for saying that Bush's strategies were in the mode of Hitler's; that the manufacturing of the Iraq menace and its consequent hysteria are intended to sustain the Republican regime and to divert American attention from a dying economy and the criminal corporate CEOs, those charged and those yet to be found out, so long in bed with Bush and Cheney, who have already done, and will continue to do, far more damage to American life than Al Qaeda will ever do.

In the firebombing of sixteen square miles of central Tokyo; in the firebombing of Dresden; in the nuclear obliteration of Hiroshima and Nagasaki, the United States of America attacked targets of no military significance and slaughtered several hundreds of thousands of civilians. Three thousand on September 11 is an obscenity, but one of a much lower order. In view of these criminal facts of American history, the largest obscenity of all is the howl of American self-pity in the wake of September 11.

The range of work collected in this volume includes reflection on the political, social, aesthetic, theological, and ethical aspects of culture. This is a book about patriotism; justice; revenge; our relationships with Israel, Muslims, and Islam; American history and symbology; art and terror; and pacifism. All of the essays are united in the belief that America is threatened by the most powerful enemy in its history, the administration of George W. Bush.

As troubling as the failure of American secular intellectuals (though not those collected here) to intervene and question the war on terrorism is, this war has also seen the capitulation of church and synagogue to the resurgence of American patriotism and nationalism. Some—for example, the editors of *First Things*—have gone so far as to suggest that the resurgence of religious faith in the aftermath of September 11, 2001, may be the start of a religious awakening. God and country are back. Again, however, the Bush administration wants it both ways. They want America to be "religious," but they want to make clear that this is not a "religious war." With extraordinary speed George Bush has become a scholar of Islam, assuring us that Islam is a tradition of peace. We find it curious, given Christianity's history, he does not find it necessary to assure us that Christianity is a tradition of peace.

We hope, therefore, the readers of this book may find the nonapologetic theological essays refreshing or, at least, different. It is no secret that many secular intellectuals have no time for serious theological work. Many assume that if everyone is well enough educated and has more money than they need, no one will need God. Accordingly the modern university has largely failed to help students appreciate those determinative religious convictions that shape the lives of the majority of the world's peoples. It will be clear that the theologians and religious scholars whose essays appear in this collection have no use for apologetic strategies designed to reassure those on the right or the left that when all is said and done, religious faith is not all that dangerous.

Religious faith is dangerous. Jew, Muslim, and Christian know that there is much worth dying for. Faiths constituted by convictions worth dying for can also become faiths worth killing for. So questions of life and death are at the heart of any religious faith worth having. But it is also the case that only a religious faith for which it is worth dying will have the resources to challenge idolatries justified by the presumption that America is blessed by God in a manner unlike other nations. "God Bless America" is not a hymn any Christian can or should sing. At least it is not a hymn any Christian can or should sing unless it is understood that God's blessing incurs God's judgment.

This is but a reminder that the babble unleashed by September 11, 2001, cannot be challenged on its own terms. Rather we must find the linguistic resources in communities that have found ways prior to September 11, 2001, not to be seduced by the false speech that is always our temptation. We quite literally, therefore, offer these essays as an "offering," and hope that they may help us begin to speak truthfully against the lies that can so easily constitute our lives.

DANIEL BERRIGAN

After

When the towers fell
a conundrum eased;
Shall these inherit the earth
from eternity,
all debts amortised?

Gravity was ungracious,
a lateral blow
abetted, made an end.

They fell like Lucifer,
star of morning, our star
attraction, our access.

Nonetheless, a conundrum;
Did God approve, did they prosper us?

The towers fell, money
amortised in pockets of the fallen, once for all.

Why did they fall, what law
violated? Did Mammon
mortise the money
that raised them high, Mammon
anchoring the towers in cloud,

highbrow neighbors
of gated heaven and God?
"Fallen, fallen is Babylon the great . . .
they see the smoke
arise as she burns . . ."

We made pilgrimage there.
Confusion of tongues.
Some cried vengeance.
Others paced slow, pondering
—this or that of humans
drawn forth, dismembered—

a last day; Babylon
remembered.

ROBERT N. BELLAH

Seventy-Five Years

September 11, 2001. I am not sure that even now, more than four months later, I know how to think about it. I have heard young people say, "September 11 is the worst thing that ever happened to America." I am tempted to reply, "In your lifetime." I will be seventy-five years old this year and I have lived through quite a few dark days in my life. Perhaps it will not be entirely inappropriate for me to try to put September 11 in perspective by reflecting on some of those earlier moments.

I was born in 1927. Although I was too young to understand it, the stock market crash of 1929 had serious repercussions for my family. As I was becoming aware of the world in the middle 1930s, Hitler, Mussolini, and Stalin were all in power, and the Japanese were at war with China. I remember being the one who brought in the paper every morning, and in those days before television, it was the newspaper that we depended on for news (though I do remember listening to speeches by Hitler and Mussolini on the radio, and the reassuring words of FDR). How many mornings I saw huge black headlines reporting the latest disaster! In March 1938 came the *Anschluss*, Hitler's annexation of Austria. In September of that year there was the infamous Munich pact, through which the British and French handed over the Sudeten border area of Czechoslovakia to Hitler; followed early in 1939 by Hitler's occupation of the whole country. And on September 1, 1939, Hitler, now acting on the basis of a secret pact with the Soviet Union, invaded Poland. The period of appeasement was over; the Second World War had begun. One might think these were events in Europe, not events affecting the United States, but those of us who lived through those events, even a twelve- or thirteen-year-old child as I was at the time, knew that these terrible events were happening to the United States because they were happening to the whole world.

Auden's famous poem "September 1, 1939" was written, as its opening line tells us, in New York, and it expresses not only what an Englishman, but what many Americans were feeling at that moment:

> I sit in one of the dives
> On Fifty-Second Street
> Uncertain and afraid
> As the clever hopes expire
> Of a low dishonest decade:
> Waves of anger and fear
> Circulate over the bright
> And darkened lands of the earth,
> Obsessing our private lives;
> The unmentionable odour of death
> Offends the September night.[1]

Although the Polish campaign was over in weeks, many more dark headlines were to come. In April 1940 Hitler invaded Denmark and Norway with little opposition. In June he overran the Netherlands, Belgium, and France with lightning speed, although most of the British army was successfully evacuated from Dunkirk. The ensuing air war over Britain was inconclusive, and Hitler turned his attention from a possible invasion of Britain to what he expected to be a lightning campaign against the Soviet Union. In early 1941 the total failure of the invasion of Greece by Italy, Germany's ally, diverted his attention to the Balkans, where again he made short work of Yugoslavia and Greece. He was now master of almost the whole of Europe right up to the Soviet frontier, but he wanted more. On June 22 the Russian campaign began, initially with enormous success, driving to the gates of Moscow and Leningrad by the end of the year.

However breathlessly we watched the fall of Europe, on December 7, 1941, something terrible at last did happen to the United States. I have recently had to remind my younger friends that the horrifying attacks on New York and Washington on September 11, 2001, pale in comparison to the defeat suffered by the United States on December 7, 1941. Pearl Harbor was a military disaster of the first order. The U.S. Pacific Fleet was effectively destroyed, even if a few carriers absent from Pearl Harbor were spared. The United States being militarily incapacitated, in the next six months the Japanese took the Philippines, Indochina, Burma, and the Netherlands East Indies. Perhaps the most shocking news was the sudden fall of the supposedly impregnable fortress of Singapore. In New Guinea the Japanese had come to within a few miles of the northern shore of Australia. That is what Pearl Harbor meant: the Japanese conquest of almost all of East and Southeast Asia. It would be hard to think of a greater defeat in American history.

And yet we won the war. After an enormous effort by the United States and its allies, including importantly the Soviet Union, the Germans surrendered in May and the Japanese in August 1945. World War II is what we all believed was the "good war," the war against an evil so enormous that there could be no question of the justice of our cause. And the end of European fascism and Japanese militarism, among the worst regimes modernity has produced, was certainly a good.

But is it so entirely clear that we won the war? Wasn't there a sense in which we were defeated in that war, and I don't mean only by the early disasters? I would say that we were defeated to the extent that we became like the enemy we opposed. Early in the war we condemned the Germans for their indiscriminate bombing of civilians. By 1943 or 1944 we were engaging in the most terrible bombing of civilians in history. Hundreds of thousands died in the firebombing of Dresden, Tokyo, and other German and Japanese cities. And then on August 6 and 9 the United States unleashed the only two atom bombs ever to be used, unleashed them on the large, crowded cities of Hiroshima and Nagasaki. As an eighteen-year-old at the time, looking forward to immediate induction into the army, I, like most other Americans, had no doubt that using the atom bomb was the right thing to do. Only considerably later did I come to see it as second only to the Holocaust among the crimes of the twentieth century.

In a roundtable discussion on terrorism in a recent issue of *Harvard Magazine*, David Little points out that the only place in international humanitarian law where the word *terror* appears is in two 1977 protocols that supplement the Geneva Conventions protecting victims of armed conflict: "The civilian population as such, as well as individual civilians, shall not be the object of attack. Acts or threats of violence, the primary purpose of which is to spread terror among the civilian population, are prohibited." Jessica Stern then responded: "But what about the carpet bombing specifically with the aim of terrorizing the civilian population? Does that fit into our definition? What about dropping nuclear weapons on Hiroshima and Nagasaki? I think that has to fit into our definition, because it's very clear from the documents the purpose was to terrorize the civilian population."[2] It would seem that the United States, now engaged in a "war on terrorism," not so long ago perpetrated the greatest acts of terrorism in human history.

While I was an undergraduate at Harvard the relief at the end of World War II quickly evaporated and the cold war, pitting the "free world," led by the United States, against atheistic Communism, led by the Soviet Union (later referred to as the "evil empire"), began. The cold war lasted more than forty years, and again we won it. Who could not rejoice at the "velvet revolutions" of 1989, the fall of the Berlin Wall, and the end of Communist domination in the former Soviet Union itself? That these great transformations occurred with a minimum of violence is almost as wonderful as the fall of tyranny itself.

So we won the cold war, but again, did we? Did we not, in some ways even more clearly than in World War II, become like our adversaries? In *The Good Society* my coauthors and I pointed out the enormous centralization of state power in the United States that began with the Truman administration. Not only were the armed services united in the Department of Defense, not only was the Central Intelligence Agency (CIA) created, but

> the National Security Council, headed by a national security advisor, created only a little later, extended the direct initiative of the President in foreign policy over the heads even of the secretaries of state and defense. A report written in 1950 by a committee headed by Paul Nitze for the National Security Council (NSC 68) became a kind of blueprint justifying the emergence of a national defense state within a state. Nitze's logic was that America had to use Soviet means to counteract the Soviet threat. The ironic consequence was to create a powerful apparatus of centralized authority outside the normal constitutional structures of democratic accountability that mirrored the Stalinist state itself.[3]

In the name of fighting Communism, the United States systematically undermined freely elected governments and supported ruthless anti-Communist tyrannies all over the world for the entire period of the cold war.

One of the earliest and most shocking examples of American disregard of democratically elected governments occurred in Guatemala,
where Jacobo Arbenz Guzmán, after being elected president in 1951,
made agrarian reform his primary concern. In 1954 he was overthrown
by invading forces organized by the CIA. In the Democratic Republic
of the Congo (formerly the Belgian Congo) in 1960 Patrice Lumumba
was elected premier in the first parliament after independence, but he
was driven from office and killed after Joseph Mobutu, with American support, instituted a military government. Mobutu's decades-long
American-supported regime systematically looted one of the largest
and richest countries in Africa, leaving it at his death without a func-
tioning government or society. In 1965, after an abortive Communist
coup involving army leaders, President Sukarno was overthrown by
General Suharto with American help. In the ensuing bloodbath hundreds of thousands, perhaps as many as a million, Indonesian leftists
were massacred. There is some indication that the CIA supplied the
names of many who were killed. In 1970 Salvador Allende was elected
president of Chile. In 1973 he was overthrown and killed in a military
coup, with American help, by General Augusto Pinochet, who ruled
Chile as a dictator until 1989, presiding over a regime that "disappeared" and murdered thousands of leftists. Mobutu, Suharto, Pinochet, and many other dictators were regularly recognized by the United
States as "leaders of the free world."[4]

This string of cold war "victories" was broken at one decisive point:
Vietnam, where the United States entered a war it could not win. The
Korean and Vietnam Wars were the two hot wars that punctuated the
decades of the cold war. We did not win the Korean War, but we did
reestablish the status quo ante.[5] Vietnam was very much part of cold
war strategy, justified by the famous domino theory, namely that if
South Vietnam fell, all of Southeast Asia would follow. It is interesting
to note that the Vietnam War was a war against terrorists, namely the
Viet Cong, insurgent guerrillas fighting the intensely unpopular government of South Vietnam, charmingly referred to by Lyndon Johnson as "the free people of South Vietnam and their government." This
"free" government, under the leadership of Prime Minister Ngo Dinh
Diem, refused to hold the elections mandated by the Geneva agreement of 1954, which had divided the country into north and south,
elections that were to be supervised by an International Control Com-

mittee. Diem was afraid he would lose. It was to this government, not because in any intelligible sense it was free but because it was anticommunist, that we committed ourselves.

Our involvement in the war, which began gradually in 1964–65 and ended ignominiously in 1975, had by 1969 required 540,000 American troops on the ground. Over the course of the war we sustained more than 50,000 dead, and the Vietnamese well over a million. In addition to indiscriminate bombing and the killing of civilians in ground warfare, we engaged in widespread chemical warfare (Agent Orange), the effects of which are still being suffered by some Vietnam veterans in this country, as well as many in Vietnam. Devastating though the war was for the Vietnamese, the consequences for American society, from which, wishful thinking to the contrary, we are still suffering, were extraordinary, marking in many ways an important social and political turning point. I will come back to these domestic consequences.

There is no question that the Soviet Union and the Communist regimes it sponsored were oppressive and on a large scale murderous, often exterminating those who had earlier been their leaders, and it is a mercy that they are gone. The crimes committed by the Chinese Communists, however, were at least as bad, and today we consider them our friends, although they continue to be one of the most oppressive regimes in the world.[6] Since the United States during the cold war helped to militarize much of the world, supported regimes drenched in blood, and severely damaged our own society, it is certainly questionable that we "won."

Now, since September 11, 2001, we have, for the third time in my life, embarked on a war, this time the war against terrorism.[7] On September 11 the United States suffered the worst attack on our own country since December 7, 1941. Like Pearl Harbor, the events of September 11 were a terrible defeat. In spite of our enormous military budget, in spite of the lavishly funded efforts of the FBI, the CIA, and other intelligence agencies, nineteen men, utterly ruthless with respect to the lives of others and willing to sacrifice their own lives, carried out a devastating and totally unexpected attack, whose consequences we will be living with for many years. In the patriotic euphoria that has swept the country since September 11, the extent of the defeat we suffered has been downplayed to the point of denial. Polls indicate that trust in government is up since September 11, after having been in decline for decades, though why confidence in a government that failed to protect us from such an attack in spite of our enormous expenditures on "defense" should be trusted is far from clear.

It is not only the loss of life and the physical destruction in New York and Washington, but also the effects on our economy and on our daily lives that have to be considered in thinking about the gravity of this defeat. An already weak economy has plunged into recession, a recession that lingers in spite of optimistic expectations of early recovery. Everything having to do with air travel has suffered severe economic setbacks, and there are ripple effects throughout the economy. A taken-for-granted sense of security in our own country has been lost, perhaps forever. "Security" is now an issue not only at airports but throughout our society. It is indicative of our new situation that the president created the Office of Homeland Security, bringing the term *homeland* into prominence in a way unusual in our history. *Homeland* usually referred to the "old country" from which we or our ancestors came. America was different; it was the chosen land, the land to which we came. Now we are just one more "homeland" among the nations. That a group of nineteen men, with only a few hundred thousand dollars at their disposal, should so gravely wound the most powerful nation on earth is a fact with which we have not yet come to terms. That all our wealth and all our power did not protect us and perhaps can never protect us from unforeseen catastrophe will take a long time to get used to.

The military campaign in Afghanistan has gone more quickly than most people expected, and that has diverted us from thinking about the full magnitude of what has happened to us. Although Afghan civilians killed by our bombing probably outnumber those killed on September 11 in the United States, the casualties have, as wars go, been light, and extremely light for American troops. As of this writing neither Osama bin Laden nor Mullah Omar have been found, and finding them is a major war aim, but otherwise we could declare that we have "won" and consider the war over. The Taliban regime was truly awful, even in a world of terrible regimes. Its ruthlessness toward its opponents, its brutal treatment of women, its horrifying desecration of religious monuments of other faiths (the figures of the Buddha carved into the cliffs near Bamiyan being only the most notable example) make it a regime whose end we can truly be glad to see. The rhetoric of the war on terrorism, however, suggests that it is intended to be much more than a brief campaign in Afghanistan leading to the replacement of the Taliban government. There are terrorists, we are told, in some sixty countries in the world, and it is our intention to "hunt them down" and eliminate them wherever they are. After much speculation that Iraq appeared to be next on the list after Afghanistan, George W. Bush, in his first State of the Union Address on January 29, 2002, specified an "axis of evil" consisting of Iraq, Iran, and North Korea.

The very idea of a "war on terrorism" has been questioned, as it does not seem to be like what we ordinarily consider a war to be: someone wins and someone loses, or there is an agreed end of hostilities. Like a war on drugs or a war on poverty, a war on terrorism would seem to have no end. It is hard to think of instances in which such wars have been won. When we consider the case of the ETA in Spain, the Tamil Tigers in Sri Lanka, or the Islamic militants in Kashmir or Palestine, the prospects of "victory" are not encouraging. Even after decades of armed struggle the British never "defeated" the IRA: it was only when peace talks brought the political representatives of the IRA into the government of Northern Ireland that a still somewhat uncertain peace was established. That example might suggest that terrorism can be "defeated" only by negotiation, not by retaliation.

It is far too early to say whether the war on terrorism will have anything like the scale or length of World War II or the cold war, but our experience with those wars may lead to more than a little caution about this one. Even at the beginning of it we have at moments sounded like our enemy. President George W. Bush at the National Day of Prayer and Remembrance service held on September 14 at what is called the National Cathedral (actually the Episcopal Cathedral of Saint Peter and Saint Paul) promised to "rid the world of evil." A reporter for the San Jose *Mercury News* called me for comments on that talk and I suggested how unlikely it is that we can "rid the world of evil." She said, "I can't even rid my own neighborhood of evil," and I replied, "I can't even rid my own heart of evil."

Early on President Bush began to refer to bin Laden as "the evil one," but, as Richard J. Mouw, the president of Fuller Theological Seminary in Pasadena, California, the largest seminary in North America for the mainstream evangelical movement, pointed out, "The problem with 'the evil one' is that in Christian thought, the only one who is totally, hopelessly evil is Satan. We don't really believe that anybody is beyond redemption until their dying breath, if they reject Christ." Calling bin Laden "the evil one" supernaturalizes him, Mouw said. He added that saying bin Laden was wanted dead or alive, as the president had done, trivializes human life. "That's not an example of moral leadership, or spiritual leadership," Mouw said.[8] Bush's language strangely mirrors that of Osama bin Laden, who also believes that he is at war with "evil." It suggests that in a prolonged war on terrorism we will in many ways resemble our opponents. The fact that we are bolstering several tyrannical regimes in formerly Soviet Central Asia as part of our campaign against terrorism is a pattern all too familiar from the cold war.

At a press conference since September 11, Bush made another comment that is revealing not only of the state of his own but also of the national psyche. When a reporter asked him, "Why do they hate us?" he replied that he really couldn't understand it, "because we're so good." Apparently Bush has not studied much American history. As Cicero reminds us, "To be ignorant of what occurred before you were born is to remain always a child,"[9] although some of what Bush is ignorant has occurred during his lifetime. In concentrating on my own seventy-five years, then, I should not overlook what has occurred before I was born. America has not been "good" for a long time before 1927. In *The Broken Covenant*, I pointed to the two "primal crimes" at the beginning of American history: the genocide of the American Indians and the enslavement of Africans.[10] I also spent a few pages on the Spanish-American War of 1898 when, for the first time, we extended our imperial conquests beyond continental North America. I did not, however, discuss sufficiently the war we undertook against Philippine independence from 1899 to 1902, during which we committed atrocities that prefigured our behavior in Vietnam.

Although American history is a history of violence, it is not, in that respect, different from the history of most nations. And it is far from the whole story of America. When a student said to me at some point in the late 1960s, "This is the worst society in human history," I told him to study a little more history. This is not the place to rehearse the achievements of American society. The most notable one is the original commitment to create a society based on the belief "that all men are created equal," and the gradual process that has extended that original ideal to include those who were originally, wholly or in part, left out, especially racial and ethnic minorities, and women.

Nevertheless, even for those included, it has turned out to be a problematic society. In *The Broken Covenant* I put it in strong terms by suggesting that our material success is our punishment, in terms of what that success has done to the natural environment, our social fabric, and our personal lives.[11] Let me reflect a bit on how life in America has changed during my lifetime. During the 1930s, when I was growing up, most Americans were just getting by during a long depression. We did not think of ourselves as a great power, though we must have known we were potentially one. The great powers who made the headlines were in Europe and Asia and many Americans, remembering the futility of World War I, hoped that we could somehow stay out of the terrible conflicts taking place abroad.

World War II changed all that. By its end we knew we were a great power, one of only two great powers left in the world after the defeat of the Axis. But in our hearts most of us were still provincials, uneasy with the role that the National Security Council was creating for us. We wanted very much to believe in our own goodness and innocence, to believe that the "free world" we were leading really was free, and that all the evil was on the other side. That is the world of the 1950s when many Americans were for the first time leaving poverty and attaining a modicum of prosperity, and to which we have looked back nostalgically ever since. In the early 1960s our goodness seemed to be affirmed by the success of the civil rights movement led by Martin Luther King Jr. When the civil rights legislation finally passed early in the presidency of Lyndon Johnson I am sure I was not alone in feeling prouder to be an American than I had ever been in my adult life, or would be again. But on the very cusp of that great change—and however incomplete it turned out to be, it was a very great change—came Vietnam.

It was Vietnam that made many Americans face the dark side of our history, which had of course been there all along, little though we liked to acknowledge it. The fact that it was a failed war, and that the great sacrifices it entailed were unredeemed by any higher purpose, was a blow to our society from which we have not, as I have said in this essay, recovered. I don't think the failed war was itself the cause of the great changes in American society that have been documented by Robert Putnam—the decline of civic and social, public and private, engagement in every sphere, which began in the period 1960–1970 and has continued since[12]—but it was the catalyst.

The revival of laissez faire capitalism in the 1970s in place of the modest welfare state we had built after World War II was another indication of the change. An older elite with some sense of public responsibility seemed to shrink from the society we were becoming and its place was taken by leaders who believed they owed nothing to anyone but themselves. I don't say that all our older virtues were lost, nor that there were not also significant advances in the years since 1970, such as the greater inclusiveness I have mentioned. For me the public acceptance of homeless people on the streets as natural rather than as a disgrace that had to be addressed, which began around 1980, is an indication of the change I am describing.

In the very midst of this transformation came the unexpected end of the cold war, leaving us not one of two great powers, but the only great power, the one superpower, not only militarily, but economically and culturally. Without ever quite intending it, we found ourselves the center of a world empire of an entirely new kind, or if not entirely new, new since the fall of the Roman Empire.[13] Unlike the European and Japanese empires of the late nineteenth and early twentieth centuries, we were not a great power with far-flung possessions, locked in contest with similar empires. We were, virtually without territorial possessions, at the center of the only empire there is. What we took as normal, we expected everyone else to take as normal—politically, economically, and culturally. And who could stand up to us? Who had the power, and I don't mean just the military power, but the social power, to tell us no?

It is into this world that September 11, 2001, came. Deeply repugnant though the attack was, should it have so surprised us? Do we really have to ask, Why do they hate us? At this late date in our history to relapse into the dream of innocence and imagine that evil is the sole possession of our enemies invites disaster.[14] Covering ourselves in American flags and vowing to "smoke out" bin Laden and "get him, dead or alive," or engaging in a far-flung and open-ended war against terrorism, addresses none of the realities in the midst of which we live.

If we are really a new kind of empire, foreshadowed only by the Rome of two millennia ago, we can imagine several possibilities. A new leadership, following the examples of Trajan, Hadrian, and Marcus Aurelius, could lead us on a "civilizing mission," for which we might gain some gratitude along with inevitable resentment. Or, more likely, we

will not last very long, but will fall from the sheer weight of the enemies—on the periphery and within—we have created. The question for
those of good will, then, is whether reform is still possible, or whether
it would be better to try to build an alternative city, within the very
pores of empire. Stanley Hauerwas has argued eloquently for the latter
course. As I approach my seventy-fifth birthday I grow ever closer to
his views.[15]

NOTES

1   The first stanza of "September 1, 1939," in W. H. Auden, *The English Auden:
    Poems, Essays, and Dramatic Writings 1927-1939*, ed. Edward Mendelson
    (New York: Random House, 1977), 245.
2   David Little and Jessica Stern in "Understanding Terrorism: A *Harvard
    Magazine* Roundtable," *Harvard Magazine* (January–February 2002): 39.
3   Robert N. Bellah, Richard Madsen, William M. Sullivan, Ann Swidler, and
    Steven M. Tipton, *The Good Society* (New York: Knopf, 1991), 77-78. A fuller
    description of NSC 68 can be found on pages 223-29.
4   Space prevents anything like a complete list of the tyrannical regimes in
    Latin America, Africa, and Asia that we supported during the cold war.
    It might be remembered that even in Europe we supported Francisco
    Franco's bloody dictatorship in Spain. At the end of World War II our re-
    lations with Franco were chilly, as he had been a de facto ally of Hitler,
    but, with the beginning of the cold war, Franco became one of our good
    friends. It is also impossible to list all the countries in which we inter-
    vened, often with devastating results, but El Salvador, Nicaragua, Panama,
    Grenada, Angola, and Cambodia might be a start.
5   One might add the Gulf War to the list of "hot wars," although it occurred
    after the cold war was over and did not approach the scale of Korea or
    Vietnam. It, like Korea, ended not so much with victory, which would
    have meant the end of the tyrant Saddam Hussein, but with a return to
    the status quo ante.
6   It is striking that Castro's Cuba remains a pariah state to us, although it
    was, though indeed repressive, never murderous on the scale of the Chi-
    nese Communists.
7   Although the war on terrorism does represent, I believe, a distinctly new
    phase, we should not forget that it is very much a consequence of the final
    stage of the cold war. Al Qaeda is a product of the Afghan war against
    the Soviet Union, during which we subsidized and armed the most ex-
    treme supporters of jihad, including Osama bin Laden. In our hatred of
    the Soviet Union we ignored any restraints of just-war theory, but sup-

ported groups that devastated the Afghan people. Now they have turned the jihad that we helped to instigate on us.

8 The quotations from Richard Mouw were reported in an article by Elisabeth Bumiller, "Recent Bushisms Call for a Primer," *New York Times*, January 7, 2002.

9 Cicero, *Orator*, xxxiv: 120. Cicero's next sentence is also of interest: "For what is the worth of human life, unless it is woven into the life of our ancestors by the records of history?" Americans don't like to think about ancestors since we tend to believe we have created ourselves. Arvind Rajagopal, who teaches at New York University, in commenting on the quote from Cicero, refers to the "child-like attitude, the seemingly willful character of the innocence about U.S. history. In my own attempts to educate my class about Middle East history," he writes, "I've been amazed at how steadfastly they ignore any attempts to disturb their ignorance—I wonder if they have come to see it as a kind of civic duty, a shucking off of the past necessary to be a good American" (personal communication, e-mail, March 2002).

10 Robert N. Bellah, *The Broken Covenant: American Civil Religion in Time of Trial* (Chicago: University of Chicago Press, 1995 [1975]), 36–37.

11 Bellah, *Broken Covenant*, 143.

12 Robert Putnam, *Bowling Alone: The Collapse and Revival of American Community* (New York: Simon and Schuster, 2000).

13 Michael Hardt and Antonio Negri, *Empire* (Cambridge: Harvard University Press, 2000). I don't find the warmed-over Marxism in this book very helpful (calling the "masses" the "multitude" doesn't signal a theoretical breakthrough). However, the way they argue for the similarity of our empire to ancient Rome rather than to recent European empires is most suggestive.

14 Richard T. Hughes, in his *Myths America Lives By* (Champlain: University of Illinois Press, 2002), offers a powerful analysis of America's myth of innocence, as well as several other American myths. Reading his manuscript influenced this essay.

15 A somewhat different but complementary analysis of American society, one that addresses Hauerwas's views more directly, can be found in my epilogue to *Meaning and Modernity: Religion, Polity, and Self*, ed. Richard Madsen, William M. Sullivan, Ann Swidler, and Steven M. Tipton (Berkeley: University of California Press, 2002).

ROWAN WILLIAMS

End of War

So much of this seems to oblige us to think about language.[1] The day after, there was a phone call from Wales, from one of the news programmes, and I faced a familiar dilemma. The caller started speaking to me in Welsh, which I understand without difficulty, but don't always find it easy to use in an unscripted and possibly rather complex discussion. I had to decide: if I answered in Welsh, the conversation would go on in Welsh, and I had some misgivings about coping with it.

I am spoken to; I have some choices about how to answer. It seemed a telling metaphor at that particular moment. Violence is a communication, after all, of hatred, fear, or contempt, and I have a choice about the language I am going to use to respond. If I decide to answer in the same terms, that is how the conversation will continue. How many times have you heard someone say, "It's the only language they understand" to defend a violent reaction to violent acts? And perhaps we should at least ask, before we reply, the kind of question we might ask if we're addressed in a language we're not quite sure about: can I continue this conversation, have I the will and resource for it?

At the same time, the question is a little unreal in some circumstances. The fantastic surge of violent energy needed to plan and carry through a colossal suicide attack is, fortunately, beyond the imagination of most of us. We can partly cope with thinking about the exchanges of conventional war, because we assume a measure of calculation on each side that is fairly similar. Increasingly (and this is something else we shall have to come back to) this is not what large-scale violence is like in our age. We face agents who don't seem to calculate gains and losses or risks as we do. It is not like the deceptively comfortable cold war notion of a balance of terror.

A Palestinian woman brought up in New York, Suheir Hammad, wrote, one week after the 11th:

> I do not know how bad a life has to break in order to kill.
> I have never been so hungry that I willed hunger.
> I have never been so angry as to want to control a gun over a pen.
> Not really. Even as a woman, as a Palestinian, as a broken human being.
> Never this broken.

And if not even as a woman, as a Palestinian, what about the rest of us? What do we know?

The truth is that if we respond violently our violence is going to be a rather different sort of thing. It is unlikely to have behind it the passion of someone who has nothing to lose, the terrible self-abandonment of the suicidal killer which is like a grotesque parody of the self-abandonment of love. It is not that we are "naturally" less violent or more compassionate. The record of European or American military engagement should dispel that illusion. But we are not acting out of helplessness, out of the moral and imaginative destitution that can only feel it is *acting* at all when it is inflicting pain and destruction.

The response of at least some people in the face of deep injury, once feeling has returned, is a passionate striking out; there is something recognisable about the language of Psalm 137—"let *their* children die horribly, let *them* know what humiliation and exile are like." It is an honest moment; but for those of us who are not totally helpless in terms of internal or external resources it is only a moment. We feel very uneasy when it seems as though there is a sustained effort to keep that level of murderous or revengeful outrage alive. The point at which we need to show more footage of collapsing towers or people jumping to their death, when we raise the temperature by injunctions never to forget—that is when something rather ambiguous enters in. We are trying to manipulate and direct the chaotic emotions of victims. There may be something like a dreadful innocence about the first surge of anger; there is no innocence about the deployment of images to try and revive it.

In a way, then, we're never going to be replying in quite the same language. We, with our military and financial resources, are never going to be exactly where the suicide bomber is. The car sticker may say "Nuke Afghanistan," but we (collectively) are generally aware that this is more than a little unreal. We (collectively) have space to calculate gains and losses. There is some space between our feelings and our choices.

A pause to clarify one or two things. In the aftermath of September 11, it was almost a cliché in some quarters to say that terrorism was bred by poverty and political helplessness, and there were two kinds of hostile response to this. There were those (usually on the right) who said that this was a false and sentimental account of the motivation of the killers: it was "blaming the victim," indulging in facile anti-American feeling; it ignored the fact that the "typical" al-Qaida activist seemed to be from a prosperous background, like Osama bin Laden himself, that issues about American presence in Saudi Arabia or Israeli policy towards the Palestinians only surfaced after the atrocities as a sort of *post factum* rationalisation. No excuses: this is simply political evil, warped extremists seeking to maximise hurt against the USA. Then there were those on the left who began to talk about "apocalyptic nihilism." The atrocity is neither a despairing last resort nor a piece of horrible malignity, but a pulling down of the pillars over everyone's head, as if to provoke God himself into action, or, as in nineteenth-century Russian anarchism, to provoke the forces of history into change.

There is something here of fair comment, because there has been coarse and facile anti-Americanism around, and there is an uncanny resonance with that kind of anarchism. But bombast about evil individuals doesn't help in understanding anything. Even vile and murderous actions tend to come from somewhere, and if they are extreme in character we are not wrong to look for extreme situations. It does not mean that those who do them had no choice, are not answerable, far from it. But there is sentimentality too in ascribing what we don't understand to "evil"; it lets us off the hook, it allows us to avoid the question of what, if anything, we can *recognise* in the destructive act of another. If we react without that self-questioning, we change nothing. It is not true to say, "We are all guilty"; but perhaps it is true to say, "We are all able to understand *something* as we look into ourselves."

The same with "apocalyptic nihilism." Nihilism breeds where things do not make sense; why and how they don't is again something we can ask about, something where we can look for recognisable experience.

The temptation is always to refuse the labour of this search; but if we refuse to undertake it, we say that there could never be any language at all in which to talk with some of our fellow human beings. It simplifies matters, but it certainly brings its own problems—not least for those who think of themselves as religious.

But to get back to the main issue: we have something of the freedom to consider whether or not we turn to violence, and so, in virtue of that very fact, are rather different from those who experience their world as leaving them no other option. But if we have that freedom, it *ought* to be less likely that we reach for violence as a first resort. We have the freedom to think what we actually want, to probe our desires for some kind of outcome that is more than just mirroring what we have experienced. The trouble is that this means work of the kind we are often least eager for, work that will help us so to understand an other that we begin to find some sense of what they and we together might recognise as good. It means putting on hold our most immediate feelings—or at least making them objects of reflection; it means trying to pull apart the longing to re-establish the sense of being in control and the longing to find a security that is shared. In plainer English, it means being very suspicious of any action that brings a sense of release, irrespective of what it achieves; very wary of doing something so that it looks as if something is getting done.

It means acknowledging and using the breathing space; and also acknowledging and using the rage and revengefulness as a way of sensing a little of where the violence comes from. I'd better say it again: this has nothing to do with excusing decisions to murder, threaten, and torment, nor is it a recommendation to be passive. It is about trying to act so that something might possibly change, as opposed to acting so as to persuade ourselves that we're not powerless.

This business of the language in which you respond is, I think, what the Sermon on the Mount is dealing with. It's so easy to represent the words of Jesus here as commending passivity; you shake your head with a smile and say, "It's a wonderful ideal, it may even be an ideal for individuals, but it has nothing to do with the real world of communal and political conflict." But we're not reading closely enough.

Jesus tells us to turn the other cheek and walk the extra mile. The backhanded slap on the right cheek, as careful readers have noticed, is the kind of gesture that assumes no response at all; it's designed to be the end of the story, because it simply affirms who is in charge. The right of a soldier of the occupying power to compel your labour is the same; once you've done it, there is no more to be said.

The slave stands there rather than going away and slowly turns his head. The peasant looks at the soldier and speaks to him, saying, "I choose to go another mile." The world of the aggressor, the master, is questioned because the person who is supposed to take no initiatives suddenly does. As Gandhi discovered, this is very frightening for most of those who exercise power. It is action that changes the terms of the relation, or at the very least says to the master that the world might be otherwise. It requires courage and imagination: it is essentially the decision *not* to be passive, not to be a victim, but equally not to avoid passivity by simply reproducing what's been done to you. It is always something of a miracle.

For the Christian, it is the miracle made possible by the way in which God speaks. The story of Jesus understood as the "speaking" of God to the world repeatedly brings this into focus. God speaks one language, and human beings respond in another. God speaks to say, "Don't be afraid, nothing will stop me welcoming you"; or to say, "Be afraid only of your own deep longing to control me." Human beings respond by fearing God and struggling to please him ("The hour is coming when anyone who kills you will think he is doing a holy duty for God," says Jesus in John 16.2); and by failing to fear their hunger within them to capture and manipulate God. The speech of God is silenced by death; but God is unable, it seems, to learn any other language, and speaks again in Jesus' resurrection.

So what are we going to say in what we do?

We could be saying, "I must struggle to learn your language. I must hold on to what I've felt of your despair and strike back in the only language you understand. So I must train myself to look past the particular deaths of innocent people to make sure that my anger has adequate expression. I must work to keep up this pitch of energy until you have been silenced, and then perhaps I can start trying to re-learn the language I used to speak."

Or not, of course.

We weren't completely sure at first, most of us, but it was, of course, violence we turned to.[2] Not surprisingly, because we felt, most of us, that there really was nothing else we could do. A long programme of diplomatic pressure, the reworking of regional alliances and a severe review of intelligence and security didn't feel like doing anything. There needed to be a discharge of the tension.

But what makes discharging tension attractive is that it is an act that has a beginning and an end. The attraction fades when we cannot see the end; and here lies the risk and frustration of the conflict that began in October. From the first, it was not at all clear what would count as victory in this engagement. The abolition of terrorism? No doubt; but what possible guarantee could there be that this had been achieved? The capture of Osama bin Laden? Perhaps; but this would not in itself begin to solve the underlying problems as to where terrorism comes from. There would be plenty to take his place if the fundamental balance of power did not change at all in the world; and the drama of a martyr's fate for bin Laden would give another turn to the screw. The overthrow of the Afghan government? We should need cast-iron certainty that the Taliban administration really bore responsibility for collusion with terror; and we should need what we conspicuously don't have, an alternative for the future of the country.

The conflict begins to become an embarrassment. It is just possible to deplore civilian casualties and retain moral credibility when an action is clearly focused and its goals on the way to evident achievement. It is not possible when the strategy appears confused and political leaders talk about a "war" that may last years. And there is a fine line between, for example, the crippling of military and aircraft installations and the devastating of an infrastructure with a half-formed aim of destroying morale. Combine that with the use of anti-personnel weapons such as cluster bombs which ought to raise some serious questions (they have been described as aerial landmines in terms of their randomly lethal character), and the whole enterprise is tainted.

Tainted, because as soon as assaults on public morale by allowing random killing *as a matter of calculated policy* become part of a military strategy, we are at once vulnerable to the charge that there is no moral difference in kind between our military action and the terror which it attacks. This is not to reach for the too easy rhetoric that says there is no distinction at all between the controlled violence of the state at war and the "private" violence of terror (or indeed any unlawful killing); but the definition of what might be "lawful" violence is always fragile.

Self-defence, action against military personnel or officials of a hostile regime—these are the benchmarks that allow some principled distinctions to be drawn. From the point of view of a villager in Afghanistan whose family has died in a bombing raid, a villager who has probably never heard of the World Trade Center, the distinctions between what the U.S. forces are doing and what was done on September 11 will be academic.

To talk about lawful violence may seem odd, but law itself assumes that force is justified in some circumstances to defend a community's health and survival. But that health and survival are themselves undermined when defended by indiscriminate or disproportionate means; the cost is too high. What we set out to defend has become corrupted in the process (and this remains the cornerstone of moral opposition to nuclear, chemical, and biological armaments).

Something of this must apply to the international community. There is a high price to pay for allowing one nation to act in the name of a global campaign against terror while fudging the question of how in international law the matter might be brought to conclusion (in what court is a bin Laden to be tried?), and while claiming the freedom to determine its methods in the conflict without regard to the considerations we have just been looking at. Part of the process of putting in place an international "policing" operation, designed to bring clearly identified criminals to trial and punishment, involves maintaining the trust of other nations, the confidence that it is more than the interest of one nation that will dictate the outcome.

A good deal of the moral capital accumulated during the first days and weeks has been squandered. From a situation where Muslim nations, even Iran, expressed shock and sympathy, we have come to a point where the shapelessness of the campaign leads Muslims to ask whether there is any agenda other than the humiliation of an Islamic population. We may think this an outrageously wrong perception, but it becomes—or should become—a rather urgent factor in calculating how to restore a sense of lawfulness that would sustain some coherent action to punish and to secure a future that will be more settled and just for everyone.

Part of the problem is the fateful word "war." As soon as it was decided that the September atrocity was an act of war and that a "war on terrorism" was to be undertaken, clarity disappeared. No one has

"declared war" on Afghanistan; executive decisions have been made
to proceed with military action. At least in the UK, there is a sense
of some public confusion. There is discussion of whether we are dealing with a "just war," and the theoretical points are rehearsed (with
varying degrees of accuracy) in the broadsheets. The language fosters
the assumption that this is a conflict with a *story* to it—hopefully, a
story with a happy ending, a victory for justice. But terrorism is not
a place, not even a person or a group of persons; it is a form of be-
haviour. "War" against terrorism is as much a metaphor as war against
drug abuse (not that the metaphor isn't misleading there as well) or
car theft. It can only mean a sustained policy of making such behav-
iour less attractive or tolerable. As we've been reminded often, this is
a long job; but there is a difference between saying this, which is unquestionably true, and suggesting that there is a case for an open-ended
military campaign.

I sometimes wonder whether we have actually seen the end of war
as we knew it. Not that universal peace is about to break out; but what
we once meant by war becomes ever less likely in our world. No longer
do we see declarations of hostilities between sovereign states equipped
with roughly comparable resources; no longer do we think of standing armies competing in the field. Gradually, since 1945, the shape of
state violence has changed. There have been vicious conflicts around
regional separatism (the Biafra conflict of the late sixties, the USSR
in Chechnya), interventions in neighbouring states to restore stability
(Tanzania and Uganda), and, most noticeably, neocolonial conflicts
aimed at securing political dominance in often distant regions (Vietnam, the USSR in Afghanistan). More apparently conventional conflicts (Israel's defensive wars against Egyptian and Syrian aggression,
the Iran-Iraq conflict) have been regularly overshadowed by the irregular variety of these military adventures.

But with this goes an erosion of what once seemed straightforward
virtues—heroism in defence of one's country or for the sake of justice,
or even costly loyalty to one's allies under pressure. Ironically, these
are the virtues now prized most in just those irregular groupings that
cause us most anxiety. Terrorism survives not only on the oxygen of
publicity but on its seductive offer to reinvent some of the most ancient and numinous of (generally male) aspirations. The mythology of
the Irish Republican Army and of al-Qaida alike promises to give your

life and death the most immense significance, heroism, martyrdom; you take control of your destiny by pledging it to a cause that is beyond moral question, even beyond the possibility of ultimate failure. *You* will not die meaninglessly; that is reserved for your victims.

The comment is often made these days that we expect wars to be fought without casualties. Hence everyone's reluctance to commit ground troops to conflict and the obsession with high-tech aerial bombardment. Obsession is not too strong a word for the fantasy-laden researchers at the advancing edge of this technology ("wars can be fought and won in half an hour"). Some attribute this fear of casualties to a culturally induced cowardice and indifference. But I wonder if this isn't too glib; we can make sense, as the terrorist or freedom fighter does, of death in a righteous or even invulnerable cause, but in a period after the end of war as we knew it it is harder to understand our military engagements in these ways. And it's quite sensible not to want to die simply in a rather ambivalent police action in a foreign country (in the UK we have come to terms with our soldiers dying in Northern Ireland because that has seemed much more directly a matter of necessary and tragic defence).

The advent of superpowers has largely eradicated the old-fashioned kind of war; and the emergence of the USA as the only true surviving superpower has led some to speak not just of the end of war but of the end of history. What makes this not good news is that it obscures any idea that there are necessary but acceptable risks to be run if justice is to prevail; that loyalty to a community's vision may require the risk of failure in the short term, of death itself. Brecht may have said, "Happy the land that has no need of heroes," but, in his desire to keep at arms' length a false glorification of war, he missed the significance and attraction of a culture that at least allows some dignity to risk. When this is unrecognisable or in short supply in the ordinary discourse of a society, people will seek it out in strange places, hungry for danger, drama, meaning. We might cast a glance at our own backyards, at the fate of the young male in an environment of systemic poverty and unemployment. The least thoughtful are swept into petty-criminal subcultures (joyriding, gangs); the more reflective may join the kind of pressure group, right or left, that promises feverish and dangerous activism. Some travel across the world in search of places and causes where heroism is possible.

It happens in our own societies; if we have a problem about grasping why al-Qaida activists so often come from prosperous backgrounds in moderately prosperous states, this is part of the answer there too. To become part of a threatened minority struggling at immense cost, even the risk of violent and horrible death, to defend justice or true faith, is one way out of meaninglessness (and it also explains a little of the overheated rhetoric that so often typifies internal religious debate these days; drama is another addictive drug in all sorts of contexts).

The technologically expert violence of a wealthy country against a wretchedly poor one illustrates the problem; it drives a solution still further away.

Yet at the same time, one of the main memories of those closest to the events of September 11 will probably be of the prosaic heroism of firefighters and police in Manhattan. Memories of that morning for me include the enormously careful calm of one of the building staff, trained as a volunteer fire officer, deliberately talking us through the practical things to do next; and of the staff who were supervising the children's day care centre on the first floor, putting their own fear on hold while they reassured the children. Small examples of what was visible in much more costly ways outside, a couple of streets away. If we are to remember that day, we had better remember this too, remember, for example, that one firefighting unit in New York lost all its members that day. It puts a different perspective on heroism for a moment. It tells us that heroism is not always bound up with drama, the sense of a Great Cause, but is something about doing what is necessary for a community's health and security. For most of the time, this will be invisible; it is only in crisis that the habits slowly and even drearily formed over years emerge to make possible what can only be seen as extraordinary and selfless labours.

Some people, in other words, practise living in the presence of death; not courting dramatic immortality through a cause, but as part of what will or may be necessary to serve the social body. They are often likely to be ignored or belittled by articulate people, they lack the romance of those who take risks for the sake of giving their lives "meaning." Just as with the contrast between secular love and religious hate, we may well be sobered by the conjunction of heroism for the sake of "martyrdom," with its attendant death and devastation, and the heroism of routine. In one way, we have been reacquainted with a local and unexciting heroism that we have ignored in our restless passion for drama.

Heroism may be more remote in a postwar world, but it has not disappeared. Perhaps we should ask how we as societies come to grips with the idea that there is something, some balance of equity and mutuality, to be sustained that may require us to train ourselves in becoming familiar with risk and death, so that we recognise what needs to be done in crisis. Without this, we either look desperately for where we can find dramatic outlets for our frustration, or else we dress up our adventures in an exaggerated rhetoric of struggle and suffering, with leaders appealing to our fortitude and endurance in a situation in which most of us are not going to be exposed to any risk at all. One effect of this, too, is the weary cynicism that overtakes our responses to political leaders. They deplore it loudly and quite understandably; but they might ask how much the forcing of a high moral tone contributes to it.

So can we stop talking so much about "war," and reconcile ourselves to the fact that the punishment of terrorist crime and the gradual reduction of its threat cannot be translated into the satisfying language of decisive and dramatic conquest? Can we try thinking more about the place of risk and even loss in ordinary civil society; and about the moral resources needed to grapple with the continuing problems of shaping a lawful international order? Can we, for God's sake, let go of the fantasies nurtured by the capacity for high-tech aerial assault? As if the first move in any modern conflict had to be precision bombing? Experienced military personnel will insist on the differences of cultures, languages, terrain, infrastructure as factors that make it impossible to identify a single strategic plan as applicable everywhere. To try to reconceive our aims in terms of police action, the maintenance of international law, deprives us of some of the higher notes in the song, but it may be more to do with the reality we face.

And if we stopped talking about war so much, we might be spared the posturing which suggests that any questioning of current methods must be weakness at best, treason at worst.

We could ask whether the further destabilising of a massively resentful Muslim world and the intensifying of the problems of homelessness and hunger in an already devastated country were really unavoidable. We could refuse to be victims, striking back without imagination.

The hardest thing in the world is to know how to act so as to make the difference that *can* be made; to know how and why that differs from the act that only releases or expresses the basic impotence of resentment.

NOTES

1   This text originally appeared in Rowan Williams, *Writing in the Dust: After September 11* (Grand Rapids, Mich.: Eerdmans, 2002), 15–47. Used by permission; all rights reserved. To order this title, contact the publisher at 800-253-7521 or visit www.eerdmans.com.

2   Williams was in Lower Manhattan when the World Trade Center was attacked.

WENDELL BERRY

Thoughts in the Presence of Fear

I. The time will soon come when we will not be able to remember the horrors of September 11 without remembering also the unquestioning technological and economic optimism that ended on that day.[1]

II. This optimism rested on the proposition that we were living in a "new world order" and a "new economy" that would "grow" on and on, bringing a prosperity of which every new increment would be "unprecedented."

III. The dominant politicians, corporate officers, and investors who believed this proposition did not acknowledge that the prosperity was limited to a tiny percent of the world's people, and to an ever smaller number of people even in the United States; that it was founded upon the oppressive labor of poor people all over the world; and that its ecological costs increasingly threatened all life, including the lives of the supposedly prosperous.

IV. The "developed" nations had given to the "free market" the status of a god, and were sacrificing to it their farmers, farmlands, and communities, their forests, wetlands, and prairies, their ecosystems and watersheds. They had accepted universal pollution and global warming as normal costs of doing business.

V. There was, as a consequence, a growing worldwide effort on behalf of economic decentralization, economic justice, and ecological responsibility. We must recognize that the events of September 11 make this effort more necessary than ever. We citizens of the industrial countries must continue the labor of self-criticism and self-correction. We must recognize our mistakes.

VI. The paramount doctrine of the economic and technological euphoria of recent decades has been that everything depends on innovation. It was understood as desirable, and even necessary, that we should go on and on from one technological innovation to the next, which would cause the economy to "grow" and make everything better and better. This of course implied at every point a hatred of the past, of all things inherited and free. All things superceded in our progress of innovations, whatever their value might have been, were discounted as of no value at all.

VII. We did not anticipate anything like what has now happened. We did not foresee that all our sequence of innovations might be at once overridden by a greater one: the invention of a new kind of war that would turn our previous innovations against us, discovering and exploiting the debits and the dangers that we had ignored. We never considered the possibility that we might be trapped in the webwork of communication and transport that was supposed to make us free.

VIII. Nor did we foresee that the weaponry and the war science that we marketed and taught to the world would become available, not just to recognized national governments, which possess so uncannily the power to legitimate large-scale violence, but also to "rogue nations," dissident or fanatical groups and individuals—whose violence, though never worse than that of nations, is judged by the nations to be illegitimate.

IX. We had accepted uncritically the belief that technology is only good; that it cannot serve evil as well as good; that it cannot serve our enemies as well as ourselves; that it cannot be used to destroy what is good, including our homelands and our lives.

X. We had accepted too the corollary belief that an economy (either as a money economy or as a life-support system) that is global in extent, technologically complex, and centralized is invulnerable to terrorism, sabotage, or war, and that it is protectable by "national defense."

XI. We now have a clear, inescapable choice that we must make. We can continue to promote a global economic system of unlimited "free trade" among corporations, held together by long and highly vulnerable lines of communication and supply, but now recognizing that such a system will have to be protected by a hugely expensive police force that will be worldwide, whether maintained by one nation or several or all, and that such a police force will be effective precisely to the extent that it oversways the freedom and privacy of the citizens of every nation.

XII. Or we can promote a decentralized world economy which would have the aim of assuring to every nation and region a local self-sufficiency in life-supporting goods. This would not eliminate international trade, but it would tend toward a trade in surpluses after local needs had been met.

XIII. One of the gravest dangers to us now, second only to further terrorist attacks against our people, is that we will attempt to go on as before with the corporate program of global "free trade," whatever the cost in freedom and civil rights, without self-questioning or self-criticism or public debate.

XIV. This is why the substitution of rhetoric for thought, always a temptation in a national crisis, must be resisted by officials and citizens alike. It is hard for ordinary citizens to know what is actually happening in Washington in a time of such great trouble; for all we know, serious and difficult thought may be taking place there. But the talk that we are hearing from politicians, bureaucrats, and commentators has so far tended to reduce the complex problems now facing us to issues of unity, security, normality, and retaliation.

XV. National self-righteousness, like personal self-righteousness, is a mistake. It is misleading. It is a sign of weakness. Any war that we may make now against terrorism will come as a new installment in a history of war in which we have fully participated. We are not innocent of making war against civilian populations. The modern doctrine of such warfare was set forth and enacted by General William Tecumseh Sherman, who held that a civilian population could be declared guilty and rightly subjected to military punishment. We have never repudiated that doctrine.

XVI. It is a mistake also—as events since September 11 have shown—to suppose that a government can promote and participate in a global economy and at the same time act exclusively in its own interest by abrogating its international treaties and standing apart from international cooperation on moral issues.

XVII. And surely, in our country, under our Constitution, it is a fundamental error to suppose that any crisis or emergency can justify any form of political oppression. Since September 11, far too many public voices have presumed to "speak for us" in saying that Americans will gladly accept a reduction of freedom in exchange for greater "security." Some would, maybe. But some others would accept a reduction in security (and in global trade) far more willingly than they would accept any abridgement of our Constitutional rights.

XVIII. In a time such as this, when we have been seriously and most cruelly hurt by those who hate us, and when we must consider ourselves to be gravely threatened by those same people, it is hard to speak of the ways of peace and to remember that Christ enjoined us to love our enemies, but this is no less necessary for being difficult.

XIX. Even now we dare not forget that since the attack of Pearl Harbor—to which the present attack has been often and not usefully compared—we humans have suffered an almost uninterrupted sequence of wars, none of which has brought peace or made us more peaceable.

XX. The aim and result of war necessarily is not peace but victory, and any victory won by violence necessarily justifies the violence that won it and leads to further violence. If we are serious about innovation, must we not conclude that we need something new to replace our perpetual "war to end war"?

XXI. What leads to peace is not violence but peaceableness, which is not passivity, but an alert, informed, practiced, and active state of being. We should recognize that while we have extravagantly subsidized the means of war, we have almost totally neglected the ways of peaceableness. We have, for example, several national military academies, but not one peace academy. We have ignored the teachings and the examples of Christ, Gandhi, Martin Luther King, and other peaceable leaders. And here we have an inescapable duty to notice also that war is profitable, whereas the means of peaceableness, being cheap or free, make no money.

XXII. The key to peaceableness is continuous practice. It is wrong to suppose that we can exploit and impoverish the poorer countries, while arming them and instructing them in the newest means of war, and then reasonably expect them to be peaceable.

XXIII. We must not again allow public emotion or the public media to caricature our enemies. If our enemies are now to be some nations of Islam, then we should undertake to know those enemies. Our schools should begin to teach the histories, cultures, arts, and language of the Islamic nations. And our leaders should have the humility and the wisdom to ask the reasons some of those people have for hating us.

XXIV. Starting with the economies of food and farming, we should promote at home, and encourage abroad, the ideal of local self-sufficiency. We should recognize that this is the surest, the safest, and the cheapest way for the world to live. We should not countenance the loss or destruction of any local capacity to produce necessary goods.

XXV. We should reconsider and renew and extend our efforts to protect the natural foundations of the human economy: soil, water, and air. We should protect every intact ecosystem and watershed that we have left, and begin restoration of those that have been damaged.

XXVI. The complexity of our present trouble suggests as never before that we need to change our present concept of education. Education is not properly an industry, and its proper use is not to serve industries, either by job-training or by industry-subsidized research. Its proper use is to enable citizens to live lives that are economically, politically, socially, and culturally responsible. This cannot be done by gathering or "accessing" what we now call "information"—which is to say facts without context and therefore without priority. A proper education enables young people to put their lives in order, which means knowing what things are more important than other things; it means putting first things first.

XXVII. The first thing we must begin to teach our children (and learn ourselves) is that we cannot spend and consume endlessly. We have got to learn to save and conserve. We do need a "new economy," but one that is founded on thrift and care, on saving and conserving, not on excess and waste. An economy based on waste is inherently and hopelessly violent, and war is its inevitable by-product. We need a peaceable economy.

NOTE

1   "Thoughts in the Presence of Fear" originally appeared on OrionOnline.
    org, the website of *Orion* magazine and the Orion Society. The essay was
    first published in book form in *In the Presence of Fear: Three Essays for a
    Changed World* by Wendell Berry (Great Barrington, Mass.: Orion Society,
    December 2001).

CATHERINE LUTZ

The Wars Less Known

Yossarian tensed with alert astonishment when he heard
Colonel Korn's concluding words. "What's that?" he exclaimed.
"What have you and Colonel Cathcart got to do with my country?
You're not the same."

"How can you separate us?" Colonel Korn inquired with ironical
tranquility.

"That's right," Colonel Cathcart cried emphatically. "You're either
for us or against us. There's no two ways about it."

"I'm afraid he's got you," added Colonel Korn. "You're either *for* us
or against your country. It's as simple as that."
—Joseph Heller, *Catch-22*

The world we live in—its divisions and conflicts, its widening
gap between rich and poor, its seemingly inexplicable outbursts of
violence—is shaped far less by what we celebrate and mythologize
than by the painful events we try to forget.
—Adam Hochschild, *King Leopold's Ghost*

The wars of the United States have been showered with prose suggesting that they burst open not bodies, but history. War gives birth to new
beginnings, the story goes, even moving the course of human events
in positive, if also tragic, ways. Given this belief in war's grandeur and
its tectonic role, what followed September 11, 2001, had to be declared
another good war. And because most of its victims were homefront
civilians, it was called a war like no other. But while the hijackers who

heinously killed so many that day may have created a new kind of violent spectacle, they were not the authors of one of the human era's uniquely horrific events. For, I wearily note, we have been here before, and we have been led to forget. Today's war without end began long ago, and it has produced both the corpses of battle and economic and physical casualties in other arenas. Because you may not read this dark tale of two kinds of violence unless there is some small light to be had, the ending will suggest the sources of hope to which I cling.

I will begin with the unrecognized long war at home, and with an airplane flight I took just after New Year's Day 2002. As it turned out, I was assigned a place on the aisle in a large jet, with young men headed to the Marines' Parris Island training camp in every other seat around me. I was not surprised that it seemed to be the first flight for many, given the military's still heavy recruitment from the struggling classes. So there were some hysterical blurts of laughter, nervous comments, and macho posturing. One especially anxious young man, a boy really, retrieved his Bible and started to pray, but soon began retching violently into an airsickness bag. I asked his seatmate if this was fear of flying, and he said, "I guess, ma'am, he's just sick about the plane and the boot camp all mixed together."

This boy-man had likely heard stories about the rituals of humiliation and physical trials that he would have to undergo at Parris Island. Though he knew that these promised to make a man of him, he could fear beatings and other, more elaborate physical hazing, and the psychological tortures of having his face smeared with lipstick and his neck strung with dead fish, mostly at the hands of his fellow soldiers. He would have signed on nonetheless because his recruiter and other devices of the annual two-billion-dollar budget devoted to military labor marketing had also promised he would enter the ranks of the super-citizen, the true patriot. And because it made military life look like a job-training program or a Dungeons and Dragons game as much or more than preparation for killing or being killed, that advertising promised safety. Oddly, this is something the military may in fact deliver. That is because the war they go to might be like most of the sixty-six acknowledged U.S. foreign interventions since 1975 in relying on aerial bombardment to first "soften" their targets (often already made pliant by intense poverty). Training accident or friendly fire deaths aside, this has meant that a total of just 525 soldiers died in battle in the last two decades, a number equal to the U.S. highway death toll that accumulates in just five days. People walking into their first day of work at poultry processing plants speckled throughout the poor Carolina counties around their boot camp should vomit at the doorway, too. For they suffer higher rates of death and disability on the job than do soldiers.

Just a few days earlier, I had sensed nausea pulse through another arena of war as well, this in an NPR story about the controversy over U.S. treatment of the Camp X-Ray prisoners at Guantánamo Bay. Like the rest of the mainstream media, the station was paying devoted attention to a "national security intellectual" who was asked whether these prisoners were treated humanely and in accordance with international law governing POWs. The academic defended U.S. government actions, asserting that the camp was being governed, as she put it, by the "customs" if not the laws of warfare, such as the Geneva Convention. When asked what these customs were, she answered that they were simply practices that were in "good taste."

The intellectual and the boy-man were both struggling with queasiness inside the machinery of war (though he was much closer to the gears than she). But its mechanisms have become increasingly invisible since at least the 1950s. It was in that early era of militarization that C. Wright Mills pointed out that the nation was coming to accept an all-encompassing "military definition of reality." If we follow the young men to their destination, though, there are some routes around that wall of normalization of a gigantic army, and a world defined by the idea of threat.

They were headed to a place very like Fayetteville, North Carolina, a city of some 120,000 souls adjacent to the army's Fort Bragg where I have conducted anthropological and historical research.[1] It is just one of the 1,324 major active-duty U.S. military bases and 3,660 such places, large and small, active duty and reserve, domestic and foreign. Like Fayetteville, many are places where pervasive child poverty, domestic violence, prostitution, environmental catastrophes large and small, and homelessness coexist with the nation's massive state of war readiness. The situation in these towns constitutes a significant part of the U.S. way of life that the military is said to protect. And it does make such a world possible, if not in the sense usually intended by that phrase: the army helps create the city's conditions of immiseration through the political economy that supports it, as I detail later in this essay. Only by magical thinking could one imagine how it could be otherwise: how having the most powerful military human history has ever seen could come without massive and disguised costs.

There are many more people like the recruits than the NPR commentator on the homefront of militarization, that is, many more people who can be considered the friendly fire casualties of war. These casualties include the people who make a poverty wage working retail jobs, the main type of work created by the post as soldiers go into town to buy burgers and fries, shower curtains, tattoos, or sneakers for their children. They include people who cannot find work at all given how many military spouses are added to the local labor pool when soldiers are brought to post, and those who are the victims of crimes committed by the resulting large number of desperate poor. They are the women beaten, stabbed, or shot by their partners, victims found in greater numbers around military posts where training in violence and male privilege are a stock in trade. They are the gay and lesbian people who are unreported hate crime targets, and who live with fewer health services given their more intense closeting in military communities.

Some of Fayetteville's poverty is not specific to a military city economy, but shared with that found across the United States. But the high national rates of poverty are also related, in a more complex way, to the military budget. One example of this relationship is found, paradoxically, in the military's generally excellent pay and benefits package, which includes universal family health care, subsidized housing, living wages, and social support systems. Military workers are then subtracted from the total forces that could otherwise be organized to demand such working conditions for all. In other words, the military creates a working class divided against itself, and contributes to the suggestion that the poor must pull themselves up by their bootstraps even as the leather they inherit rots away under their touch. In this way, the military budget helps create the tale of two cities found everywhere across the United States: miserable pools of poverty and weather-beaten cottages on one side, and six-thousand-square-foot mansions dripping with commodities on the other, many of which house those who profit directly or indirectly from war.

To understand Fayetteville and the connections between its predicament and the economy of war, I have looked at its historical archive

A Tale of Two Houses, 2000. Photographs by elin o'Hara slavick.

and spoken with its residents. Some are civilians and some soldiers, and many have penetrating insights into war and its effects. There is the challenge that one man described, even after he had spent several decades in the army, of reconciling the Ten Commandments with his military training. There are the many women who described being a kind of war refugee, leaving their hometown to avoid the overwhelming climate of objectification they lived with under the glare of the city's many strip bars and the young men who pursued them. And there are the new soldiers, the great majority of whom give college benefits as their primary reason for enlisting. The military offered what seemed beyond their reach in high school, where they were often "tracked" far below wealthier peers who did not have to exchange their freedom for college tuition. The stories I heard included those of homeless people, some one quarter of whom are veterans: one of their shelters was razed when the city decided to build a $22.5 million military museum celebrating war and its heroes on its site.

Most people in the United States, including those now working in the military, have never seen battlefields. But one man's example demonstrates the importance of seeing the bodies of war, even if via media, and refusing the argument that it is in bad taste to show them. A Fort Bragg soldier who helped establish the city's Quaker House—a peace witness and draft counseling center—dates his awakening to the immorality of the war in Vietnam to one evening's television news. He was stunned to see, as he remembered it, "a big helicopter [with] a net under it, just full of bodies and they killed all these people that day and they said, 'Well now it's just a disposal problem, we have to get rid of these bodies.' And I don't know what they did, they buried them or burned or what they did. Just seeing something like that on TV, it's just like a click. You know this ain't right. No."

If most of us have not truly seen war, we nonetheless have lived with its haunting. Our lives have been made under the threat of nuclear Armageddon, and with the work of forgetting required by what has been done in our names in faraway places. This includes the destruction of Chilean democracy in 1973, collusion in the murder of labor organizers, priests, and nuns in Central America in the 1980s, and support for the Indonesian army and paramilitaries that ravaged the people of East Timor. In our name, Micronesian atolls and their people were irradiated by above-ground nuclear tests and an apartheid system was installed at Kwajalein atoll, which has been the target for missiles regularly launched from California's Vandenburg Air Force Base to arch their way across the Pacific and into its cerulean lagoon. The dead and disappeared have haunted us because we are a war culture, our government massively involved in ordering the killing, training others to kill, and threatening to kill. We have been doubly haunted because we are a warrior culture without warriors: we have instead technicians of death, who shoot through the distancing grid of instrument panels or bureaucratic plans. We are a nation of sofa spectators who see war through that same grid, or through fiction movies or old war footage on the History Channel, the latter films long ago prescreened and approved for release by the Department of Defense or its more honestly named predecessor, the War Department. We have been doubly haunted, in other words, because after all of the killing, the bodies are hidden away and denied.

While we live with war as entertainment, we also pay war taxes to support the multibillion-dollar military budget. The only true war profiteers are the executives of corporations like Raytheon and General Electric whose "net earnings" are an order of magnitude larger than even the average corporation's bloated skimming. Many in the working and middle classes get some small return on those taxes in the form of lower commodity prices that the violence ensures—fuel at bargain prices because the U.S. military keeps regimes like the Saudis' in power in exchange for cheaper oil, imported clothes whose prices would be higher if the United States did not train and equip the militaries that repress labor organizing in countries where the clothing is made. But even these slim returns to U.S. citizens prove an illusion when assembly jobs have been exported from cities like Fayetteville and moved to these very countries to take advantage of the cheap labor ensured by U.S. military aid.

This brings us from the question of the long homefront to the long battlefront of history. The first problem in this transition from the inside to the outside of the nation and its history is the illusion created by nationalism. This is the notion that safety consists primarily in defending state borders and interests defined as a singular, people's interest. These assumptions make it difficult to ask why the ubiquitous monuments to U.S. soldiers who have died in battle are not joined by others:

to ask about the missing monuments to the dead of the Middle Passage, the fallen of the Industrial Revolution and its long cancerous tailwind, or the literally millions of deaths by automobile. That is because it is assumed that the nation cannot kill its own people (no matter Yossarian's insight that war does exactly that). Is it also because we take for granted that these latter forms of carnage are mistakes, that only war is intentional if unwanted, and only it has shaped the nation?

That said, it is important to ask about continuities between the current war and earlier ones. They begin with the racial hatred that has preceded, stoked, and been inflamed by nearly every one of the last centuries' wars. They run from the campaign against Native Americans and the enslavement of Africans in the United States to the genocides in Namibia, Nazi Germany, and Rwanda. In *War without Mercy*, John Dower powerfully highlighted how exterminationist methods on the battlefield and concentration camps at home were reserved for the Japanese in World War II, while the Germans were carefully separated into the good and bad among them, and how Japanese and German imperialism had racial charters as well.[2] Our current war likewise has been enmeshed in bigotry, including bin Laden's cry against the infidel. But it is the Afghani people who had to flee their homes, as the English did not when one of their own planted a bomb in his shoe and tried to murder a jet full of people. And the chief suspect in the anthrax terrorism that emptied the halls of Congress and killed six people is a military biological warfare specialist who works at Fort Detrick, Maryland. Not only do his superiors and neighbors need not worry that their training, tolerance, or mere proximity to him condemns them to punishment, but the suspect himself seems to be escaping with impunity.

Continuities of past wars with this present one are evident in the cold war, which was also advertised as a new and endless kind of clash. It was to be a war, it was said, where the enemy would no longer fight in the open, a war requiring the sacrifice of some freedom and principle. It would require vigilance against spies and collectivists at home as well as projection of armed might abroad. It, too, birthed a search for the enemy within and slaughter in places far away, and it, too, stole the fruits of our labor.

The cold war was also a war by and against terror—if by this we mean striking fear and horror into the hearts of a whole population by threatening to kill civilians and, occasionally, doing so for demonstration effect. These terrorists were found in the highest offices of the U.S. and Soviet governments where they planned atomic and proxy wars. They were called realists, however, and their long reign of nuclear terror—in which their two nations together targeted hundreds of millions of people in skyscrapers and hovels—was called defense or even peace, and its architects men of honor. It is hardly surprising but still outrageous that the hardened missile silos, subterranean bunkers, nuclear submarines, and other infrastructure of atomic holocaust that still form part of our landscape remain misnamed. And so Henry Kissinger's assistants today can sift through his gilt-edged invitations to sip champagne in the parlors of power despite his faith in nuclear weapons and his hand in the terrors sown in Chile, Vietnam, and East Timor.[3]

The new war that George Bush wages can draw on the decades-long public relations campaign suggesting that the larger the U.S. arsenal, the safer we are. It can draw on the established idea that war elevates moral character in those who wage it and those who support it. It seems not to matter to their credibility that the elites now carrying out the war are entirely safe and that they have just emerged into their suited warrior roles from the board rooms of oil, construction, and military industrial corporations that stand to profit from the war. It seems also not to matter that the war's target has moved breathtakingly quickly from the planners of the September 11 attacks to a host of nations joined in a crazy quilt of antagonism, the axis of evil. What will be next we can only imagine, but it will surely be worthy of Joseph Heller.

What of hope, then? I have found it in dialogue and in history. Those encouraging conversations have been with people whose activism against the war I try to emulate, and those others who are trying to find their way to a moral stance toward the killing. Even those who repeat the phrase "We have to do something" seem almost always more thoughtful and less vengeful than the voices from the electronic boxes. From the days immediately after the attacks on New York and Washington, I have heard more people refuse the simplicities and the certainties of those who control the airwaves and whose framing devices overwhelmingly ask when and where the United States will strike, not how exactly this method proposes to accomplish a safe future.

In the second week of last September, I attended a class as a guest speaker. The professor leading the class described to her students how angry she was at the hijacking perpetrators and asked people to say if they were as well. Many hands went up along with mine. When I asked the students why they were mad, however, their multiple and nuanced reasons were not the instructor's. One was angry that the New York and Washington victims had not been protected despite a three-hundred-billion-dollar military budget, another that human beings continue to stoop to violence, another that her world had lost its security. While the Bush administration tried to reduce this all to a single feeling with one swift sword attached, these thoughtful, passionate varieties of anger then seemed to me openings to reflection and a response more ethical than indiscriminate force. They were ready to hear that the parallel to September 11, 2001, was not Pearl Harbor, because in 1941 it was a colonial outpost in a once-sovereign Hawaiian nation. They were ready to ask whether this was to be the opening salvo in a new round of worldwide violence like those that erupted in 1914, 1939, and 1947, and whether there was a way around the repetition of some of the foolish choices of the past. Even some of those who now have multiple U.S. flags pasted on or flying from their cars and homes and clothes mean simply to memorialize the dead, not face down enemies, foreign or domestic. But the symbol's danger is its muteness, which allows each flag to be gathered together by the administration and claimed as its own belligerent charter.

For years, people searching for alternatives to war have drawn some of their resolve and sustenance from history, as Howard Zinn and others have so eloquently motivated them to do. However familiar this history might be to some, it bears repeating as a litany of confidence in what is possible: from the success of Mahatma Gandhi's nonviolent resistance movement in evicting the British Empire from India to the more than three hundred soldiers of the Israeli army who refused to fight in the occupied territories of Palestine as 2002 opened. It includes the vibrant antimilitarist tradition in the United States from the Quakers and Mennonites to that embodied in the Constitution. That document divides state power to make war-waging more difficult because its framers were deeply wary of standing armies, one of them, Samuel Adams, even warning, "It is a very improbable supposition that any people can long remain free, with a strong military power in the very heart of their country." The flame was carried by slavery's passive resisters, escapees, and abolitionists, by the campaign against universal military training and ROTC in the World War I era, and by the civil rights movement whose legions faced down the terror of the Ku Klux Klan with spiritual armor. It was in the massive rebellion against the Vietnam War that occurred within and outside the military, a rebellion that was linked with a call to end the racism that promoted violence there and at home. And it includes the commitments of people like Philip Berrigan who has spent years in jail for standing in the path of U.S. weapons of mass destruction, and Dorothy Day's still-growing Catholic Worker movement, which births intentional communities dedicated to pacifism and justice.

The powerful antinuclear movement helped shrink the Soviet and U.S. nuclear arsenals and delegitimate their use, and mass-membership international human rights organizations were behind near-universal accord on conventions against land mines, chemical and biological weapons, state torture, and child soldiers. The International Criminal Court offers the possibility of trial and imprisonment for those who commit crimes against humanity. While the United States has often been alone in rejecting these treaties, or standing with the small group of nations it otherwise calls rogue states, these and many other alternatives have become available and are being used to delegitimate some of the most obscene forms of warfare. Hope is in the worldwide mass movement that has drawn attention to the victims of contemporary forms of economic violence. Finally, it came with the more than 100,000 people who marched on Washington, D.C., and San Francisco on April 20, calling for an end to the war on all its fronts.

When so much power is arrayed against the forces of life, it seems important to return to the places where war is planned and listen to the people who live in the shadow of that planning and closer to its costs. Their insights can still matter, especially while the discourse of democracy still holds some small sway and suggests that our views should guide what the state does. Human imagination and historical example suggest what safer and better world is possible.

The long homefront and its future fate hinge on our reconnecting both sides of the fence that separates the Fort Braggs and the Fayettevilles, seeing the links between our war taxes and the division of our house against itself, and forcing into juxtaposition the sites of carnage with the sites of good taste and euphemism. It hangs on seeing what is done in our name both at home and abroad, and on refusing the war planners, whether in the United States or Israel or Al Qaeda. As we do so, we place the bodies and the mourners and the militarization-induced poverty where the realists must see them, and see us seeing them. Is it wrong to imagine the war's strategists and the oil moguls stumbling over the dead, staining their fine clothes, on their way to a more humane, rehabilitative, and law-bound prison than the one established at Guantánamo Bay? Is it too difficult to see how the two kinds of public housing in Fayetteville—its barracks and its bantustans—are of a single piece? Can we take hope in the knowledge that—because we cannot have a gargantuan military without a hobbled homefront—we shall eliminate both problems simultaneously in the new world we struggle to make?

NOTES

1 Catherine Lutz, *Homefront: A Military City and the American Twentieth Century* (Boston: Beacon Press, 2001).
2 John W. Dower, *War without Mercy* (New York: Pantheon Books, 1986).
3 Christopher Hitchens, *The Trial of Henry Kissinger* (London: Verso, 2001).

FREDRIC JAMESON

The Dialectics of Disaster

Looking back at September 11 discloses a dissociation of sensibility, in which on the one hand we remember unrealistic visuals, of a special effects or computer graphics type, showing airplanes striking tall and massive edifices, and on the other we recall an amalgamation of media sentiment and emotion, which it would be inexact to call hysterical, since even this hysteria struck many of us, from the outset, as being utterly insincere. To get at the real historical event itself, you feel, one would have to strip away all the emotional reaction to it. But even to get at that emotional reaction, one would have to make one's way through its media orchestration and amplification. People don't appreciate a theoretical discussion of their emotions (Are you questioning the sincerity of my feelings?). I suppose the answer has to be, No, not the sincerity of your feelings; rather, the sincerity of all feelings. There is a famous moment in Proust when the narrator, seeking to enhance the grief he feels at his grandmother's death, suddenly finds he feels nothing at all: the famous "intermittencies of the heart," which the existentialists dramatized by asserting that, whatever the feeling in question (anger as well as grief, love as much as hate), we never feel enough; the emotion is never full enough; it comes and goes.

So the media hype, and the subsequent media patriotism—which one can surely qualify as obscene without too much fear of contradiction—is grounded on some lack of being in the heart itself. The media is, to be sure, an organism with its own specific biological requirements—to seize on a story of this kind and milk it for all it's worth to exhaustion; hopefully then, as in this case, sublating it into a new story with the same rich possibilities of development. The human individuals (announcers, newspersons, talk-show hosts, etc.) are then parts of this collective organism who eagerly collaborate in its developmental processes and service its wants.

But something needs to be said about the public's reaction; and I think it is instructive to step away for a moment and to deny that it is natural and self-explanatory for masses of people to be devastated by catastrophe in which they have lost no one they know, in a place with which they have no particular connections. Is nationality really so natural a function of human or even social being? Even more than that, is pity or sympathy really so innate a feature of the human constitution? History casts some doubt on both propositions. Meanwhile, think of the way in which a psychologically distressed individual sometimes fixates on some *fait divers* from a distant place or country—a bizarre accident in Kansas, for example, or a peculiar family tragedy in China—which the sufferer cannot get out of his head and on which crystallize all kinds of intense and troubled feelings, even though no one else seems interested at all. Is the only difference some media affirmation of collective unanimity, of a vast tidal wave of identical reactions? One can say these things now, despite media intimidation and the scapegoating of the unpatriotic nonmourners, because even the bereaved families have begun publicly to denounce the "ghoulishness" of such arrangements as the "viewing platform" lately erected on the Twin Towers site.

It is not particularly difficult to grasp the mechanics of a collective delirium of this kind, and of what we may technically call a collective fantasy without meaning to imply in any way that it is unreal. Aristotle already described it, in accounting for the peculiar effects of a unique collective spectacle of his day. Pity and fear: fear comes from putting myself in a victim's place, imagining the horror of the fire and the unimaginable height outside the windows; pity then sets in when we remember we are safe ourselves, and think of others who were not. Add to all this morbid curiosity and the soap opera structure that organizes so much of our personal experience, and you have a powerful vehicle for producing emotion, about which it is difficult to say when it stops being spontaneous and begins to be systemically used on the public. When that happens, is one to suppose that a real event has imperceptibly been transformed into a spectacle (Guy Debord) or even a simulation and a simulacrum (Jean Baudrillard)? That is, to be sure, another offensive way of "doubting" people's sincerity. But once a nameless and spontaneous reaction has been named and classified, and named over and over again so insistently by all the actors of the public sphere, backed up by thinly veiled threats and intimidation, the name interposes a stereotype between ourselves and our thoughts and feelings; or, if you prefer (Sartre's idea of seriality), what we feel are no longer our own feelings anymore but someone else's, and indeed, if we are to believe the media, everybody else's. This new inauthenticity casts no little doubt on all those theories of mourning and trauma that were recently so influential, and whose slogans one also finds everywhere in the coverage. One may well prefer Proust to these obligatory appeals to mourning and trauma, which have been sucked so deeply into the disaster news as to make one wonder whether, from the psychological descriptions and diagnoses they purport to offer, they have not been turned into a new kind of therapy in their own right. Therapy is, to be sure, an old American tradition; and I can still vividly remember the suggestion of a clinical psychologist on the radio, not only that the survivors needed therapy, but that all Americans should receive it! Perhaps it would not be any more expensive than George Bush's tax cut; but in any case the therapist will now have been reassured. All Americans are now receiving therapy, and it is called war (or more officially, "the war on terrorism").

One can restrain one's paranoia and still admire the timeliness with which these events rescued what his advisors call "this presidency." My irreverence for the media goes so far, I have to admit, as even to doubt the fundamental lessons it has sought to draw for us: that America changed forever on September 11, that America lost its innocence, that things will never be the same again, et cetera. The history of the superstate is as bloody as anyone else's national history; and these observations about innocence and experience (they were also affirmed during the Watergate scandal) have more to do with media innocence than with any personal kind; more in common with the widespread diffusion of public violence and pornography than with a private cynicism that has probably existed since the dawn of human history. What is shocking then is not the information itself, but that one can talk about it publicly.

If anything has changed forever, et cetera, it is that, as has also been widely observed, a minority president has been legitimized. His outrageous fiscal mission has been submissively adopted; and his zany (and expensive) arms proposal, along with the more sinister extension of the surveillance state, are promoted in the name of a universal revival of patriotism, certified by just that feeling of universal shock, grief, mourning, and the resultant indignation, that we have been examining.

I do want to add one more observation about the alleged universality of this collective feeling, for it corresponds to one of the most influential Utopian fantasies about communication in the modern age, and one more likely to be developed on the Left than on the traditional Right. This is the notion of universal intersubjectivity, based on the promise and potential of the newer media. I think it is implicit in the very notion of communication as such, conceived as a channel or contact between two isolated and individual subjectivities (as, for example, in Habermas's influential philosophy). If you can imagine somehow reunifying two monads which have been effectively separated in the first place, then why not go on to posit some collective network which unifies them all in their multiplicity? (It is a Utopian fantasy that at once dialectically reverses itself into the dystopia of the protocommunist insect community or anthill of the collective mind without individuality.) If such a thing is possible, I think it can only be imagined negatively; the positive versions, the coming of the benign aliens in *Close Encounters of the Third Kind*, for example, are cloying and without conviction. As Sartre often said, a collectivity is unified only by an external threat or danger, an external enemy, something certainly witnessed in the present instance. I've suggested elsewhere that such a moment—those Utopian potentialities of the media developed everywhere in media studies from Habermas to fantasies of the Internet, and from John Fiske to leftist speculations about mass democracy—is to be glimpsed in the day or two that followed the Kennedy assassination; in retrospect (and in the hindsight of the present event) it would also seem to have been dependent on the relative inexperience of the media in such matters, their clumsiness, the technological naiveté in which they sought to rise to the occasion: here, too, then, we may modify the received wisdom—not America, but rather its media, has definitively lost its innocence.

As for the attack itself, it is important to remember that historical events are never really punctual—despite the appearance of this one and the abruptness of its violence—but extend into a before and an after of historical time that only gradually unfold, to disclose the full dimensions of the historicity of the event. To be sure, it has been pointed out that the Americans themselves, with the help of the Pakistani secret police, invented bin Laden during our covert participation in the Soviet war in Afghanistan. That he should therefore subsequently turn on his creators seems to offer a textbook example of dialectical reversal (we shall see, however, that the lessons of the dialectic are even more relevant than this).

Yet the seeds of the event are buried far more deeply than that, and suggest that we need to revise the current overestimation of religion's role in society today. This is less to deny that there is a religious revival in course today all over the world than it is to suggest that what is called religion today (in a variety of forms, from left to right) is really politics under a different name. (Indeed, maybe religion has always been that.) What is called religious fundamentalism is then a political option, which is embraced when other political options have been shut down: most notably, left politics and communist parties all over the Islamic world, if not the third world generally. But although the collapse of the Soviet Union certainly discredited the official communist parties, along with socialism itself, in the West, this event should not be assigned any primary ideological role (the disappearance of Soviet money and technological support was far more crippling to the older left-wing movements). Instead, we have to enlarge our historical perspective to include the wholesale massacres of the Left systematically encouraged and directed by the Americans in a period that stretches back virtually to the beginnings of the cold war. We are aware of our complicity in numerous Latin American repressions, but have only gradually come to grasp our involvement in Africa (Raoul Peck's new film *Lumumba* will be a timely revelation for many people), let alone in Asia itself. Yet the physical extermination of the Iraqi and Indonesian communist parties, although now virtually forgotten, were crimes as abominable as any contemporary genocide. These are instances in which assassination and the wholesale murder of your opponents are preeminently successful in the short run; but whose unexpected consequences are far more ambiguous historically. It may well be that the traditional Left remains paralyzed by the trauma, as seems to be the case, for example, in "postdictatorship" Chile. But this simply means that a left alternative for popular resistance and revolt has been closed off. The so-called fundamentalist religious option then becomes the only recourse and the only available form of a politics of opposition; and this is clearly the case of bin Laden's movement, however limited it may be to intellectuals and activists.

But what of the relationship of this movement to the State? Is it "sponsored" by someone, to use the favorite U.S. government term? There is evidently something deeply ironic in the quizzical scrutiny of one group of wealthy businessmen by another. We have to remember that the last half-century was uniquely free of major wars: the two "Vietnams"—those of the United States and of the USSR—were limited conflicts, and even the truly horrendous war between Iraq and Iran, longer than World War II, was not a "world" conflict. One does not have to endorse Hegel's infamous comment, that wars are necessary for the spiritual health of societies, to see how the absence of generalized physical destruction creates a certain problem for capitalism, in the survival of old plant and inventory, and the persistent saturation of key markets. For the health of capitalist societies these enormous unused inventories need to be destroyed every so often for even the productivity of capitalism itself to develop in a way that avoids the sterilities of finance capital. Meanwhile the Reagan/Thatcher tax revolutions, designed to eliminate the welfare state, had as their specific political tactic the sharp reduction of taxes on the wealthy and on the corporations, something the new Bush regime has renewed with a vengeance, under the pretext of economic recession. More paradoxical is the deleterious effect on the system of this financial accumulation in private hands (the hands of those Theodore Roosevelt called "malefactors of great wealth"): something far more dramatic than the occasional million of the robber barons of yesteryear. These immense fortunes of the present day—scarcely drained by post-Reaganite taxation and left intact by the feeblest of death duties—then make a mockery of what used to be celebrated as the separation of ownership and control (and what was latterly and more spuriously touted as stockholders' democracy). The gingerly debates on campaign finance reform have only lifted a modest corner of the veil on the true immensity of this financial power in private hands, which allows individuals to become something like a state within a state, and endows them with a margin of political and even military autonomy.

It is crucial to remember that bin Laden is one of those people. Exotic trappings aside, he is the very prototype of the accumulation of money in the hands of private individuals and the poisoned fruit of a process that, unchecked, allows an unimaginable autonomy of action of all kinds. What is still a matter for conspiracy theory over here, where (as far as we know) *The Pelican Brief* is less the rule than the cronyism within the established business and government institutions, can be witnessed in the full flower of its development in Al Qaeda, which constitutes less a new and interesting party-organizational form for the new world of globalization than it does a rich man's private hobby.

Still, this concrete commando-style operation also struck symbolically at one of the rare centers of globalized finance capitalism. That it was anti-Western was always clear enough and reflected in the Muslim decorum and family values which become the logo for a repudiation of immoral Western permissiveness and consumer culture. The opponents of an antiglobalization politics will certainly be quick to identify bin Laden's politics with the antiglobalization movement generally and to posit "terrorism" as the horrible outcome of that misguided antagonism to the logic of late capitalism and its world market. In this sense, bin Laden's most substantial political achievement has been to cripple a nascent left opposition in the West. The rush to dissociate ourselves from terrorism, however, should not mean abandoning the fundamental theoretical critique of globalization. Rather, it should now include a critique of that very ethical politics that the pseudo-Islamic side of the bin Laden movement so ostentatiously deployed. Politics is not ethics: a proposition that does not mean that it is amoral and nonethical (rather, it is collective and beyond matters of individual ethics), but is, on the contrary, designed to explain why political extremism can so often be found to be motivated by categories of ethical purity.

Poor Stockhausen, who in the paroxysms of a Bataille-like death frenzy, saluted the World Trade towers' destruction as the greatest aesthetic gesture of the twentieth century, thereby at once becoming a pariah. Stockhausen was, however, not wrong to insist on the essentially aesthetic nature of the act, which was not truly political in any sense. His outburst suggests that we also need to augment the ethical critique, as well as the standard strategic account, of the terrorist act—that it is a desperate attempt to address and even to expropriate the media—with this other aesthetic and image-society-oriented dimension.

As for *terrorism*—a loaded and ambiguous term if there ever was one

—its prehistory—propaganda by the deed—lies in the failures of late-nineteenth-century anarchism, as well as in the "successes" of 1960s activism, whose program called for efforts to force the state to disclose its true repressive and "fascist" nature (the second part of the program, however, the mass uprising of the people against this fascist state, hung fire).

This has been, indeed, precisely the dialectical success of bin Laden's operation as well: to motivate and generate an immense remilitarization of the state and its surveillance capabilities all over the world, and to unleash new and deadly interventions abroad, which are equally likely to motivate and to fuel new forms of mass hatred and anti-Western resistance.

Yet in this dialectic, in which each term of the opposition reinforces the other one, there does not have to come a moment of synthesis. Marx himself spoke of the way in which world-historical conflicts end "either in a revolutionary reconstitution of society at large, or in the common ruin of the contending classes." It is the prospect of that common ruin which must now fill us with foreboding.

JOHN MILBANK

Sovereignty, Empire, Capital, and Terror

Concerning the immediate aftermath of the events of September 11, the initial question one should ask is exactly why there was outrage on such a gigantic scale? After all, however unusual and shocking this event may have been, people are killed in large numbers all the time, by terror, politics, and economic oppression. Within a matter of days after the attack on the World Trade Center, the United States already may have killed more people in response to the attacks than died in them, through increased and tightened sanctions in the Near East which bring pressure on governments through the deliberate terrorization of civilian populations. So why this unprecedented outrage? There may be two answers here.

The first answer is the threat to sovereign power that is involved. It is, after all, sovereign power that is supposed to have the right over life and death, whether in Islam or in the West. The sovereign state can execute people. It can pass laws that increase the lives of some and decrease the lives of others. It can fight wars. It can impose sanctions that kill. Individuals who take upon themselves this right of life and death are considered to be criminals. But to kill on this scale throws everything into confusion. Is this a crime? No, it seems, because killing on this scale is something only the state is supposed to be capable of. Is it then an act of war? Well, if so, then is it a different kind of war, because only sovereign states can wage war. It actually seems to be worse than normal war waged by a state, because it is a threat to the very idea of the state itself, and so to sovereignty itself.

One must here ignore the pieties about the dreadfulness of terrorism. The West and Israel itself engage in or covertly support many acts of terror all over the globe, and indeed terrorism has only arisen as a tactic of minority resistance in imitation of the new late-nineteenth- and twentieth-century deployment of unabashed physical and psychological terror against civilians as a primary instrument of war in contradiction to all traditional Christian teaching and even practice, up to a certain point. (These horrific new tactics were arguably first taken up during the American Civil War.) The terrorism that is seen here as being uniquely evil is the terrorism that assumes a power that is supposed to belong to states alone. I am not at all saying that the people who blew up the World Trade Center buildings were anarchists. No, they were perhaps indeed Islamic totalitarians who wished to establish something like an Islamic International (this applies to Al Qaeda; whereas the Egyptian Hamas organization aspires to Islamic nation-statehood). But their *mode of action* threatens the very idea of the state. So that is my first answer.

But answer two is that there was a hidden glee in the official outrage on the part at least of some, though certainly not of others. The attack seemed to give an opportunity to do things that some factions in the West have wanted for a long time. What are these things? An assault on so-called rogue states; a continuous war against "terrorists" everywhere; a policing of world markets to ensure that free-market exchange processes are not exploited by the enemies of capitalism. But, above all, the attack provided an opportunity to reinscribe state sovereignty.

The modern secular state rests on no substantive values. It lacks full legitimacy even of the sort that Saint Paul ascribed to the "powers that be," because it exists mainly to uphold the market system, which is an ordering of a substantively anarchic (and therefore not divinely appointed in Saint Paul's sense) competition between wills to power —the idol of "liberty," which we are supposed to worship. This liberty is dubious, since it is impossible to choose at all unless one is swayed one way or another by an influence: hence a supposedly "pure" free choice will only be a cover for the operation of hidden and uniform influences. People who fondly imagine themselves the subjects of their "own" choices entirely will, in reality, be the most manipulated subjects and the most incapable of being influenced by goodness and beauty. This is why, in the affluent Anglo-Saxon West today, there is so much pervasively monotonous ugliness and tawdriness that belies its wealth, as well as why there are so many people adopting (literally) the sing-song accent of self-righteous complacency and vacuous uniformity, with its rising lilt of a feigned questioning at the end of every phrase. This intonation implies that any overassertion is an impolite infringement on the freedom of the other, and yet at the same time its merely rhetorical interrogation suggests that the personal preference it conveys is unchallengeable, since it belongs within the total set of formally correct exchange transactions. Pure liberty is pure power— whose other name is evil.

The nation-state itself creams off and piles up this pure power in the name of a people. Every modern state therefore is inherently semiracist because it proclaims the supreme interest of a discrete populace, defined by legacy as well as territory. This semiracist holding together of a people requires an exterior—a potential enemy. As Carl Schmitt argued, the occasional emergency of war is crucial for the (one must add, modern) state's legitimacy. But globalization puts the modern state into crisis. There is now the prospect of no more exterior, no more real foes. Sovereign power is consequently threatened. If it remains merely domestic, it will wither away in the face of multiple loyalties. If it exports itself and drives toward the global state, then it still needs an enemy who is other. Without an external enemy, the enemy must now be internal, lurking everywhere. Without the possibility of the occasional emergency of war, there must be perpetual war against an internal danger. As Jean Baudrillard has said, globalization inevitably evokes its own shadow: the irruptive challenge of suppressed singularity, which when all other resources are lost to it, can still make the symbolic gesture of sacrificial death (suicidal self-sacrifice or the sacrificial murder of others; the two being often combined, as on September 11).[1] A monotonous totality both requires this opposition and tends to provoke its unexpected instance.

Because of its history of expanding frontiers—its internal wars against native Americans, African Americans, British loyalists, Spaniards in the South and West, the dissenting Confederate states, southern and Central America, dealers in alcohol and drugs, and Communists in the 1950s, the United States has in a sense been long preparing for this new sort of global conflict. As Michael Hardt and Antonio Negri have argued in their *Empire*, American neo-Roman imperialism works by a constant subsumption and inclusion of "others," such that difference is apparently welcomed, yet actually subordinated to an unremitting uniformity. This subsumption coincides with an obliteration of the older distinction between colonies as the extracapitalist sources of "primary accumulation" and the fully capitalized home markets. Now all comes to be within the unrestricted one world market.

This contrasts with older European imperialism, which held the other at a subordinated distance, permitting its otherness, even while subordinating it for the sake of an exploitation of natural and human resources. And one should I think add to Hardt and Negri that, in the case of Britain and France, there were also many utopian imperialist schemes that went beyond even this subordination and tended to deploy the peripheries and "savage" to mock the center and "civilized" (see for example Rider Haggard's *King Solomon's Mines*). Such nuances are often overlooked in pseudo-left-wing American "postcolonial" discourses, which actually assist the ideology of the American Right by implying the original "innocence" of the United States as a once-colonized nation, and it's natural solidarity with all the colonized. (The frequent simplifications concerning Ireland, and the downgrading of the Anglo-Saxon as opposed to the Celtic contributions to the history of liberty—both are real—fall within this paradigm.)

These implications tend to conceal the fact that American neocolonialism is yet more insidious than the older variety. It does not attend to cultural difference (like, for example, the British law code for India, assisted by the historicist and comparativist work of Henry Maine); it pursues no substantive goals of the political and social good (however deluded the ones of old empire may often have been) and seeks instead both for pure economic exploitation and for the absolute imposition of American signifiers. Under French and British colonial law child labor was banned; now within the "American Empire," but of course with total European connivance, it is everywhere rife. One can also note here that where British imperialism *was* purely economic, it tended also to be more corrupt and oppressive, as in the case of China and the opium trade (see Kazuo Ishiguro's novel *When We Were Orphans*), or the ruthless policy of divide and rule pursued in the Near East, which the United States and the UK now perpetuate.

While Hardt and Negri concede that neoempire in certain ways outdoes old empire in vileness, they still subscribe to a dialectical myth that renders this more nakedly capitalist phase of empire somehow a necessary staging post on the way to socialist utopia. Surely we need instead more sober reflections on the temporary need for some sort of more benignly parentalist assistance for the South from the North? So much of the South is devastated in its internal resources and in any case so bound up with the North that only global solutions enabled by a West newly committed to global equality will be viable. Tony Blair at times appears to have such a vision: unfortunately these times are utterly vitiated by his continuing devotion to the untrammeled market.

Instead, any enactment of this vision would require a withdrawal by the North from its unqualifiedly capitalist commitments. But what we now see is the very opposite: a fearful extension of American Republican Imperialism, in terms of a logic that is impeccably Machiavellian. The unity of the republic, snatched by fate out of time for the sake of its own negative freedom (and the negative freedom of its citizens insofar as this is maintained through their absolute submission to the republic) can only be secured through constant reunification in the face of a threat to this freedom. Given that the republic is isolationist and has no interest other than its own freedom, it is not able to mediate with the other, even in an old-European hierarchical fashion. Instead, it can only withstand by subsuming, by expanding at least its frontiers of cultural reach. Commentators who have tended to think that Bush was jolted out of isolationism by the catastrophe miss the point that isolation and hysterical expansion are two halves of the American Republican dialectic.

Moreover, the American sense that what is isolated and expanded is unquestionably the *acme* of human political achievement, frozen forever in an ideal constitution, disallows the self-denying ordinances, the sense of temporariness, of passing expediency, and of fearful desire to avoid *hubris* that is expressed, for example, in Kipling's poem "Recessional." American imperialism never supposes that the Captains and the Kings must one day depart.

This is why, in an emergency that tends to release the unspoken truth, there has been so much apparently insane language concerning "infinite" processes: an infinite war, infinite justice, infinite retribution—sustained in George Bush's terrifying address to Congress. There he declared, for the first time perhaps since Hitler's announcement of the Third Reich, a kind of state of perpetual emergency. He announced a new sort of war without aims or a foreseeable end, often to be fought in secret. Those not with the United States and Britain in the war were declared to be against them and allied with terrorists. This is potentially a license for totalitarianism, and already, for the sake of fighting a vague conflict explicitly projected to last almost forever, it has become unquestionable that basic legal procedures and respect for people's privacy should be suspended.

The existence of a state of emergency was witnessed in the statement by Donald Rumsfeld (about which many of his colleagues exhibited understandable unease) that non-Afghan Taliban should be "*either* killed or taken prisoner.*"* This was more or less a license to the Northern Alliance to kill these people like dogs, on the very dubious assumption that they were somehow implicated in the attack on the Twin Towers. Of course even if they had been, the proper response would be to arrest and try them; yet implicit in Rumsfeld's statement was an exceptional suspension of all normal legality: *both* the norms of criminal legality *and* the norms of military legality. Because one is dealing with a threat to sovereignty as such, law as such no longer applies, since the merely formal, decisionistic basis of law in a state that exists mainly to undergird the market cannot appeal to a natural equity beyond itself. Without the state, there is, for the modern outlook, no good and evil, and therefore against the enemies of the state, neither morality nor law applies. They are neither warriors for another power (or an internal counterpolitics), whom one must respect as individuals, nor transgressors of the law whom one must respect as malefactors deserving punishment and the instigation of repentance.

No, they have sunk beneath humanity, as Dick Cheney later confirmed. Captured "terrorists" he declared "don't deserve to be treated as criminals. They don't deserve the same guarantees and safeguards that would be used for an American citizen going through the normal judicial process." This exclusionary logic has been impeccably realized in the confinement of Al Qaeda suspects in animal cages exposed to the elements off Cuba. This stark denial of the *imago dei* for "terrorist suspects" tends to expose the concealed racist basis of the usual talk of "human rights." This "universal" notion was originally invoked by the West in order to intervene in the internal affairs of nonwhite countries, from Turkey in the case of the Armenian massacre, onward. But as soon as the white West is threatened, it becomes clear that rights are things that archetypally belong to "American citizens" under "normal," which means local and not at all universal, circumstances. This is all a very far cry from Harry Truman in 1945, who insisted, against Churchill's unreflecting proposal to shoot the Nazis in a corner, that "this would not sit easily on the American conscience."

The suspension of all norms of legality is further confirmed by the stipulation that future secret executions of those covertly convicted of terrorism can be watched by the relatives of victims of September 11. Here one is confronted with the purest barbarism: in the past, or in the Islamic present, public executions possess at least the primitive rationale of visible justice and warning, while unwitnessed modern execution exposes a certain proper shame and hesitancy on the part of the state, but *selectively* witnessed executions obliterate the line between punishment and vengeance, since all that matters here is the death of the other power threatening "domestic" power and lives. How is one to interpret this as anything other than a kind of sop to a mass psychopathology?

Such emergency measures are not really being proposed because of the unique character of terrorism, but rather because of the perception of a new threat to sovereignty and capital. Hence the new European anti-terrorist laws, which define as terroristic any actions intended "to destroy [European] political, economic or social structures" and include "the illicit capture of state or government installations, the means of public transport, infrastructures, public places," seem designed more to inhibit militants than to catch terrorists. As Alima Boumediene-Thiery put it in *Le Monde*, "Bin Laden and his friends aren't in the habit of walking about without papers with bombs in their pockets; nor of occupying *usines* and banks: they direct them."[2]

So one is confronted with an unspeakably bizarre turn of events whereby, in a matter of months, one single terroristic assault has led to the permanent suspension of ancient Anglo-Saxon liberties, including habeas corpus, in both Britain and the United States. How does this shockingly abrupt transformation relate to the idea of a war of civilizations, which has for some time been in the air?

Within the perspective of Samuel Huntington, who first spoke of this type of war, Islam has been seen as the other, outside the Western legacy and somewhat immune to Western post-Enlightenment values. However, Islam should be thought of as both other and yet not other.

Revived Islamic civilization is in some ways a challenge to the Western secular state, but it is also much more like a rival twin than we care to imagine. Recent scholarship is showing just how Islamic the West itself has been. When the University of Oxford was founded in the late twelfth century, some scholars there took over an essentially Islamic project for the experimental control of nature that was at first to do with optics and alchemy. The Cartesian turn to the subject, the idea of knowledge as detached representation of spatialized objects, the exposition of being as univocal, all have their long-term origin in, ironically, the Oriental thought of Avicenna (ibn Sina). To say, as many do, that Islam was only accidentally, and for a time, the bearer of a Mediterranean civilization to which it was essentially alien is quite untrue. Even though philosophy was less easily assimilated within Islam than in Christendom, Avicenna and other philosophers were still concerned with "prophetology," or the nature of inspiration, and this profoundly inflected their rendering of Aristotelian and Neoplatonic understandings of the soul. In this crucible, protomodern ideas concerning subjectivity were forged and then handed over to the West.

In the year 1277, the Christian West reached its crisis: certain drastic edicts issued by the archbishops of Paris and Canterbury meant that it decided more or less to outlaw the common Hellenistic legacy of Aristotle fused with Neoplatonism, and blended with allegorical readings of the Hebrew Bible, which it shared with Islam, Judaism, and Byzantium. A common culture of mystical philosophy and theology, focused around analogy and ontological participation—which has also tended to favor social participation—was rendered impossible. The West went in one direction and Islam in another, since Islam, too, inclined in this period to outlaw this perspective. Islam became a doctrinally orthodox, scriptural, and legalistic civilization to the exclusion of dialectics and mystical theology (apart from newly enhanced Sufistic tendencies).

The conventional view is that from that point forward, the West became secular and Islam became theocratic. But that seems to me to be a half-truth. In fact, by abandoning the shared mystical outlook, Western Christian theology started to look more and more itself like Islamic orthodoxy; it started to read the Bible more like the Qur'an, allowing only the literal meaning and construing that meaning more narrowly than it had. The new stress in the fourteenth century, that only God's will makes things true and right, echoed earlier Islamic *Kalam* theology and some of the ideas of Al-Ghazali. The West's attitude toward evil, with ironically the Cathars safely defeated, started to become more Manichean, again taking over the unfortunate Iranian contamination of Islam by the primordial Zoroastrian tradition. But, above all, in the political domain, the Islamic linking of the absolute will of the Caliph with the will of Allah, and with the right to fight holy wars, was taken over by Christian thought. As earlier in Islam, so now also in the West, a merely de facto grounding of state sovereignty in absolute right to do what it likes is linked to its mediation of the will of God. Thus the early Western nation-state started to fight holy wars within Christendom itself. Modern Islam and Christianity are not after all so dissimilar in certain ways.

What I am wanting to suggest here is that theocratic notions of sovereignty are not simply something archaic within Islam that stands over against our Western modernity. In many ways theocratic notions are specifically modern in their positivity and formality (as Carl Schmitt indicated). Bush in a crisis has appealed to the supposed divine destiny of America, and it is modern Judaism that has lapsed into a statist, Zionist form.

There is now a terrible symbiosis arising between Zionism and the American Protestant and un-Christian literalistic reading of the Old Testament in the Puritan tradition, which equates Anglo-Saxondom with Israel. Both ascribe to an idolatrously nontypological and non-eschatological reading of God's "free election of Israel," as if really and truly God's "oneness" meant that he arbitrarily prefers one lot of people to another (as opposed to working providentially for a time through one people's advanced insight—as Maimonides rightly understood Jewish election); and as if he really and truly appoints to them, not just for a period, but for all time, one piece of land to the exclusion of others. (Regina Schwartz's *The Curse of Cain*, which tries to distinguish true from idolatrous monotheism in the Hebrew Bible, is highly relevant here.) There is also an unfortunate tendency within contemporary theology to play down the Christian "going beyond the law," which incoherently and anachronistically seeks a kind of alignment with post-Biblical Rabbinic law, as if this somehow had obviously more status for Christianity than Islamic law (even if we may well often find the former to be nearer to Christian charity).

Meanwhile, the Islamic Wahhabi, to whom bin Laden and the Al

Qaeda belong, are themselves in some ways very modern. They are opposed to all iconic images, all auratic manifestations of religion; they
are urban, middle-class, fanatically puritanical. They are prepared to
compromise the Islamic tradition insofar as it stands firmly against
usury. And they are thoroughly in love with technology. Bin Laden
in the desert with his gun is surely an American antihero: perhaps a
sectarian first cousin to Joseph Smith. For it is not an accident that
the Mormons—that archetypical American sect, according to Harold
Bloom—express such explicit kinship with Islam.

But of course the West and Islam have construed the legacy of theocratic sovereignty in very different ways. The West has invented a secular sphere that is neutral and unmystical: the sphere of a pure balance of power whose control is still nevertheless, in the last analysis,
divinely sanctioned. Strict Islam knows only an expression of sovereignty through sacred laws. One may not much care for either variant.
But on what basis can one decide that an Islamic sacral state, especially
if it took a more sophisticated form than that envisaged by the Taliban, is not permissible? In reality our apparent concern for women
and others persecuted by these unpleasant people is fantastically hypocritical: as recently as 1998 the Californian oil giant UNOCAL, with the
backing of the United States, was trying to enlist Taliban support in
building an oil pipeline through Afghanistan from the former Soviet
territories to the north. Meanwhile, the manifestations of *asharia* law
in Saudi Arabia have not appeared troublesome to Western economic
interests.

The only possible basis for refusing the legitimacy of an Islamic state
would be if Islamic men, and especially Islamic women, themselves decided that they no longer wanted such a thing. This decision would
amount though to a new construal of Islam, and a redefinition of Islamic community apart from the sanction of coercive law. Islam would
then have to proceed in a more Sufistic direction. It is certainly not in
principle up to the West to decide, but I do not think that the West
as it is presently constituted can tolerate this forbearance and all its
implications.

Yet properly speaking, this is a debate that Islam should be able to
conduct with itself without external impediment. Such a debate could
even help us in the West to realize that genuine religious pluralism and
tolerance means far more than merely respecting the private beliefs of

the individual. Communities also are collective realities that we should respect, within certain bounds of discrimination.

A perpetual war against terrorism can be seen as an effort to resolve the crisis of state sovereignty in the face of globalization. Since in a real sense both the Western and the different Islamic state forms face the same crisis, one can go further and say that both terrorism and counterterrorism, which will quickly become commingled and indistinguishable, are attempts to resolve this crisis. To see globalization on one side and anti-globalization on the other (as Baudrillard perhaps tends to do) is too simple.

But there is also another aspect to the crisis of globalization—the economic rather than political. The West, especially the United States, has expanded its economic hegemony since the end of the cold war. Once there was no longer any need to pander to third world regimes in order to counter Soviet influence, the United States, mostly supported by Europe, proceeded to set up economic structures that operated entirely in its own interests, with the result that global inequality has vastly increased as well as environmental damage, which is sometimes the direct result of U.S. intervention, as in Columbia at the present moment. These structures have included the liberalization of markets and the removal of all inhibitions on stock exchange speculation, as well as the scandalous patenting of genetically altered (and thereby probably contaminated) crops allied to the outlawing of the natural varieties produced, particularly in South America.

But now these hegemonic economic structures show signs of impending implosion: supply has been outrunning demand; computer technology has been overinvested; Western interests in older manufacturing have been possibly rashly sold off; and domestic shares and economically crucial information has gotten into the hands of people who are potential enemies. The United States and Europe are consequently faced with a need to implement more internal regulation—but also with the specter of having already let things slip beyond their control. We seem to have reached the moment in history prophesied by Franz Steiner in his essay "On the Civilising Process," when so many forces of danger have been unleashed in a "civilised" society without taboos, that these dangers must be relentlessly policed. Steiner conjectured that this would simply drive the dangers "inwards," so that as humans become more and more subject to terroristic counterterror, the more they will all tend to become pathological, potentially terror-istic subjectivities.

The assumption prior to this new turn has been that the market and freedom simply line up with Western dominance. Now, however, we are beginning to see how a small number of hostile, politically moti-vated investors can reap devastating effects. September 11 was a kind of chiasmus—a crossing over and reversal. During the 1990s, West-ern power became more and more abstracted and virtual in charac-ter: dominating the pathetically real and material lives of people in the South. Now suddenly the West was reduced to the Paleolithic. We saw that the abstract was still partly stored in two fragile standing totems with less resilience even than neolithic standing stones. This still-fixed capital was simply knocked over. But meanwhile, in the face of the failure of Western information to stop this catastrophe, the terrorists, whoever they are, were manipulating information in order to seize the maximum abstract advantage.

Given the sheer convenience of war and military emergency to forces wishing to resolve the twin crises of Western sovereignty and West-ern capitalism, one has to ask to what extent these forces were, sub-consciously or consciously, urging war before September 11? The cur-rent war is a war against terrorism we are told, which has suddenly become a global and immediate threat, though we were not generally told this before the catastrophe. And in fact there is much evidence that global terrorism has been recently in decline rather than to the contrary. Therefore there is every reason to suspect that this war is not simply a war against terrorism, but is also a war against multiple targets, designed to ensure the continued legitimacy of the American state and the global perpetuation of the neocapitalist revolution of the 1980s.

Ever since January 2001 at the very least, crisis has surely been in the air. Bush withdrew from international agreements on ecology, weap-onry, debt, and the pursuit of justice—most ironically of all he refused to acknowledge that any American could ever be a war criminal, thereby undercutting the legitimacy of international juridical proce-dures against someone like bin Laden. Meanwhile Communism in the East had been reemerging, anticapitalism was reasserting itself in Western Europe and under the banner of antiglobalization it was start-ing to coalesce with resistance movements in the South. Right along the Atlantic seaboard from Britain to Portugal a growing irritation with America in the face of economically disastrous flooding probably linked with global warming was evident, but was scarcely reported in the United States at all. Anti-Americanism in France and Italy was increasing at an alarming rate. In Great Britain the conservative party faced possible extinction and public opinion, moving to the left of Tony Blair, now favored action to reduce drastically corporate greed.

More seriously still, the socialist president of Venezuela (and friend of Fidel Castro), Hugo Chavez, had been flexing considerable political muscle in the face of the general failure of neoliberal regimes in his subcontinent. In the face of American and European opposition, he had encouraged the OPEC countries to sustain a middling level of oil prices where market demand would have forced a drop. This, obviously, had implications for Middle Eastern politics and for the U.S. hegemony in that region. For some time now, reliance even on Saudi oil had become dubious.

Suddenly then, American and capitalist hegemony looked surprisingly fragile—although of course this should not be exaggerated. But it must have appeared fragile enough to powerful right-wing think tanks, who are in any case prone to apocalyptic scenarios: a frightening possible convergence of a protesting South America, Islamic nations rich in oil, revivified communism, and a Europe more wobbly and more prone to anti-U.S. sentiment than at any time since World War II.

Finally, the United States was and is itself a potentially unstable polity. Cultural and political shifts in South America would have ripple effects among Latino populations in the United States; low election turnout reveals a vastly indifferent and often alienated population; an eighteenth-century constitution produces constant stasis and deadlock that cannot deliver normal modern state infrastructures and welfare provisions that form a buffer against dangerous discontents of the underprivileged; the cultural gap between coastal and middle America could erupt into something serious; edgy rival oligarchies do not trust democracy to deliver security, but believe they have to manipulate the outcome of elections (as occurred in November 2000). In the face of this potential hydra, it is clear that the U.S. establishment and the Bush administration were deeply divided and inconsistent. Pure isolationism had been one response, yet it was clear to many that this is a very risky course. Those advocating a more aggressive and interventionist strategy on the assumption that American supreme power must never be challenged (a doctrine initiated by Madeleine Albright: the Democratic Party is as guilty as anyone else in all this) were delivered, by good fortune or otherwise, a supreme present on September 11.

Not only could national security henceforward override democracy without question, but the immediate threat of terror for the moment pulled Europe, Russia, South America, moderate Arab States, and China in line behind the United States. They have been enlisted with varying degrees of enthusiasm and begrudgingness behind a military action that will assault all those who resist the sway of the global market, as well as behind police deployments to ensure that the market and flow of information are not themselves used against the market and against this flow. In addition, a new unity of Americans, rich and poor, behind a resurrected patriotism, has been put into place. The fractures lurking ever since November 2000 are for the moment sealed, although any manifest failure of "the war" might cause them to appear again with a vengeance.

At the very center of this strange and multiple conflict stands oil. Detailed and objective analyses by *Le Monde* and many other reliable sources show that what is currently being played out in Afghanistan is not a war against terrorism nor a response to the attack on the Twin Towers, but *le nouveau grand jeu de Kipling*. Multiple interests are trying to seize control of one of the largest pools of natural resources in the world in the former Soviet and largely Islamic territories to the north. There is also an attempt by the gulf states to reestablish the ancient silk route to China, which would link these states all the way to Islamic Chinese communities; an attempt that the West is clearly anxious to resist. Perhaps this is partly why even Iran has now been declared by Bush to be a problem state, even though this statement has immediately led to a resurgence of conservative Islamic elements in its government. Hence the economico-political stakes are enormous and also deeply confused. I have already mentioned that the United States initially sought to cooperate with the Taliban in building oil pipelines. But they proved to be far too unreliable, especially after the 1998 bombings in Kenya and Tanzania.

It has become instead imperative for the United States to lay oil and gas pipelines through a more manipulable Afghanistan, and one can note that Iran would provide a far more direct route. In the face of a rebellious OPEC, the United States badly needs a new pool of tame oil suppliers besides the increasingly edgy Saudis. At the same time this new North-South resource route will cut through the middle of the potential Islamic East-West trade and political axis. The new Afghan wedge that is being established involves also a new cooperation between the United States and Russia: the naive British were surprised to discover after the retaking of Kabul that they were not much welcome; and Russian forces were creeping back in. The trade-off for the Russians is, of course, license to pursue their own brutal policies in Chechnya; just as the trade-off for India is a stepping-up of its quarrel with Pakistan.

Oil, therefore, is the clear focus of a crisis that has wider political and economic dimensions of the kind that I have described. As long ago as December 2000, experts in the United States were suggesting that an American-Russian action against bin Laden and the Taliban in Afghanistan was being planned. "The war" is therefore not simply in response to September 11, which may even have been a preemptive strike by some Islamic forces. There are also unanswered questions about the somewhat implausible tardiness of the U.S. reaction to the terror strike at every level.

However, one does not need to suppose any sort of conspiracy theory for my main theses to stand, even if this cannot as yet be entirely ruled out. Reactions to September 11 in the U.S. government were admittedly various and variously motivated. Even George Bush kept on changing his tune as to whether a police or a military response was the more appropriate. However, one does have to ask why so universally and immediately the attack was compared to Pearl Harbor, when, after all, it was only a terrorist attack, albeit of an unprecedented appalling kind. One man destroying New York with a nuclear bomb would still be a criminal and not a warrior, and one treats all warriors with more respect than criminals. Usually one avoids seeing terrorists as engaged in war, because that is just how they want to be seen and starting a war is generally their aim. In the annals of terrorism, Al Qaeda has now been uniquely successful: the West has played their game at every turn. For as Baudrillard says, they aim to pose against the regime of formal exchange and technological war without losses, the symbolic capital of death for a singular and substantive cause, gambling on the likelihood that, pushed to the limit of questioning, the West must still trade in the capital of death if it is to legitimate itself, which has indeed proved to be the case. Yet, as Baudrillard further contends, the West tends to lose in this exchange: the extermination of innocents with zero loss of combatants on a somewhat arbitrarily chosen stage (Afghanistan) cannot really outweigh the suicidal targeting of a supremely significant site. For this reason it must inevitably foster many more potentially self-sacrificial terrorists in the future, and in this way the West is itself sucked down a suicidal path, and led away from formal equilibrium.

Thus, while indeed in one respect "the war" is not simply to do with September 11 and is commanded by the West's pursuit of its own economic interests, in another respect its specific mode has been dictated by the need to react symbolically and cathartically in the face of public outrage, and in this respect the terrorists have truly dictated the pace and character of recent events. A balanced analysis must do justice to both the economic and the symbolic aspects, and try to comprehend just how they interact.

In neither aspect, however, is one really talking about the tracking down of evildoers, as we have been led to believe. Supposedly "the war" in Afghanistan was pursued against bin Laden, and yet it doesn't seem likely that if he were ever caught he would be treated in accord with the Geneva Convention. If terrorism were *really* the issue, then much the safer thing would be to stick to the discourse of crime and the practice of regular policing and due juridical process. Anything else, as the bitter experience of the French and British shows, only tends to increase the support of terrorist groups and legitimate their operations. The ethical evil of terrorism is that, more than certain modes of conventional warfare, it directly instrumentalizes human life. But as Kenneth Surin and Rowan Williams, the Anglican Archbishop of Canterbury, have pointed out, this means that any response that tends to do the same thing is uniquely ineffective: in losing the ethical high ground, it *also* tends to lose the strategic high ground.[3] This has already happened to America, who has now bombed and killed innocent villagers supposed to be "harboring" terrorists (the results could not be seen on American television); who, together with Britain, has bombed a prisoner of war camp at Qala-i-Jhangi fortress from the air; who has caused all the major aid agencies to flee Afghanistan for the duration of the conflict, and who has delayed the arrival of humanitarian aid even after the fall of Kabul—thereby cumulatively causing thousands of innocent deaths. Even were those who say that only "massive force" stops terrorism (and they are unlikely to be proved right in the long term because of the delayed "blowback" phenomenon), the implication would be that only a permanently terroristic state can stop terrorism—once again wiping out all moral distinctions between the respective parties. Baudrillard rightly points out that this leveling effect between crime and punishment is vastly reinforced by the power of filmed images (when they are available), which tend to convey violence and its results rather than the reasons for violence. In this way they assist the human propensity to sustain a spiral of revenge.

The use of cluster bombs, of heavy bombers where there were no hard targets, and the attack on unquestionably non-Taliban places like the village of Gardez show that one is not even speaking about "collateral damage" here. Most crucial of all has been, not capturing bin Laden, nor even overthrowing the Taliban, but rather exhibiting a show of terror intended to cow the entire region for the foreseeable future and bend it and parallel terrains to the Western will. From the war against Spain to capture the Philippines, through Hiroshima and Vietnam and the Gulf conflict (where bombing has secretly continued), the United States has deployed the terrorizing and murder of civilians (five million dead in the Vietnam conflict in the whole of Southeast Asia), the massacre of disempowered individual combatants, and the use of poisonous or torturing weapons (condemned ever since antiquity by civilized nations) as a primary instrument of military and political policy. Cumulatively, this reveals the relatively genocidal tendency of specifically Republican imperialism (commencing domestically with the treatment of native Americans—who, in Virginia at least, had been significantly chary about the original break with Britain), and it amounts to an atrocity almost on a level with the Holocaust and the Gulags—raising the suspicion that U.S. and indeed European domestic democracy is a kind of harmless theatrical indulgence for the globally privileged. And this circumstance reveals to us that the trouble is not "totalitarianism" pure and simple, but the emptiness of the secular as such, and its consequent disguised sacralization of violence. There is a desperate need for the United States to reach behind its current Machiavellian, Hobbesian, and Lockean norms for its deeper and more truly radical legacy of Christian (and at times Jewish) associative agrarian and civic Republicanism, which has truly to do with just distribution and the inculcation of social virtue. Among much of the American populace, the spirit of this legacy is still extraordinarily and creatively alive, as anyone who has lived in the United States can testify. Yet it is today rarely able to achieve any conscious political articulation.

But if we have, in the case of America's latest imperialist war, renewed instances of unjust *jus in bello*, is there not surely a just *jus ad bellum*? Well, the oft-used analogy here with medieval wars against pirates is not really right. Pirates in the Middle Ages were in many cases treated like criminals, in a period in which war itself was seen as a kind of police action—at least justified war. And because pirates were mostly afloat, they were a kind of isolatable antistate in any case. Terrorists, by contrast, live like criminals in the pores of society, and cannot readily be reached by military means. There cannot be a just war against terrorists, because they are neither a sovereign state, nor do they necessarily represent a true rebel cause that will justify talking about civil war in some sense. Thus it is not surprising that, as the fairly conservative politician Wayland Kennet pointed out in Britain, there was only a "rhetorical declaration of war" in Afghanistan, rendering it an illegal conflict from the point of view of international law.

Were this a war against terrorists it would not be a just one, primarily because it would be a lunatically "disproportionate" action. A case against Al Qaeda should have been brought before the International Court in the Hague, which could have sponsored many effective means to reduce their influence. In any case, not the perpetrators (still at large after thousands of deaths and the sowing of the seeds of untold future misery and future terroristic movements) but a sovereign state—which was ready to hand over the supposed perpetrators, and with whom the British Foreign Office recommended a deal— have been attacked. As I have already said, the idea that Britain or the United States cares about the iniquities of the Taliban is ludicrous: they helped to create them; they are happy to tolerate the convenient Islamic atrocities of the Saudis; and having totally failed to carry out their own ground war, they were ready to let the Taliban be displaced by the equally obnoxious Northern Alliance.

One must assume that the powers that be are cynically aware of all this. So one must also assume that the war against terrorism is a cover for other operations and purposes of the kind that I have described, as well as being an unpremeditated symbolic response to an overwhelmingly symbolic event. Indeed, as Rowan Williams points out, since terrorism is a now permanently possible form of behavior, the idea of a "war" against it is as absurd as the idea of a "war on drugs."[4]

Unfortunately, the chance for the Western state and the Western market to ensure its continued hegemony in the face of dire symbolic and real threats is also the chance of specifically modern Islamic fanaticism. Bin Laden's following among those who in other circumstances would deplore him has probably been vastly increased by the recent actions of the West and Israel.

A war against a civilization cannot be won. And Islam could prove to be more united, less decadent, and more resilient than we imagine. Prophecy is perilous, but we may have reached the point where the only way out of a catastrophe that could potentially destroy the West is to abandon our global idolatrous worship of sacralized absolute sovereignty, and the formally neutral market, with their empty pursuit of power, in West and East alike.

Both empty secular power and arbitrary theocratic power, in their secret complicity, show us no way forward. Neither enlightenment nor "fundamentalism" can assist us in our new plight. Instead we need to consider again the Biblical and Platonico-Aristotelian metaphysical legacy common to Christianity, Judaism, and Islam. We should ponder ways in which this legacy may provide us with a certain area of common vision and practice, while at the same time respecting social and cultural spaces for exercised difference.

Such a common vision would eschew all idolizations of formal power, whether in the case of individual "rights" or of absolute state sovereignty. Instead it would trust that human wisdom can intimate, imperfectly but truly, something of an eternal order of justice: the divine *rapports* of Malebranche and Cudworth. A shared overarching global polity would embody this intimation in continuously revisable structures dedicated to promoting the common good insofar as this can be agreed upon. It would also embody this imperfection through the maximum possible dispersal and deflection of human power.

Perhaps then the noble and at times heroic perpetuation of the local and embedded also could be a proffered gift to the whole globe, which would reciprocate with a measured influence and support, instead of an obliterating equivalence. Perhaps then we would cease to sacrifice the substantively particular to the generally vacuous, ensuring that there was no need for the particular to incite in response the suicidal sacrifice of everything, forever.

NOTES

1 Jean Baudrillard, "L'Esprit du Terrorisme," trans. Donovan Hohn, *Harper's*, February 2002, 13–18 (reprinted in this volume on pages 149–61).
2 Alima Boumediene-Thiery, Alain Krivine, and Giuseppe di Lello Finuoli, "Europe: vers l'état d'exception?" *Le Monde*, November 29, 2001.
3 Kenneth Surin, "September 11th and the Ethics of Violence," in *Strike Terror No More*, ed. Jon L. Berquist (St. Louis: Chalice Press, 2002); Rowan Williams, *Writing in the Dust: After September 11* (Grand Rapids, Mich.: Eerdmans, 2002).
4 Williams, *Writing in the Dust*, 37.

VINCENT J. CORNELL

A Muslim to Muslims

Reflections after September 11

Oddly, my first thought is of what a Moroccan scholar of Fez once said about a Berber tribe that used to raid the city's fields and orchards: "They are not the Beni Mtir; they are the Flying Catastrophe!"[1] Despite all of our arguments to the contrary, Samuel Huntington appears to be right. His "Clash of Civilizations" has become the first war of the twenty-first century.[2] And the name of the Flying Catastrophe is Islam.

Seven months later, events in Palestine and Israel remind us that this is supposed to be where it all began. CNN, Fox, and Al-Jazeera remind us of the Fifty-Four-Year Catastrophe that never ends. Broken hopes and shattered dreams of friendship between Muslims and Jews lie dead in the rubble of Palestine. Israeli tanks crush cars and houses in Nablus, Bethlehem, and Jenin. Thousands are homeless in Jenin alone. The heavy hand of collective punishment follows the brutal but ultimately impotent logic of revenge. Palestinian despair and anger confront Israeli guilt and fear. The only winners are the extremists. Hamas activists and Jewish Settlers dance *dabkas* and *horas* of self-righteous bigotry, believing that God is on their side. The Palestinian population bomb is made flesh through murderous acts of self-immolation. If we go down in flames, we'll take the whole world with us. Is this the beginning of the end? Said the Prophet Muhammad, "Islam came as a stranger, and it will be a stranger once again." The same can be said of the religions of Moses and Jesus.

Two important fallacies of September 11, 2001, are directly related to April 11, 2002. Arab and Muslim political activists tell us that American support for Israel created the hatred that led to the attack on the Twin Towers. Talking heads from the Israeli government tell us that America has finally tasted the terrorism that Israelis have long experienced. Accepting these arguments means accepting counterfeit coin for legal tender. The Sufi poet Jalal al-Din Rumi said that counterfeit coin could never be taken for real coin if there weren't real gold in it. There is indeed great and well-founded frustration and anger throughout the Muslim world because of America's unequivocal support for Israel's policies. This is especially true today, as the Israeli army invades the Palestinian territories and destroys the Palestinian Authority, conveniently cloaking their assault in Bush's "war on terrorism" rhetoric. It is also true that Israelis have lived in a constant state of war since the founding of their nation in 1948. This has engendered a fortress mentality that influences much of Israeli policy. The false coin can be found in the theories of causality and definitional equations bandied about by each side. Support for Israel, we are told, leads to Islamic hatred. All forms of terrorism are supposed to be alike. What the public really needs to know is what is not said in the media. PLO apologists do not tell us that Palestinian extremists have no intention of accepting the legitimacy of either Israel or the Palestinian Authority. Israeli apologists do not tell us that Israeli extremists want every Arab out of Palestine. Neither do they tell us that some of these extremists are in the present Israeli government. For the past eighteen months, every step that has been taken for peace has been countered by an atrocity on the Palestinian side or a provocation—and now an atrocity—on the Israeli side. Extremists on both sides want to disrupt the peace process. In 1993, I spoke with Ramadan Abdallah, just before he became the head of Islamic Jihad for the Liberation of Palestine. He made no pretense at hiding his contempt for Yāsir Arafat, both personally and politically. It doesn't take a Middle East expert to understand that the only way to power for Islamic Jihad is over the ruins of Arafat's Palestinian Authority. Everything that weakens Arafat strengthens Islamic Jihad. Peace is the end of their dreams. Chaos is their means to power. Power over Palestine is just a way station in the master plan to create an Islamic state in Palestine and Israel. Ironically, the closest ally of Islamic extremists has been Ariel Sharon. The feud between Sharon and Arafat has devastated the Israeli and Palestinian peace movements and has left the field to the extremists. The invasion of Lebanon in 1982 and the invasion of Palestine in 2002 are the work of the same person. Sharon will be no more successful in ensuring Israel's security today than he was then. Yitzhak Rabin was willing to take risks for peace. He knew not to respond in kind to the extremists' attempts to disrupt the peace process. While Rabin was alive, those who desired peace had hope. The extremists were on the decline. Then a Jewish extremist assassinated him. Two assassinations stand out in the twentieth century for opening the door to seemingly endless chaos and despair: at the beginning of the century, the assassination of Austrian Archduke Franz Ferdinand in Sarajevo; at the end of the century, the assassination of Israeli Prime Minister Yitzhak Rabin. Justice for Palestine depends on the realization that Rabin was killed, not by a Muslim or a Palestinian, but by a Jew.

For Muslims, the greatest mistake would be to believe that September 11 was about Israel and Palestine. Extremists on both sides feed on America's moral and eschatological obsession with the Holy Land. Both sides exploit the memory of the Crusades. Christian fundamentalists, dreaming of the Second Coming, echo the call to arms of Pope Urban II, conveniently forgetting that Christian knights massacred the Jews along with the Muslims when they conquered Jerusalem. A popular Arab song about the Al-Aqsa Intifadah asks, "Where is the anger of the Arabs? Where is Salah al-Din (Saladin)?" There is too much anger in the Middle East already. Salah al-Din, after conquering Jerusalem, wasted no time in making a peace that left the remaining Crusaders in their Palestinian kingdoms. Where is Salah al-Din indeed? Al Qaeda did not destroy the World Trade Center in the name of Palestine. Bin Laden and his followers are fighting against Western globalism and the American presence in the Arabian Gulf, not only for the Palestinian people. In the latest bin Laden video, one of the September terrorists reads a manifesto while wearing a Palestinian headscarf. But the graphic next to him says in Arabic, "Expel the polytheists from the Arabian Peninsula." If the doves of peace settled in Israel and Palestine today, Al Qaeda's war with America would continue.

The Prophet Muhammad said, "The first person against whom judgment will be pronounced on the Day of Resurrection will be a man who has died a martyr. He will be brought forth and God will make known to him the blessings He has bestowed on him and he will recognize them. God will say: 'And what did you do about them?' He will say: 'I fought for you until I died a martyr.' God will say: 'You lie! You only fought that it might be said about you, "He is courageous."'

And it was as He had said. Then he will be ordered to be dragged along on his face until he is cast into Hell fire."[3] Do the ideologues of Hamas, Islamic Jihad, and the Al-Aqsa Martyrs' Brigades recount this tradition when someone volunteers to become a human bomb? I don't think so. Or do they recount another famous tradition, in which the Prophet said, "When Allah decreed the creation, He wrote down a pledge which He kept unto Himself. And it said: 'My mercy prevails over My wrath?'"[4] I am sure that they do not recount this tradition. Is this enough to convince readers that extremists have hijacked "true" Islam? Most non-Muslims would probably hope so. But the people for whom these teachings are intended would probably not listen to them. The ideologues of fundamentalism are well aware that the nature of one's religion depends on the scriptures that one reads.

If an American Muslim tells you that she did not suspect that the perpetrators of September 11 were Muslims, she is not telling you the truth. The universal response of Muslim America to the 1995 Oklahoma City bombing was, "Oh God, please let it not be a Muslim!" On that occasion, American Muslims got a break. The arrest of Timothy McVeigh allowed us to continue believing that Muslims could do no wrong: "See? Muslims aren't the only terrorists." We had a rare opportunity to ask ourselves where our communities had been going these last forty years. We refused to recognize the intolerance and lack of cultural understanding that had grown unchecked in our mosques. We refused to acknowledge the influence of extremists, raised under oppressive Middle Eastern and South Asian regimes, who used the First Amendment as a cover for doctrines that made a farce of the U.S. Constitution. Like all minority groups, we were loath to acknowledge the severe tensions that existed within our community. We hid behind the apologetic American definition of Islam that is brought forth at all interfaith gatherings: Islam means peace. Although the Arabic word for *peace (salam)* comes from the same root, *Islam* does not mean "peace." *Islam* means "submission." Theologically, it means submission to God. But historically, it has meant many other kinds of submission as well: submission to authority, to tradition, to culture, and sometimes even to the baser human instincts, which are cultivated in the name of religion. Sufis have long maintained that the corruption of the religious scholar and the distortion of religious knowledge are the most profound and difficult moral tests that Islamic society must undergo. The Prophet Muhammad was aware of this problem. He was aware of how the interpretation of religion depends on human perceptions. The Prophet related that God said, "I am whatever My servant thinks of Me."[5] What do we American Muslims know of God today, when in our mosques and Islamic centers we talk more about politics than spirituality?

Many contemporary Muslims tend to think of God as an instrument of power. Not as the theologians' Creator or Motivator of the Universe, but as a personal power source (or, for Muslim engineers and computer scientists, an omnipotent supercomputer) that can be called on to defeat or outstrategize their opponents. This is especially the case among the advocates of Islamic extremism. If you pay your dues to God by maintaining basic rituals and practices (including wearing the *hijab* veil if you are a woman), God will requite you by smashing your enemies. It's the kind of equation that appeals to the engineers and computer scientists who are drawn in unusually large numbers to Islamic fundamentalism.

Shortly after September 11 Christiane Amanpour of CNN interviewed apologists for Osama bin Laden at an exclusive secondary school in Pakistan. For these children of the elites, geopolitics followed the plot of a Marvel Comics book. Bin Laden was tough. Bin Laden was cool. Bin Laden gave the West what it deserved. He struck blows against the Empire in the name of all who resist Zionism and Western imperialism. But what did the West do to harm these young cricket-players? Without the social and economic changes wrought by colonialism and postcolonial imperialism, their parents could never have earned the tuition that allows them to indulge in fantasies of empires lost and then redeemed. The West they claim to despise even wrote the curriculum of the school in which they study. In terms of core values, they have more in common with Londoners than with their own people. It is ironic that the majority of Pakistanis do not share bin Laden's views. In the face of grinding poverty, they still refuse to trade their common sense for a false ideology. Nine hundred years ago, the Muslim theologian al-Ghazali wrote, "A change from one kind of intellectual bondage to another is only a self-deception, a stupidity. What position in God's world is baser than that of one who thinks that it is honorable to renounce a truth that is accepted on good authority, and then relapses into an acceptance of falsehood, which is still a matter of blind faith, unaided by independent inquiry? Such a scandalous attitude is never taken by the unsophisticated masses of men. For they have an instinctive aversion to following the example of misguided genius. Surely, their 'simplicity' is nearer to salvation than sterile genius can ever be."[6] In the early nineteenth century, a similar point was made by Thomas Jefferson, the ideologist of American rationalism, whose election as president caused an earlier group of "American Taliban" (Protestant Christian "Taliban" in this case) to flee to distant shores: "Man once surrendering his reason, has no remaining guard against absurdities the most monstrous, and like a ship without rudder, is the sport of every wind. With such persons, gullibility, which they call faith, takes the helm from the hand of reason, and the mind becomes a wreck."[7] Al-Ghazali and Jefferson spoke well, but the Qur'an said it better, and even more to the point: "Is the recompense for good anything other than good? So which of the favors of your Lord will you now deny?"[8]

The fundamental problem with Islamic extremism is not that it is otherworldly, but that it is so worldly. It seeks a perfection that Islam, as represented by the Qur'an, rejects as impossible. By seeking to re-constitute the lost empire of the Caliphate, Osama bin Laden and the extremists of Al Qaeda not only chase a mirage, they also forget the seemingly mundane but crucial spirituality on which the religion of Islam was founded. "Is the recompense for good anything other than good?" asks the Qur'an. Islamic extremism is about power: govern-mental power, social power, economic power, gendered power—domi-nation. God is power. Islam is power. Power controls. Islam controls. Islamic extremism follows the maxim of La Fontaine: "The reason of the strongest is always the best."[9] Or put another way, the logic of power is always the best. The logic of Islamic extremism is the logic of power. La Fontaine's maxim is the moral of a fable in which the "un-reasonable" logic of the wolf trumps the "reasonable" logic of the lamb. It is not the strength of the logic that counts, but the power of the logi-cian. Reason matters little in the game of power. Ask any Palestinian. Palestinian despair stems in part from the fact that the reasonable ar-guments of the oppressed seem to matter little in the court of public opinion. For more than twenty years, right-wing Islam has used the logic of the wolf to dominate mosques and Islamic centers through-out the United States and Europe. Liberal Muslims have countered by using the logic of the lamb. As a result, liberal Muslims have lost not only their mosques, but their children as well. These are the children of Asia, Africa, the Middle East, Europe, and America who joined the Taliban in the aftermath of September 11. In their game of jihad, their imagined ace in the hole is the Divine Protector. "Verily, for the friends of God there is no fear, nor shall they grieve."[10] The logic of having God on one's side (shared by George Bush's "God Bless America" rhetoric) is the most powerful logic of all. God trumps the logic of all other powers. With God on my side, I am no longer weak. I am at the center of the circle of power. Such is the wolf-logic of Islamic extremism.

Culture, like law, is an instrument of control. The concept of authenticity helps maintain cultural control. At a recent conference on Muslim-Christian relations hosted by the Archbishop of Canterbury, the Mufti of Bosnia, a liberal Muslim jurist who was educated at the University of Chicago, spoke of the problem of the "assimilated Muslim" who is in danger of losing his authentic "Islamic" identity. Not a single Christian at the conference—whether Protestant, Catholic, or Orthodox—saw any problem with the "assimilated Christian." Among monotheistic religions, assimilation has historically been a Jewish problem, because Judaism is defined both culturally and theologically. Despite its great diversity, Judaism is still thought of as a monoculture. Judaism does not claim to be a universal religion. Islam is supposed to be universal, but most contemporary Muslims do not act as if Islam is a universal religion. Ironically, by idealizing the concept of the Islamic nation, Muslim extremists have judaized Islam. By defining Islam as a "nation"—a complex of culture and tradition—politically oriented Islam mirrors the isolationist self-image of Judaism. This is one of the reasons why Palestine is so important to contemporary Muslims. Not only is Jerusalem a holy place—the first direction of prayer for Muslims and the starting point for the Prophet's vision of ascension to heaven—but Palestine as a whole is part of the Islamic "nation." According to the ideologists of Hamas and Islamic Jihad, Islamic law must govern the entirety of Palestine. Palestine is also part of the Arab core of the Islamic nation. Veiled Muslim women in Cairo demonstrate against Israel's invasion of Palestine by holding up signs that read "Arab Palestine." The Arabism of Islamic extremism harks back to the first century of Islam—not to the era of the Prophet and his companions, but to the era of the Umayyad Caliphs (681-750), when Islam was an Arab religion and converts to Islam had to become the clients of Arab tribes. For bin Laden and his followers, to convert to Islam means to "become Arab." Like John Walker Lindh, the new Muslim must wear "traditional" clothing, adopt Arab customs, and affect a pseudo-Arab accent. In the distorted mirror of Al Qaeda's Islam, to be Muslim is to be Oriental, not Western. The worldview of Islamic extremism is the mirror image of Western Orientalism. It is a religion of difference, of boundaries that are as much cultural as theological. It comprises the ideological myth of the "Islamic nation."

When the Qur'an says, "Verily, the religion of God is Islam," it proclaims universalism.[11] For the Muslim who holds a universal perspective, there can be no war between "Islam and the West." Qur'anic Islam is not a culture. As a universal religion, it perfects the cultures that embrace it. The jihad that a Qur'anic Muslim must fight in a globalized world is a struggle over transnational values expressed through individual behavior, not a struggle between nations. There is no reason why a Muslim cannot be fully American, fully English, or fully Danish and be as much a Muslim as one who is Arab, Pakistani, or Iranian. Contrary to what many American Muslims have been led to believe, there is nothing intrinsically "un-Islamic" about Western culture. Every sin that can be found in the United States can be found in the Islamic world as well. So can every virtue. Most of the same sins and virtues could have been found in the Islamic world centuries before the United States ever existed. Nevertheless, Muslims, Christians, Jews, and the secular alike might agree that the imperial power of the American media to project the worst of American culture—its rampant materialism, its degradation and trivialization of sexuality—is a deadly feature of the globalization of the American disease in the late twentieth century. But Qur'anic universalism does not allow a "clash of civilizations." Instead, it calls for debates within the person and between individuals. The struggle over values is a struggle *within* society and *within* civilization, not between societies and between civilizations. Most of all, it is a struggle within the individual soul. This, as the Prophet Muhammad has said, is the battlefield of the "Greater Jihad." Every suicide bomber, contemporary jihadist, and political Islamist has overlooked the struggle for his or her soul by seeking the causes of his suffering outside of himself. This is why the Qur'an asks, "So which of the favors of your Lord will you now deny?"

The Saudi news magazine *al-Majallah* recently conducted a poll in the Arab world on the subject of suicide bombing. Approval of suicide bombing ranged from a low of 44 percent in Lebanon to a high of 96 percent in Iraq. Only in Lebanon did a majority of respondents come out against the practice. The April 8, 2002, issue of *Time* magazine carried an opinion piece by Eyad Sarraj, a psychiatrist and founder of the Palestinian Independent Commission for Citizens' Rights. Entitled "Why We Blow Ourselves Up," the article details how thirty-five years of Israeli occupation and the broken promise of the Oslo Accords have led to a sense of humiliation and a desire for revenge among Palestinian Arabs. "Shame is the most painful emotion in the Arab culture," writes Sarraj, "producing the feeling that one is unworthy to live. The honorable Arab is the one who refuses to suffer shame and dies in dignity."[12] A potential suicide bomber asserted, "Would you fight for your country or not? Of course you would. You would be respected in your country as a brave man, and I would be remembered as a martyr." This statement, claims Sarraj, echoes the teaching of the Qur'an, where God promises both men and women paradise for taking this "ultimate test of faith." By making statements such as these, Sarraj ignores basic Islamic doctrines and acts as an unwitting apologist for extremism. The practice of suicide bombing contradicts several fundamental Islamic tenets. The suicide bomber who wishes to be remembered for being brave disobeys the tradition that condemns the martyr who forfeits his life in order to appear brave before his family and friends. Even more serious is Sarraj's assertion that Palestinians are so ashamed that they feel unworthy to live. Hopelessness and despair have long been regarded as major sins in Islam, because they imply a lack of faith. The desire to take one's life out of despair is a sign of disbelief. The Prophet said, "There was among those before you a man who had a wound. He was in such anguish that he took a knife and made with it a cut in his hand, and the blood did not cease to flow until he died. God the Almighty said: 'My servant has himself forestalled me. Thus, I have forbidden him paradise.'"[13] If Sarraj's analysis of Palestinian psychology is accurate, the effects of Israeli occupation have caused the Palestinian people to forget some of the most important principles of their religion. Rather than being an "ultimate test of faith," self-immolation for the wrong reason is a serious perversion of faith. Turning suicide bombing into a religious virtue poses a grave challenge to Islamic ethics. This is true even before one raises the moral question of killing Israeli or American civilians under the pretext of collective responsibility. Not to mention the omnipresent prejudice among Muslims that sees all Jews as enemies. What has become of the concept of "People of the Book"? In the tenth century c.e., 'Abd al-Rahman III, the Caliph of Islamic Spain, appointed a Jew named Hasdai ibn Shaprut as the vizier of a state that claimed to represent Islam throughout the world. Does this make 'Abd al-Rahman III an unbeliever? Unfortunately, many contemporary Muslims would think so. After a year and a half of the Al-Aqsa Intifadah and Israeli reprisals, Jewish advocates for peace in Israel can no longer find Palestinian interlocutors. Palestinians who wish to engage with Jews in dialogue for peace run the risk of being branded as collaborators. Collaborators tend to wind up dead in today's Palestine. What a pity for Palestine that this is so. What a pity for Israel. What a pity for Islam.

Americans are constantly being told that everything has changed since September 11. The political consequences are easy to see. The current "war on terrorism" means that the killing of civilians for the purpose of terror will not be tolerated. The battle for public opinion is the only jihad that the United States and its allies will allow. No matter what the provocation or the justification, the present U.S. administration will not tolerate the targeting of civilians by suicide bombers. There must be no more 9/11s. There must be no more Passover massacres. People who appear uncivilized do not get invited into the community of nations. Resistance to occupation does not justify murder. For the time being, it will do little good to point to the atrocities made by those who claim to defend order, to the secularized actions of those who wrap themselves in the cloak of "civilization." American Muslims know that now is the time to act circumspectly. We are more deeply aware than ever before of our precarious status as a religious minority. American Muslim intellectuals are caught in a particular quandary. How are we to address the extremism that exists within parts of our community without becoming apologists for the current administration? How are we to critique ourselves without playing into the hands of right-wing ideologues who seek to dismiss all of Islam as a form of religious fascism? How do we make our internal debates about Islam relevant to the rest of the Islamic world, as well as the non-Islamic world? For the past twenty years, Muslim conservatives have used "American Islam" as a pejorative term that denotes laissez-faire Islam or an Islam that serves the interests of U.S. foreign policy. News accounts of the capture of the Al Qaeda leader Abu Zubaydah report that he accused his Pakistani captors of being "American Muslims." The very term begs the important question: Is there a fundamental incompatibility between Islamic values and "American" values?

The challenge for the American Muslim intellectual after September 11 is to provide a vision of Islam that is compatible with American constitutional values and still remains true to the Islamic historical tradition. This is not an easy task. To do so, the Muslim intellectual must find a way to bridge cultural and ideological differences that at their extremes are diametrically opposed. On the left, the secular humanist will brand all discussions of faith, theology, and doctrine as either trite or irrelevant. On the right, the culturally oriented Muslim will resist all attempts to change the values he has brought from his homeland. It matters little that many of these values differ according to country of origin. They are still part and parcel of what it means to be Muslim. The critical examination of Islamic history demonstrates that all attempts to create a total and unified Islamic system have been failures. In Islamic history, the desire for earthly unity has seldom been realized. The most innovative and fruitful periods of Islamic civilizational development have been when the doctrines and philosophies of diverse peoples could compete in a "free market of ideas." Without the challenge of Greek thought, there would be no Islamic philosophy; without the challenge of Christian thought, Islam would have no systematic theology; without the challenge of Babylonian and Indian thought, Islamic science and mathematics would never have prospered; without the challenge of Aristotelian thought, Islamic jurisprudence could never have become a model of Islamic reason. No culture or religion is born in a void. The challenge of the future can only be faced by an Islamic worldview that embraces diversity, equality of the sexes, and the freedom, not only to be right, but also to be wrong. Failure to meet the challenges of a diverse, multicentered, and religiously pluralistic world will ultimately lead to an Islam that is irrelevant to contemporary life, and might even herald the decline of Islam as a world religion. To maintain an Islam that is both spiritually and socially relevant, Muslims must, as the Sufi Abu al-Qasim Junayd said, "distinguish what is eternal from that which is created in time." Religions can approach the world in many different ways, but there is no religion without spirituality. One cannot follow the teachings of the Qur'an without thinking about God. In contemporary Muslim political discourse, God is mentioned but not engaged. Islamic theology and philosophy, as they existed in the classical Islamic past, barely exist today. This is because new methods of theological and ethical inquiry have not been developed that can incorporate modern epistemologies into the Islamic worldview. Instead, one finds political philosophies where God is viewed instrumentally and romantic discourses of traditionalism that seek to build Islamic civilization on idealized models of the past. The political philosophies of Islamism provide an Islam that is bereft of soul. Islamic romanticism perpetuates the myth of static traditionalism, which turns Islamic civilization into an artifact that should be placed in Epcot Center somewhere between "Morocco" and "Thailand." For American Muslims, the ultimate challenge since September 11 is to define Islam in the context of a pluralistic American political culture whose roots lie in Protestant Christianity and whose branches reach in the direction of secularism. This is the challenge that has stimulated the most debate among American Muslim intellectuals in the months since September 11. Crisis has become the catalyst that has freed American Muslims to ask questions that had been ignored for too long.

NOTES

1   *Huma mashi Bani Mtir, huma al-bala' li kayteer!*
2   See Samuel P. Huntington, *The Clash of Civilizations and the Remaking of the World Order* (New York: Touchstone Books, 1998).
3   Related by Muslim, Tirmidhi, and al-Nasa'i.
4   Related by al-Bukhari, al-Nasa'i, and Ibn Majah.
5   Related by al-Bukhari, Tirmidhi, Muslim, and Ibn Majah.
6   *Al-Ghazali's Tahafut al-Falasifah* [Incoherence of the Philosophers], trans. Sabih Ahmad Kamali (Lahore: Pakistan Philological Congress, 1963), 2–3.
7   Thomas Jefferson to James Smith, 1822. In *The Writings of Thomas Jefferson, Memorial Edition*, ed. Andrew Libscomb and Albert Bergh (Washington, D.C.: Thomas Jefferson Memorial Association, 1903–1904), 15: 409.
8   Qur'an 55, *Surat al-Rahman*, 60–61.
9   Michel Serres, "Knowledge in the Classical Age: La Fontaine and Descartes," in Serres, *Hermes: Literature, Science, Philosophy*, ed. Josué V. Harari and David F. Bell (Baltimore: Johns Hopkins University Press, 1982), 15.
10 Qur'an 10, *Surat Yunus*, 62.
11 Qur'an 3, Al 'Imran, 19.
12 Eyad Sarraj, "Why We Blow Ourselves Up," *Time*, April 8, 2002.
13 Related by al-Bukhari.

FRANK LENTRICCHIA AND JODY MCAULIFFE

Groundzeroland

. . . the more clearly we see terror, the less impact we feel from art.
—Don DeLillo, *Mao II*

It was late in the evening of September 11 and a network special on the day's events was coming to a close. A famous news anchor was saying—these were his final words, solemnly delivered—that tomorrow, when New Yorkers awaken, they will awaken to an altered skyline. Not words about the memory of the dead and the imagination of their terrifying destruction. Nothing to the effect that "our hearts go out" to the ruined families and friends of the dead. Instead, words about a rupture in the perceptual field. A "defamiliarization," as the aesthetic theory of the Russian formalists would have it: that was the deep horror we were left to contemplate by the famous news anchor, who we must not rush to conclude was a shallow, unfeeling man. Let us recall that for most of us—the very greatest majority of us—the thousands slaughtered are abstract. We have no personal connections with them. We never really did, or ever really will, *grieve* for them, though we may think we do so in the world made by Oprah, where human beings assume God's role of feeling everybody's pain.

The famous anchor was in effect predicting that New Yorkers would have an experience of the sort prized by the most advanced imaginative writers and art theorists of the last two centuries. In the perceptual world something new would collapse into view. And tomorrow's newness—awful, to be sure, in more than one sense—would be signified by an absence of two heretofore boring buildings; a hole in the familiar. Those New Yorkers without connection to the dead, the injured, and the displaced would grieve (and fear) not for the dead, the injured, and the displaced, but for themselves, undergoing now the terror of the new.

And the rest of us, who do not live in New York? We would like to be invited to make a pilgrimage. We would take our children and our disposable cameras. Acquire the tickets. Then wait in line for as long as it takes to enter and to view. It would please us greatly if Mr. Giuliani, America's mayor, would announce on CNN that we are all welcome to visit Groundzeroland.

This much do we learn from Anthony Tommasini, a classical music critic for the *New York Times,* whose provocative report was widely reprinted in American dailies: on September 16, 2001, Karlheinz Stockhausen, the German pioneer of electronic music and a figure of international renown, was asked at a news conference in Hamburg for his reaction to the terrorist strikes in the United States. He responded by calling the attack on the World Trade Center "the greatest work of art that is possible in the whole cosmos," and went on to speak in apparent awe of the terrorists' achievement of "something in one act" that "we couldn't even dream of in music," in which "people practice like crazy for ten years, totally fanatically for a concert, and then die."

This is our fascination: the transformation of the World Trade Center into a narrative of spectacular images. Terrorism for the camera. The small section of smoking rubble, that pathetic piece of the Pentagon, a squat and ugly building, holds no appeal. But Stockhausen is not interested in the images. It is the event itself that entrances him. The event itself is what he means by "the greatest work of art that is possible in the whole cosmos." His incendiary artistic analogy is seriously intended, and he pursues it: "You have people so concentrated on one performance, and then five thousand people are dispatched into eternity, in a single moment." In the face of such achievement, might Stockhausen be the lesser artist? A touch of envy—envy of terrorism—appears to creep in. "I couldn't do that. In comparison with that, we're nothing as composers."

Stockhausen had been taking questions before the commencement of a four-day festival of his work in Hamburg. His concerts were abruptly canceled; his daughter, a pianist, informed the press that she would no longer appear under the name Stockhausen; international reaction was swift and predictably harsh. In the midst of controversy, he tried to explain: "Where has he brought me, that Lucifer," he asked, referring to a major invented character who regularly figures in a series of seven operas that have engaged him in a twenty-five-year project.

Tommasini acknowledges that Stockhausen "has long been fired by the idea that art should transform us 'out of life itself' . . . otherwise 'it's nothing.'" And Tommasini will allow that "any artwork, from a short Schubert song to a long Dostoevsky novel, can have a transforming effect," but he thinks that a line was crossed. "Stockhausen has dangerously overblown ambitions for art." He's been "losing touch with reality," he's an "egomaniac" and a "raving has-been" who needs to be "confined to a psychiatric clinic."

The extremity of the avant-garde composer's remarks drives the music journalist to a place that the music journalist rarely goes: to theoretical pronouncement. "Art may be hard to define, but whatever it is, it's a step removed from reality." In one breath, Tommasini, a modest man, says that he can't define it; doesn't know what it is; nevertheless will define it; will tell us, in effect, that he knows exactly what it is, when he writes the words "a step removed from reality." He goes on: "A theatrical depiction of suffering may be art; real suffering is not. . . . Images of the blazing twin towers, however horrifically compelling, are not art." (Tommasini, too, is apparently compelled by the blazing towers; the poor Pentagon does not qualify.) Stockhausen's thoughts to the contrary, who was not thinking of the electronic images but of the thing itself, are for Tommasini decisive proof of madness. Art is representation ("depiction"); to claim otherwise is not only to announce one's insanity, it is to impugn what is presumed to be at the core of art: its so-called humanity.

Or perhaps it is to announce, as aesthetic revolutionaries have frequently announced over the past two centuries, that the war on tradition is a war against what would seem to be the inescapable fact about art—that it is inherently artificial (not life): by definition "once removed." Aesthetic revolutionaries historically wage polemical war on behalf of the authentic, which they habitually define as an overcoming of precisely traditional art's "once removed" character. The famous intention of Wordsworth, for example, to write a language "really spoken" by the rural unprivileged, as opposed to the artificial writing of the poets of his youth, or the intention of his inheritor Robert Frost, by avant-garde standards, like Wordsworth a staid conservative, to "drop to an everyday level of diction that even Wordsworth kept above," and to "entangle," in Frost's words, a living voice in the "syntax, idiom and meaning of a sentence"—these artistic desires of Wordsworth and Frost are alike desires to jump the gap between word and thing (writing and voice) and thereby defeat the mediated or representational character of literature as it has been theorized since Aristotle, who two thousand years before his *New York Times* inheritor argued in the fourth chapter of *The Poetics* that "objects which in themselves we view with pain, we delight to contemplate when reproduced with minute fidelity: such as the forms of the most ignoble animals and"—now an example to the point of September 11—"of dead bodies."

The pain-giving object would appear to be the definitive case for Aristotle, who in his theory of the transformative power of representation argues in effect that when an object is relocated from the place in the world where it has its pain-giving being to the realm of an artistic medium, where it is "reproduced" as an image, the pain-giving object becomes pleasurable because we are spared direct interaction with the thing itself. We may merely contemplate it. And our delight lies just there ("We delight to contemplate") in the contemplative act facilitated by representation; an act presumably made highly unlikely, if not impossible, when we face the real thing in its awful presence.

By the powerful traditional standard set by Aristotle, the pain-giving events themselves of September 11 in New York, as Tommasini argues, are not art. For those on the scene, and their kin and acquaintance, the strike on the towers was only horrific. But the images, on Tommasini's own testimony, are something else. They are "horrifically compelling." In other words, in our contemplative security from the real, the images trigger pleasure—call it engrossed compulsion, the kind of spiritual pleasure attendant upon loss of self, as we are absorbed by the transfixing object of our attention. And this very contemplative pleasure, governed by imitation, argues Aristotle, is a deep spring of art. On traditional theoretical grounds, images of Ground Zero in lower Manhattan may indeed deserve to be called art. How difficult is it to imagine—all that shocking footage artfully edited to become a truly absorbing short film? Absorbing need not entail pleasant. ("And the award for short subject goes to . . .")

Does it make any sense to speak, as Stockhausen did, of the aesthetic character and effects of those violently transgressive acts? The events themselves, not their artful representation? To consider the merits of such an idea would require that we put aside the virtually unavoidable sentimentality that asks us to believe that art is always somehow humane and humanizing; that artists, however indecent they might be as human beings, become noble when they make art, which must inevitably ennoble those who experience it.

After returning home from his Hamburg debacle, Stockhausen issued this statement on his Web site: "In my work, I have defined Lucifer as the cosmic spirit of rebellion, of anarchy. He uses his high degree of intelligence to destroy creation. . . . I used the designation 'work of art' to mean the work of destruction personified in Lucifer." At the press conference, Stockhausen had been asked if he considered Lucifer's "work of art" to be a criminal act and he answered that it was of course a criminal act because the innocent who were killed had not been given a choice. He added, "But what happened spiritually, this jump out of security, out of the self-evident, out of everyday life [not out of life itself, as Tommasini reports], this sometimes also happens in art . . . or it is worthless." (*Note: also.*) Stockhausen, presciently, asked the assembled journalists not to publish his responses because people "might not understand this."

The Devil, the Arch-Criminal who made Stockhausen speak so scandalously, is not just another character bearing a point of view not necessarily shared by his author, but the very figure of artistic ambition (the Arch-Criminal Artist) with which his author identifies. As the mythic destroyer of creation, Lucifer is the destroyer of Somebody Else's creation, Somebody Else's law: *oppressive* is understood as the implied modifier of *creation* and *law*. Lucifer, the spirit of rebellion and anarchy, is the model of the artist, and long has been, not for Stockhausen alone but for the tradition to which he belongs. *Romantic, prophetic, apocalyptic, revolutionary*—these are the familiar terms used to describe the tradition of the transgressive work of art summed up by Stockhausen as the work of destruction: the destructive power of art that underwrites aesthetic value but is not itself that value. (Stockhausen, like Lucifer, is not a nihilist.) Aesthetic value is the destruction which enables consciousness, or what the Romantic poet Shelley meant when he said that art "strips the film of familiarity" from the world as we know it—the evil of familiarity; a stripping—like an altering of a skyline?—which is a deep cleansing of perception and prelude to the establishment of new consciousness; in Stockhausen's words, an act of imagination with spiritual impact on us—a jump out of security, the self-evident, out of everyday life.

Removed from context, Stockhausen's remarks on aesthetic theory are a banality of avant-garde thought. Had he said that the *footage* of the World Trade Center disaster was the greatest work of art possible, his remarks would probably have received only modest attention, to the effect that this is just the kind of thing that this kind of artist is likely to say—an especially insensitive example of *épater le bourgeois*. But Stockhausen referred to the event of mass slaughter and not its filmic reproduction as the greatest work of art, just five days after September 11. His concession that "of course" this was a criminal act because the innocent had no choice, followed hard by his ruthless conjunction ("but what happened spiritually"), seems a *pro forma* preface to what most excites him: a satanic act that would, *like* an aesthetic act, renovate consciousness through and through.

The terrorists achieved what Stockhausen's kind of artist aspires to. They succeeded in awesome fashion in stripping the film of familiarity from the American view of the world. They seized, they transformed (but for how long?) consciousness. Stockhausen's ambition for his own music, to "break through the routine of time," "to get out of the normal human cycles" in order to "train a new kind of human being," is the cultural ambition of the artist-prophet (a powerful nineteenth-century idea), who viewed himself and his work as a source of truth and justice, and who was to be followed through a cycle of destruction and rebirth; the re-creation of humanity by aesthetic means. In this setting, the terrorist events of September 11 are isomorphic with Stockhausen's aesthetic theory and it is not difficult to understand why he would be swept away, as an artist, by them.

Three discriminations:

> 1. As any avant-garde artist might, Stockhausen sees the devotion of high artistic seriousness (like Flaubert, like Joyce) in the complete commitment of the terrorists, which he likens to practicing "like crazy for ten years, totally fanatically for a concert." Like terrorists, serious artists are always fanatics; unlike terrorists, serious artists have not yet achieved the "greatest" level of art. *Note:* "greatest" is not a claim for uniqueness but a claim for the terrorists' continuity with what serious

artists in Stockhausen's tradition always try for: *great, greater, greatest* signify ascending degrees of influencing mass consciousness; at the superlative stage of art, and terror, consciousness is not merely influenced: it is transformed.

2. As for that key word *transformation:* Stockhausen's madness, according to Tommasini, who will not mind standing here for the reasonable point of view, lies in his taking of transformative possibilities in art at face value; transformation not, in Aristotelian fashion, of the object, in order to provide a congenial occasion for contemplative reflection and pleasure, an occasion for cognition unimpeded by emotion, but transformation of the attending consciousness itself; an occasion for the emergence of a New Man and a New World. And transformation is not qualifiable. There cannot be, as Tommasini seems to want, a small, safe transformation, with the majority of consciousness (and world) untouched and secure in all the old familiar places. Transformation is either total (and revolutionary) or it is not transformation; failure of transformation is failure of art and terror. In true transformation, we are possessed and catapulted out of the ordinary—taken over by original vision with no wiggle room for rational escape. Such aesthetic experience may be apocalyptically political, or it may be the sort of experience pointed to in Tommasini's reference to a "short Schubert song": an experience of ravishment (interior apocalypse), which for its modest duration takes us away and renders us useless for the affairs of everyday life.

3. When Stockhausen slips and says that what happened in New York on September 11 "also" may happen in art, or art is worthless, he tells us that his intentions as an artist are as ambitious as those of the terrorists, that he wants art to have that kind of force. In this way would he be a terrorist of art. The terrorists did the thing that he would do but hasn't yet done, having not yet reached in his music the plateau of "the greatest." And he tells us clearly, but perhaps not yet himself, still swept up as he is by the seductive idea of September 11, that the event at the World Trade Center is not art. Stockhausen's logical slippage, marked by his "also," is just this: his idea of art is a subset of the category of transgression; the category includes many acts—criminal and punishable by law, as Stockhausen's music is not—that are not art. Which is to say: transgression and its desired effect, transformation, are not uniquely artistic phenomena. Stockhausen's transcendental ambition to transgress and transform is only the latest indicator of what ambitious artists have most feared for the last two centuries—their cultural inconsequence, looming now more than ever, in the Age of Television.

No one has yet seriously proposed that Stockhausen, for having composed what he's composed, should be incarcerated. Tommasini does urge incarceration, but that in a clinic for the insane; incarceration deserved not for what Stockhausen composed but for what he proposed in his theory of great art.

"Getting shot is for real . . . there's no element of pretense or make-believe in it," Chris Burden, the performance artist, speaking of *Shoot* (1971). A real-time activity (an actual shooting); a body subjected to risk and serious pain (Burden's); a violent act whose goal, nevertheless, is to trigger "mental stuff," says Burden, in those who take it in. Illusion is false. Here is total disdain for the mainstream West's Aristotelian theater of representation. Though of course an audience is desired; that's the contradiction. This is not antitheater after all. Something is to be done to those who take it in. A wish to communicate not *about* the real, but to communicate the real itself; thrust it bodily through the space separating performer and viewer. Performance art is ontological-didactic theater.

Or consider the big event—site specific, environmental. An elaborate spectacle requiring advanced technology. A theater of images, set in an unconventional location, requiring a huge cast and crew and, in its audience, competence in visual grammar: a theater on behalf of perception—not text or story. Robert Wilson says, "Listen to images." Performance art in the 1990s is art more and more with an agenda. A theater of lessons, visually encoded.

In spite of their *intentions*, which not even Stockhausen called aesthetic, the suicide terrorists who struck New York may be said to have made—with the cooperation of American television—performance art with political designs upon its American audience. The site, the WTC, was unconventional and politically loaded: the symbolic center of American capitalism. Advanced technology was mastered and put into play. The cast was huge; bodies were subjected to serious pain. All of this in real time, with no element of pretense or make-believe in it. Thanks to the cameras, which bin Laden could confidently assume would be there, images of a spectacular sort were generated, framed, and replayed endlessly. Thanks to the presence of the camera, which guaranteed a vast audience, this act of performance means something, achieves the paradoxical fusion of "life" and "art," "event" and its filmic representation in minute and faithful reproduction.

In more traditional terms: there were authors (bin Laden, Atta, etc.);

there was plot—a structure of events with deep narrative inevitability; there were thousands of characters—but with no choice in turning down the role, with no knowledge that they'd been cast to die. And there was an audience with no choice not to experience terrorist narrative once that narrative found its true medium of communication, the media without which terrorist art is ineffective, and which complicitously completes its totalitarian trajectory: to saturate consciousness in the United States with the thought of terror, with no sanctuary left for the blessed banalities of ordinary life. They would make Americans forever insecure; cause us to join the rest of the world, at last, and end, at last, our long holiday from history. They would change us.

And the mainspring of this aesthetic experience is an absence, a rubble pit in lower Manhattan; that rupture in the perceptual field which marks the original art of the suicide pilots.

When Gottfried Semper designed the Bayreuth Festival Playhouse, which opened in 1876, he placed the audience on one single "classless" level, a feature anticipated by Wagner himself (the director of design) in keeping with his anticommercial, antibourgeois, pro-"folk" theoretical stance. Semper would build community by leveling the tiers of the traditional theater, erasing class difference, and creating a "mystic gulf" between the audience and the stage. On December 30, 2001, Mayor Giuliani opened a viewing platform for the folk over the mystic gulf that is Ground Zero, a stage to which he urged Americans, and everybody, to come and experience "all kinds of feelings of sorrow and the tremendous feelings of patriotism." Though concerned that some would come for "the wrong reasons," whatever they might be, he was sure most would go for "the right reasons," whatever those are. "Tourist sight" or "hallowed ground"? Or "tourist sight" and "hallowed ground"? Heavily supported by the New York tourist and convention bureau, the platform proposal "glided through unusually dense thickets of red tape." Restaurants and hotel beds have been empty too long.

Herbert Muschamp of the *New York Times* articulates what sounds like a manifesto of an artistic movement with a political agenda in his description of the design of the platform: "The design does hold meaning. It embodies stoic principles. It treats the need for design as a reduction to essentials. The result has substance. Stop the mystification, the

grandiosity, the use of architecture to disconnect our history from ourselves. Give the city back." Give us back our exceptionalism. Because
the long American holiday from history is far from over.

The platform's purpose is to connect tourists to their history at a site
that perfectly conjoins terrorism, patriotism, and tourism. A ticket is
available, as yet for no charge, for those cold, sad pilgrims who would
like to connect to their history, without mediation and with maximum transparency, without waiting in line: a ticket stamped for a specific time, for a specific fifteen-minute interval. Andy Warhol's whisper
echoes in the time limit on the platform, that magic fifteen minutes,
the promise of future fame for everybody: the leveling of class difference. FastPass to Magic Mountain. FastPass to Groundzeroland.

People don't know what they're looking at. The platform will tell
them. Pictures are snapped; souvenir hats and pretzels are bought; T-
shirts are sold; designer sunglasses are hawked. The first fortunate pil-
grim gets his name in the paper just as he did when he snagged first
place in line for the World Series. Tourists come from Japan to see
"this reality," what one grieving mother described as "my child's body
all over that place." Collectors or curators "relying on aesthetic judgment," randomly but not accidentally, select objects to be stored for
future exhibition. They call them "artifacts," *art*ifacts of terror, and by
virtue of their selection and acquisition, the city of New York in effect
lends credibility to Stockhausen's perception of the terrorist attack as
"the greatest work of art that is possible in the whole cosmos." The
madman approaches vindication.

The only problem is how can the traces of her child's body all over
the place be removed from the artifacts without destroying them. In
some cultures, the curators would be perceived as vultures engaged
in an act of desecration, an act of grave-robbing. The value of an object selected by curators immediately becomes "incalculable," whereas
unselected objects end up in the junkyard, without value, or sold for
recycling—lacking the "power to stir the imaginations and the souls
of visitors." One firefighter, outraged at first at a curator taking digi-
tal photographs of the gravesite of his brothers, was soon transformed
into a curator himself with the understanding of "an archive, a memorial," destined perhaps for the Smithsonian, so that others will understand.

The tourists think their presence is a gift to the grieving. One man's grief is another man's right to reality. Surrounding offices into which determined tourists try to break, enforcing their right to see, are choice skyboxes to the towerless void, this "fake New York." Seeing the pit on television, seeing the representation, does not provide sufficient meaning. The pilgrimage must be made to the so much bigger, so much more surreal Groundzeroland. They claim their right to look. Democracy gives them the right to look, to take back the view that was stolen from them.

In his novel *The Sheltering Sky*, Paul Bowles draws a sharp distinction between tourists, deserving of scorn, who journey for a fixed period of time, and travelers, brave adventurers who might never return. Travelers might find true reality in Evan Fairbanks's twenty-five-minute video of the attack—history playing at the New York Historical Society —the only mediation that of the documentarian's soundless camera. Where is the grassy knoll—on TV, in the pit, or in the mind?

If George Bush is right that we should show patriotism by going on vacation and spending money, then visiting Groundzeroland is a patriotic act. The sublime power of American consumer culture to absorb and commodify even such a devastating blow as this transgressive act of destruction and murder is final proof of that culture's fundamental indestructibility. Walk up the ramp to the platform without filter and, for a golden fifteen minutes, see the erasure—see what isn't there— and see what cannot be erased: the meeting ground for the producers and consumers of popular culture. Experience the Warholian conflation of violent, tragic, mass media news with the patriotic glory and glamour of death. Pose for a picture: mix disaster and death with stardom and beauty. Feel the scale. Absorb it. Go down in history. Move on. Understand it all. Find closure.

MICHAEL J. BAXTER

Dispelling the "We"
Fallacy from the Body of Christ

The Task of Catholics in a Time of War

Within hours after the attacks of September 11, academics were busy
doing what academics do: talking about words. For example, the word
war, which President Bush used to describe the attack. What exactly
does that word mean? So too with the word *terrorism*. And the word
cowardice. And *extremist, tragedy, religion, freedom,* and *civilization*. In
those days and in the months since, the words which have commended
my attention are *we, our,* and *us*. Why did they do that to *us*? How did
they breach *our* security systems? What should *we* do in response? In
these sentences, what is the subject? Who is the "we"? The answer is
that it is "we *Americans*."

This identity of *we Americans* I accept with serious reservations, especially in a time of war. My reservations about using the word *we* (and
related first-person pronouns) in conjunction with the word *American*
are due to the fact that this usage bespeaks a kind of collective purpose,
a shared project, a community that is, I would argue, a fiction. The argument here is complex, but it can be summarized briefly as follows:
genuine political community is not possible in the United States owing
to the absence of a shared understanding of the good life—an understanding that must be rooted in a substantive account of the purpose
of life, and, ultimately, of the Author of life: God. But the United States
is a political order formed on the exigencies of moral and religious
pluralism, in which such a common understanding is not available. Indeed, politics in the United States is designed to translate moral and
religious convictions into interests, which are set over against other
interests, which are then adjudicated so as to achieve whatever relative forms of justice and peace are attainable given these differences.
The aim is not true justice and peace grounded in the good. The aim
is rather a relative justice and a tolerable peace, which is the best that

can be achieved amid the various parties in a religiously and morally pluralistic society.

This social setting and political vision produces a certain kind of moral relativism, the kind which says that it is wrong for parents to destroy their unborn offspring if the parents believe that it is wrong, but not wrong if they believe that it is not wrong; the rightness or wrongness of abortion depends on the belief system of each individual, his or her preferences, his or her choice. This kind of moral relativism also bestows on people the so-called right to die, a right, it can be argued, that with time will be expanded to include not just the terminally ill, but also the very seriously ill, and the mentally ill, the burdensomely ill, the old and decrepit, the unwanted. A trenchant criticism of how this kind of moral relativism is promoted in a liberal democratic culture has been delivered by Pope John Paul II. In recent encyclicals, in particular *Veritatis Splendor* and *Evangelium Vitae,* he argues that democracy as a form of government is not a good in and of itself, that its goodness depends on the virtues of its citizens, and that when those are lacking, it can promote or protect heinous evils.[1] Advancing this line of reasoning, he refers to the tyranny that can arise in the name of the will of the majority, a tyranny that preys on the weak and disabled, the poor and the innocent; and to the extent that the state protects or promotes this tyranny it can be regarded as, to use John Paul II's phrase, a "tyrant state."[2] It is no secret that these remarks were aimed at the United States of America.

The pope's warning about liberal democratic political orders in general and the "tyrant state" in particular should make Catholics wary of using the words *we, our,* and *us* in reference to the United States of America. Catholics should be wary, in other words, of falling prey to the "'we' fallacy." This notion is floated by Christopher Hitchens as a way to track what he calls the "consensus-fabricating syntax" that too often marks the speech and writing of mainstream reporters and political commentators, as is evident in all the talk of *our* interests, *our* credibility, *our* will, *our* nuclear weapons, the *our* in each case creating a false impression of familiarity and common interest among (to use yet another consensus-fabricating phrase) "the American people." Hitchens makes this point in a review of Noam Chomsky's *The Culture of Terrorism.*[3] He credits Chomsky for naming this problem for what it is, "the manufacture of consent" (this was long before their famous parting of the ways over what should be done about the attacks of September 11), but he traces the insight back to Lionel Trilling and, before him, to Walter Lippmann. He also could have given partial credit to Randolph Bourne, whose insights on these matters have been dusted off and brought back into circulation in many quarters these past several months, as they should be whenever this nation goes to war.

The essay that makes Bourne so contemporary was written during World War I. Entitled simply "The State," the essay decries the way in which during wartime, a nation's population is transformed into a single herd that conforms to the aims and purposes of the state.[4] In times of war, Bourne observes, the state realizes its "ideal," which is "that within its territory its power and influence should be universal." It makes a claim on "all the members of the body politic," for "it is precisely in war that the urgency for union seems greatest, and the necessity for universality seems most unquestioned. The State is the organization of the herd," Bourne continues, and "war sends the current of purpose and activity flowing down to the lowest level of the herd, and to its most remote branches." Thus the state becomes "the inexorable arbiter and determinant of men's businesses and attitudes and opinions."[5] As an open supporter of various leftist movements of the time, Bourne was concerned with the ways in which control is exercised over the population by means of the police, courts, prisons, and other state-sponsored institutions. But he is particularly insightful about the subtle mechanisms by which conformity is ensured through a complex network of symbols, attitudes, and customs that produce what he calls "State-feeling" or "State-enthusiasm."[6] Old symbols are taken out and dusted off. Old slogans are brought back into circulation. "Public opinion, as expressed in the newspapers, and the pulpits and the schools, becomes one solid block. And 'loyalty,' or rather war orthodoxy, becomes the sole test for all professions, techniques, occupations." As Bourne points out in a related essay, this is true in the academy, when the "herd-instinct" becomes the "herd-intellect."[7] And it is also true in the churches, "when Christian preachers lose their pulpits for taking more or less in literal terms the Sermon on the Mount."[8] The mechanisms that produce this "State-feeling" are so subtle, so well dispersed, reaching each cell in the body politic, that conforming to it feels natural and right, so much so that it feels natural and right to kill

for it. Of course, one never quite says, to oneself or others, "I'm killing for the state"; it is always for noble ideals, such as freedom, justice,
security. In such a context, the state enjoys a show of support that is
rarely displayed in peace time, leading Bourne to declare, in the words
for which he is most remembered, "war is the health of the State."[9]

In the six months since the September 11 attacks, this dynamic of
"state-feeling" has emerged once again, rescuing the state from absorp-
tion in the trivial (the vote tally in Florida or the shenanigans of Gary
Condit) and returning it to the status of a set of institutions worth
dying and killing for. At the University of Notre Dame, for example,
where I live and work, flags went up everywhere in the days after September 11. Dorms were draped in Old Glory. Little flags appeared on
the tables in the faculty lunchroom. Red, white, and blue ribbons were
pinned to little cards printed with the Prayer of St. Francis and distributed at the Center for Social Concerns. A flag went up in front the
Basilica of the Sacred Heart. At the first home football game after the
attacks, virtually every fan in the stadium was handed on the way into
the stadium an image of the stars and stripes cut out from the back page
of the *South Bend Tribune*. The Catholic high school down the street, St.
Joseph's, had students put the same cutout in all the windows facing
the busy street. Perhaps the most striking example of this merging of
church and nation was symbolized by the cover of a church bulletin
that was distributed at the Basilica of the Sacred Heart, on October 7,
2001, the day the bombing campaign began. Taking up the entire cover
page was a large cross with a banner of the stars and stripes draped
over it, a blue sky in the background, and a skyline toward the bottom.
Emblazoned over the image was the Prayer of St. Francis, beginning
with the words, "Lord, make me an instrument of your peace." When
I inquired as to who was responsible for the bulletin cover, I was informed that this cover was recommended by the service that provides
bulletins for churches across the country. And so it goes.

All of which indicates that Catholics have in effect denied their own
membership in the Body of Christ in favor of membership in the body
politic called the United States of America. This rejection of Catholic identity on the part of Catholics rarely occurs overtly or explicitly.
Rather, Catholic identity is simply *merged* into American identity, as if
the two are perfectly harmonious, as if there is absolutely no conflict
between them. And thus Catholicism gets subordinated to the aims

and purposes of the nation, signified by the way in which their religious symbols are blended so harmoniously with national symbols, especially the flag.

This is not to say that Catholic leaders have made no gestures of moral discernment as to the justice of the war in Afghanistan. There have been some. But they have been overwhelmingly in support of the present war on traditional just-war grounds, with no acknowledgment that such judgments must be provisional and with no serious consideration of what to do if such judgments change.

Take, for example, the statement issued by Cardinal Anthony Bevilacqua on October 8, one day after the United States and its allies launched the air attack on Afghanistan.[10] The statement reads, "According to Catholic teaching, a military response in defense of our people is justified as long as: a sufficient time has been allowed to exhaust all other peaceful means; that our intent is not aggression for its own sake but rather the achievement of justice and peace; our target is never the innocent people but only those responsible for terrorist attacks and their resources." It then states that the intention is for justice and peace (though it does not explain how), that this military action is against terrorists and not the Afghanis (though it does not insist that noncombatant immunity be preserved), and it laments the probable further loss of life (though it issues no warnings that the evils resulting from U.S. attacks not become disproportionate to the war's aims). Curiously enough, it does not address the principle of last resort, even though it lists this as a criterion. Had it done so, it would have been difficult to argue that the action taken by the United States only twenty-six days after the September 11 attacks was actually a last resort; given the logistics, it is hard to imagine an air assault of this magnitude being launched with more dispatch. The statement does not consider all the principles of a just war, and those that it does consider are not considered very rigorously. Nevertheless, the statement served an important purpose: it gave the Bush administration the green light for the action that had already been undertaken.

A similar problem can be found with a statement issued by Cardinal Francis George of Chicago on the next day, October 9.[11] This statement holds that "this is a just war, not a holy war nor a war of religions." It supports this claim by explaining that it is in response to a "brutal and unjust attack which killed thousands of innocent people," and that "our political and military leaders are using no more force than is necessary, acting to protect all innocent lives and engaging in diplomatic as well as military means toward resolving this conflict." It also notes that food is being dropped for the refugees in Afghanistan. There is little more in the way of substance. Nowhere is the principle of last resort mentioned. Nor is there any mention of the principle of an attainable goal, which would have been difficult to support, given that the stated goal was (and as of this writing still is) to stamp out all terrorism all over the world. Nor is there any mention of the principle of proportionality. And yet, the effect of this statement, too, is to give the clear go-ahead to the war just undertaken.

Other statements by other prelates have sent similar messages: this war is just. But what these statements lack is any account of the need for continuing judgments about the justice of the present war, thus giving the impression that these judgments, made within days or weeks of the beginning of overt attacks (covert operations were underway long before), are good for the duration of the war, however long that may be.

On this score, the statement issued by the National Conference of Catholic Bishops in November 2001, "Living with Faith and Hope after September 11," is better.[12] Unlike previous statements, it shows no signs of a hastily patched together press release. The statement provides a full list of both the *jus ad bellum* and *jus in bello* principles of traditional Catholic just-war theory, proposes them as a moral framework for continued reflection on the war, engages in an extended analysis of the political issues connected to Middle East tension, and urges Catholics and others to continue discerning the moral nature of the war. In these respects, we have a more serious acknowledgment that the war could change in character such that it would become unjust. But in one respect, it too is not complete. It gives no indication as to what should occur if at some point this war *were* to be judged unjust. What if such a judgment were to be made? What would the church do then? What would we have to say to Catholics in the military service? Should they refuse to participate in the war if it were to become unjust? And what is being provided for them now, in helping them to discern which actions within the war are unjust and with which they should therefore not cooperate? What virtues would be needed for Catholics and others for this kind of reflection? What institutional mechanisms are in place to sustain the practices needed? What is being done in the military chaplaincy to aid in this kind of critical discernment? What about the rights of conscientious objectors in the military? And about working to achieve recognition in civil and military law for selective conscientious objection?

These are important questions, but the Catholic Church in the United States has done very little to address them. The problem stretches back to 1983, when the Catholic bishops in the United States issued their pastoral letter *The Challenge of Peace*. Sharply critical of the Reagan administration's nuclear weapons policy, this letter was hailed for signaling a turning point in the church's witness for peace in the United States, but its summons to peacemaking has turned out to be largely ineffectual. On this score, the significance of the bishops' letter of 1983 should be read in light of the Gulf War (or, as it could more aptly be called, the Great Petroleum War of 1991), which Catholics supported in overwhelming numbers, as they have the subsequent embargo, even though the pope was critical of it then and has been ever since. A similar show of virtually unqualified support is operative now. Catholics have displayed very little in the way of conscientious objection to the present war in Afghanistan.

Conscientious objection. This phrase is often associated with pacifists, whose views are not very warmly received these days. But it must be noted that *conscientious objection* is also a crucial phrase in Pope John Paul II's encyclical *Evangelium Vitae*, a central contention of which is that people are obligated to conscientious objection rather than to participate in the intrinsically evil acts of abortion and euthanasia.[13] The operative principle here is that noncooperation with evil is a moral duty. This principle has been endorsed not only by John Paul II, however, but also by Gandhi, whose position on cooperation with evil was roughly equivalent to the pope's.[14] A similar consensus between the two can be found, by the way, concerning the practice of contraception.[15]

My point is this: the teaching of the Catholic Church on any number of so-called life issues—abortion, the death penalty, euthanasia, the waging of war—runs counter to the theory and practice that prevails in the political order we call "the United States of America," but Catholics have nevertheless managed to accommodate themselves all too well to this political order. This becomes disturbingly clear during wartime when the church ceases to be a body in and of itself and becomes, in keeping with Bourne's description, just one more cell within the body politic of the state. This is why Catholics rarely if ever ask themselves a question that must be asked in the United States in this day and in wartime: Why should Catholics defend a political order that protects by law the so-called right of parents to destroy their unborn sons and daughters?

Questions such as these are not raised often or seriously enough. But it is quite possible to raise them, as demonstrated by two of the most remarkable Catholics of the past century, one who espoused a just-war position, the other a pacifist. The first is Elizabeth Anscombe, not of the United States but of England, a student of Ludwig Wittgenstein and throughout her career a philosopher at Oxford and Cambridge. In the fall of 1939, shortly after England declared war on Germany, she wrote a brief, very powerful essay, "The Justice of the Present War Examined." Arguing on the basis of traditional just-war principles, Anscombe stood against the war waged by the British government for three reasons: (1) the government's intentions were not just but clearly opportunistic, (2) it was planning to murder large numbers of civilians by means of indiscriminate obliteration bombing, and (3) the probable evil effects of the war outweighed the probable good effects given that the Allies were bent on waging a war without a clear goal. The essay was published as a pamphlet, but before it could be widely disseminated her bishop ordered the pamphlet withdrawn from publication, to which she complied. Given the present wartime circumstances, her introduction is particularly pertinent:

> In these days the authorities claim the right to control not only the policy of the nation but also the actions of every individual within it; and their claim has the support of a large section of the people of the country, and of a peculiar force of emotion. This support is gained, and this emotion caused by the fact that they are "evil things" that we are fighting against. That they are evil we need have no doubt; yet many of us still feel distrust of these claims and these emotions lest they blind men to their duty of considering carefully, before they act, the justice of the things they propose to do. Men can be moved to fight by being made to hate the deeds of their enemies; but a war is not made just by the fact that one's enemies' deeds are hateful. Therefore it is our duty to resist passion and to consider carefully whether all the conditions of a just war are satisfied in this present war, lest we sin against the natural law by participating in it.[16]

Anscombe's pamphlet exemplifies much more of a well-reasoned, conscientious stand than anything mustered by the bishops who suppressed it, more too, for that matter, than the bishops of our day who have so quickly and sketchily assured their flocks of the justice of this present war.

The second remarkable Catholic is Dorothy Day, cofounder of the Catholic Worker Movement, editor of *The Catholic Worker* paper, and author of several books, including the autobiographical account of her journey to God, *The Long Loneliness*, one chapter of which is entitled, "War Is the Health of the State." The reference is to Bourne's essay and it is a purposely provocative one, given that Bourne's left-leaning sympathies would not be well received in some quarters when the book was published in 1952 at the height of the cold war. Like Anscombe, Day stood against her country's declaration of war, but unlike Anscombe she did so as a Christian pacifist. "We Continue Our Christian Pacifist Stand," she entitled an editorial of *The Catholic Worker* in January 1942. She wrote:

> Seventy-five thousand copies of *The Catholic Worker* go out every month. What shall we print? We can still print what the Holy Father is saying, when he speaks of total war, of mitigating the horrors of war, when he speaks of cities of refuge; of feeding Europe . . .
>
> We will print the words of Christ, who is with us always, even to the end of the world. "Love your enemies, do good to those who hate you, and pray for those who persecute and calumniate you, so that you may be children of your Father in heaven, who makes His sun to rise on the good and the evil, and sends rain on the just and the unjust."
>
> We are at war, a declared war, with Japan, Germany, and Italy. But still we can repeat Christ's words, each day, holding them close in our hearts, each month printing them in the paper. In times past Europe has been a battlefield. But let us remember St. Francis, who spoke of peace, and we will remind our readers of him, too, so they will not forget.
>
> In *The Catholic Worker* we will quote our Pope, our saints, our priests. We will go on printing the articles of Fr. Hugo, who reminds us today that we are all "called to be saints," that we are other Christs, reminding us of the priesthood of the laity.
>
> We are still pacifists. Our manifesto is the Sermon on the Mount, which means that we will try to be peacemakers.[17]

Not surprisingly, the circulation of *The Catholic Worker* dropped after this editorial and throughout the World War II right up to its end, when Day condemned the use of the atomic bomb on Japan. Subscriptions never returned to their prewar level.

In their pastoral letter *The Challenge of Peace,* the Catholic bishops of the United States commended Dorothy Day for her commitment to nonviolence.[18] But this commendation rings hollow given their performance over the past six months, which reveals their allegiance to, as Day would put it, "Holy Mother State" over Jesus Christ, their—our— true Lord and King. Of course, this stance does not answer the question, What should we do about terrorism?—at least not in the terms in which it is usually posed. For the *we* for Dorothy Day is not *we Americans* but we Catholics, we disciples, we who have been baptized and thus transformed into "other Christs." In which case the answer to the question is that we counter the works of war by practicing the works of mercy, feeding the hungry, giving drink to the thirsty, welcoming the stranger, visiting the sick and imprisoned. There are scores of Catholic Worker Houses and other communities that engage in such practices and that have reiterated the stand taken by Dorothy Day at the outset of World War II: "We are still pacifists. Our manifesto is the Sermon on the Mount, which means that we will try to be peacemakers."

In conclusion, it might make sense to describe one or more such communities as a way to display the kind of life to which "we" are called as members of the body of Christ. But this would beg the question of what to do about terrorism, for these communities are still rather far removed from the threat of terrorism, and are being protected, like it or not, by the Armed Forces of the United States of America. So instead, I would like to turn to another community whose life and work is shaped by the works of mercy, a community of Trappist monks in Tibhirine, Algeria.

The community was founded in 1938 under the patronage of Notre-Dame de L'Atlas at Tibhirine, a name meaning "the gardens."[19] In the decades that followed, the small community of monks established their traditional life of prayer and contemplation and also served the people of the nearby village, who were Muslims. One brother set up a medical clinic and served the villagers for some five decades. Some of the other monks agreed to assist the villagers with aspects of the financing and distribution of their olive oil production. The monastery as a whole was trusted by the villagers. There was mutual respect, love. But on Christmas Eve 1993, the monastery was invaded by a band of militant Islamist rebels, notorious for their violence and readiness to assassinate their enemies. In this encounter, the leader of the rebel group informed the abbot of the monastery, Father Christian de Chergé, that the community must leave the area.

De Chergé said that they would not be leaving, to which the leader said, "You have no choice." De Chergé replied, "Oh, but we do." Over the next several years, the monks consistently refused to acquiesce to the demands of the rebels. At the same time, they refused the protection of the Algerian military. Then on March 24, 1996, seven of the monks were kidnapped and held by armed rebels, and on May 24, they were massacred by their captors. Their decapitated heads were found on May 30, 1996. The monks knew that this fate was in all likelihood awaiting them.

In this day and age, especially in the months since September 11, the problem facing the civilized world is often presented in terms of religious pluralism or differences and the solution is often presented in terms of religious tolerance or civility, an understandable response to religiously inspired violence. But there may be a trap awaiting those who follow this line of reasoning. For when the problem of religious tolerance is cast in terms of statecraft, the solution comes in the form of the modern liberal state; and this solution, which is the solution of "we Americans," all too easily transforms into yet another ideology for violence. The monks show us another way, born out of their identity as members of the Body of Christ, a way that embraces differences to the point of being willing to die rather than obliterate the other, all the while trusting in a God who has mercy on us all.

This other way is most dramatically articulated in a circular letter that Father de Chergé wrote before his death addressing his family, friends, fellow monks, and even his would-be assassin. After clarifying that the extremism of the Muslim militants in Algeria does not represent true and genuine Islam, he explains that there in Tibhirine, in relating with his Muslim neighbors and in learning their faith and religion, he has learned some important things about the Gospel, things that we—we Christians, we Catholics—need to learn again and again. He writes:

> I have proclaimed it loud and clear, I believe, to everyone who knows me that I found here the clue to the Gospel that I learned at my mother's knee, my first church, and in the respect of Muslim believers.
> My death would seem to vindicate those who summarily dismiss me as naïve, an idealist, (saying): "Let him say these things now!"

But they ought to know that at last my long-lived curiosity will be satisfied.

For then I shall be able, if it pleases God, to submerge my gaze in the Father's, to see his Islamic children, illuminated by the glory of Christ, by the fruits of his passion, endowed with the gift of the Spirit, whose secret joy is always to establish communion and to restore likeness, by acting among differences.

For life lost, totally mine and totally theirs, I give thanks to God, who seems to have wanted it to be utterly so, for this joy, through and despite everything.

Within this thank you where once and for all, all is said about my life, I include you, my friends of yesterday and of today, and you, my friends from here, along with my mother and my father, my sisters and my brothers and all who belong to them, (life) yielded a hundredfold as was promised!

And you, too, my last-minute friend, you who know not what you do.

Yes, for you too I wish this thank you, and this *adieu* which is of your planning.

May we meet each other again, happy thieves, in paradise, should it please God, the Father of us. Amen!

Inshallah![20]

NOTES

1 *Veritatis Splendor*, n. 99, 101; *Evangelium Vitae*, n. 18–20.

2 *Evangelium Vitae*, n. 20.

3 See Christopher Hitchens, *For the Sake of Argument* (London: Verso, 1993), 216–21.

4 Randolph S. Bourne, "The State," in *War and the Intellectuals: Collected Essays, 1915–1919*, ed. Carl Resek (New York: Harper and Row, 1964), 65–104.

5 Bourne, "The State," 69.

6 Ibid., 77, 78, 70.

7 The essay to which I refer is "The War and the Intellectuals," in Bourne, *War and the Intellectuals*, 3–14; see 7.

8 Ibid., 71.

9 Ibid., 71.

10 Anthony Cardinal Bevilacqua, Archbishop of Philadelphia, "Statement Regarding U.S. Attack in Afghanistan," October 8, 2001. Viewed online November 28, 2001, at www.archdiocese-phl.org/abo/archstat/acbafgha.htm.

11 Francis Cardinal George, O.M.I., Archbishop of Chicago, "Statement from Rome on U.S. Military Action in Afghanistan," October 9, 2001. Viewed online November 28, 2001, at www.archdiocese-chgo.org/cardinal/state ment/stat_01_100901.shtmp.

12 National Conference of Catholic Justices, "A Pastoral Message: Living with Faith and Hope after September 11," November 14, 2001. Viewed online November 28, 2001, at www.nccbuscc.org/sdwp/Sept11.htm.

13 *Evangelium Vitae*, n. 73.

14 M. K. Gandhi, *Non-Violent Resistance*, ed. Bharatan Kuma rappa (New York: Schocken Books, 1951), 102–76.

15 Lovis Fischer, *The Life of Mahatma Gandhi* (New York: Harper and Row, 1950), 240.

16 In *War in the Twentieth Century*, ed. Richard Miller (Louisville, Ky.: Westminster/John Knox, 1992), 125.

17 In *The Selected Writings of Dorothy Day*, ed. Robert Ellsberg (New York: Knopf, 1983), 261–62.

18 National Conference of Catholic Bishops, *The Challenge of Peace: God's Promise and Our Response* (Washington, D.C.: United States Catholic Conference, 1983), n. 117.

19 For an account of the life and witness of this monastic community, see John W. Kiser, *The Monks of Tibhirine* (New York: St. Martin's Press, 2002).

20 This particular translation of de Chergé's letter can be found in *Origins* 26 (June 13, 1996): 50–51.

SUSAN WILLIS

Old Glory

They just want to show their patriotism because that's all they can do.
—A flag salesman in Durham, North Carolina, interviewed on
BBC World Service, December 6, 2001

In the wake of the attack on the World Trade Center, America responded with the rapid deployment of the American flag. The urge to
display the flag was ignited by the Iwo Jima–style image of the three
firefighters who raised the flag over the rubble at the Lower Manhattan site and whose photograph was then emblazoned across the
front pages of the nation's newspapers. Desire to perpetuate the heroic
image has since impelled the development firm Forest City Ratner to
commission a statue in the likeness of the photo, which will be installed at the New York City Fire Department headquarters. Subsequent calls that the statue reflect the multiethnic makeup of the victims
of the attack—and America generally—have resulted in the decision
to create a statue where two of the original white flag raisers will be
replaced by representative black and Hispanic figures.

Many Americans who support the inclusion of nonwhite figures fail
to realize that New York City's firefighters—like its police force—are
almost exclusively white. Mayor Giuliani, everyone's hero of the day
and *Time*'s "Man of the Year," reigned over this country's most ethni-
cally diverse city with the most racially exclusionary uniformed brigades. The nation's desire to transform the statue of New York's firefighters into an emblem of diversity gives symbolic reversal to the
city's racist policies. It also makes the statue a displaced icon of a different fighting force that is racially diverse: the U.S. military. In the
guise of New York's firefighters the statue embodies the nation and

facilitates a shift from the local to the international, from the work of recovery to the work of war. As a sliding signifier, the statue enables the nation's attention to move from Lower Manhattan to the new Iwo Jima in Kabul and Kandahar.

The desire to inculcate the statue with the spirit of multicultural-ism also serves to assimilate America's nonwhite population under the universal blanket flag euphoria, in contradiction to the fact that the de-monstrative display of flags has been a predominantly white response. Notwithstanding the Arab merchants who quickly attached the Ameri-can flag to their homes and businesses in the hopes of heading off attacks by rabid bands of U.S. patriots, most black and Hispanic neigh-borhoods have been relatively flag free. Incorporating black and His-panic figures into the composition of the firefighter statue may well give recognition to the numbers of nonwhites who serve the country, but its larger purpose is to launder the image of the flag itself and the country for which it stands—both better known by these same popu-lations for sponsoring racial profiling, neighborhood sweeps by "la Migra," and doing everything possible to avoid reparations for slavery.

While the attitude of many nonwhite residents and citizens of the United States is one of letting white folks do their thing, the mean-ings attached to flag waving have a lot to tell us about the America that emerged phoenix-like out of its ashes to remake itself for the twenty-first century. This survey of flag scenarios looks beyond the various clichéd versions of "United We Stand" to consider ideologies implicit to empire and free-market consumerism—all unfurled with the flag.

Not only is the flag displayed at fixed positions, on homes, freeway overpasses, and storefronts, it has also become a circulating signifier. The flag raised Iwo Jima style over New York's Ground Zero was sub-sequently shipped to Afghanistan where it was raised over the Kanda-har airport. Passed from the hands of the firefighters to those of the marines, the flag designates a shift in America's interests away from a host of domestic needs left pending after September 11, and toward a politics aimed at military operations overseas, whose repercussion on the domestic is, then, the militarization of the homefront under the guise of Homeland Security. The fact that this particular flag can gener-ate certain specific meanings in its New York incarnation and very dif-ferent ones over Kandahar makes it a supersymbol. Indeed, in its power to evoke healing and perseverance over New York and retribution over

Kandahar, this flag shows itself as an empty signifier, capable of designating a host of referents without being perceived as contradictory. As empty signifier, this flag concentrates the power inherent in the commodity to become a fetish. Like the Shroud of Turin, this flag speaks for a form of patriotism raised to the level of religion. As a physical object, it offers itself as relic—a replacement for a more properly materialist sense of history. As relic, it embodies the fundamentalism of the Bush White House, where there is little distinction between ardent political conservatism and Christian evangelical values. One can imagine that the firefighter's flag will continue to circulate, following the antiterrorist special forces brigade to all the world's hot spots. With each unfurling, the flag will consecrate yet another site crucial to America's efforts to secure the global production and distribution of oil. The existence of this flag will finally bestow meaning on all the flags we purchase at Wal-Mart and on eBay. It proclaims the possibility of the unique object, the object that valorizes our investment of hopes and desires in our pitiful series of knockoffs.

Immediately following the collapse of the Twin Towers with numbers of investment concerns in disarray and the economy spiraling into the recession nobody was yet willing to acknowledge, we were told to shop. Shop to show we are patriotic Americans. Shop to show our resilience over death and destruction. Shop because in consumer capitalism shopping is the only way we can participate. Contrary to our president's call to shop, many Americans chose, instead, to give blood as eucharistic bonding of our life and body with those stricken and maimed. The desire to make physical connection with others, to describe community in the exchange and circulation of blood contrasts with the consumerist model of society where people are articulated as individual consumers rather than members of a collectivity. While the donor model of community strikes a contrast, it is already being recycled into consumerism as a number of dystopian writers (Leslie Marmon Silko, for one) have begun to imagine a world where the poor are farmed for their organs, a situation become reality in China, where wealthy consumers can bid on the organs of death-row inmates.

Americans overwhelmed blood-donor sites even when it became apparent that the rubble would yield few survivors—indeed, few bodies. Awash in a sea of blood that couldn't possibly be used within the time that blood can be stored, blood banks urged donors to postpone their donations. The request that people delay the gratification associated with giving flies in the face of a nation trained to expect the sorts of gratifications associated with consumerism where pleasure is supposed to be spontaneous and continual. No wonder many turned to displays of the flag as the only available mode of proclaiming community. Remarkably, the great majority of Americans did not purchase a "real flag," one made of cloth to prescribed dimensions and typically hoisted up a flagpole, but chose instead to tape a paper version on their car window or mount a plastic one on their car antenna. Did they anticipate that the flag craze would undergo the obsolescence of all commodities, making the paper or plastic flag most appropriate? Or did they intuit that in a society wholly defined by consumerism plastic is most representative; indeed, there can be no real object (except the superfetish circling the globe with the special forces). Finally, the display of flags underscores the importance of quantity over quality. Engulfed and smothered in flags, we consume them visually. Much of the American landscape gives the impression that we all shopped at a Wal-Mart where the only item on the shelf is the flag.

While the flag is an empty signifier, the context of its display endows it with meaning. For instance, flags displayed in the Garden District of New Orleans, all of them cloth and flagpole appropriate, absorb the meanings generated by their ambient context defined by upper-middle-class comfort and good taste. The trolley ride down St. Charles Street evokes a journey down Embassy Row, with every embassy flying the same flag. As testament to America's global reach, the view down St. Charles Street bespeaks America's new alliances in the fight against terrorism wherein every nation's troublesome dissidents become a pretext to adopt America's search and destroy policy. Russia's war against the Chechens, China's repression of its Muslim population in Xia Jiang Province, and Israel's drive to exterminate the Palestinians—all implicitly fly the American flag of approval.

Many Americans in more humble districts and abodes not nearly so grand as the mansions of the Garden District have refrained from the hubris of mounting a disproportionately huge flag on the front porch and instead chosen to incorporate a flag in the larger landscape setting of the house. Flags can be seen sprouting from garden beds and a few hanging from trees—both sites probably frowned upon by the guardians of flag etiquette. Of the flags displayed in gardens, the great majority are intimately connected with the homeowner's mailbox. Draped around the mailbox post, attached to the red mailbox "flag," or popping out of the ground next to the mailbox, flag and mailbox declare a symbiotic relationship that bespeaks the nation's political unconscious. In connecting flag to mailbox, we give symbolic recognition to the dead and endangered postal workers whose exposure to anthrax was belatedly and inadequately addressed by the selfsame government that claims to act in the name of the flag. In contrast to the employees of the Hart Senate Office Building, who were carefully screened for anthrax, their offices undergoing costly and lengthy fumigation, postal workers were summarily overlooked even though it was obvious that the mail that brought anthrax to Senator Daschle's office passed through the hands and buildings of postal workers. In turning our mailboxes into flag shrines, we acknowledge that our country treats its workers unequally and we make a symbolic gesture to restore parity by giving recognition to those who otherwise died disregarded and in vain.

By far the most preferred site for flag display is the automobile. Taped to the inside rear window, tattooed into the paint, or streaming from tailgate or antenna, the auto flag makes every roadway into a Fourth of July parade route. Flags on cars can give rise to patriotic forms of road rage as the drivers of noticeably flag-bedecked autos attempt to cut off drivers deemed less patriotic by the telltale absence of a car flag. A passive-aggressive form of road rage is manifested by the pickup truck convoy, traveling at 10 mph and forcing a long line of motorists to begrudgingly queue up. The various forms of flag-induced road rage bespeak the ideological blackmail not only brought to bear on America's allies but on all of us as well with the slogan, "If you're not with us, you're against us."

In the days immediately following September 11, many Americans in places far removed from Ground Zero took to the roads in a frustrated attempt to get away from the twenty-four-hour news coverage and in search of other shell-shocked Americans. Since we are held together by our interstates and conduct much of our daily lives from behind the wheel of our cars, it's not odd that we would take to our cars in the effort to connect. With public transport at a halt, the private car was our only access to the freedom of mobility. The foray out on the road was apt to dramatize all the socially symbolic meanings we attach to cars generally—and by extension to the flags they fly. Predictably, the biggest, most numerous, and most noticeable flags are mounted on pick-ups and suvs. Even while radio and tv pundits continue to disclaim the feeble voices from the left that suggest a link between the removal of the Taliban and their questionable efficacy as stewards of the trans-Uzbek pipeline, Americans show with our car-mounted flags that we know the "war on terrorism" is the code phrase for the preservation of our interstates, cars, suburbs, and the petrochemical octopus that feeds and clothes us.

 While all our displays of the flag partake of ritual practices and meanings (if only in the way we mount our flags and later decide when it's appropriate to take one down), there is one use of the flag that far outstrips all others for ritual import. This involves the six thousand flags—most probably diminutive—reported to have been blasted into space with American astronauts aboard space shuttle Endeavor. The astronauts also brought aboard three large flags—one each from the World Trade Center, the Pentagon, and the Pennsylvania State Capitol—in an effort to consecrate these for more earthly missions. The number of small flags was meant to symbolize the then-purported six thousand victims of the attack on the World Trade Center. That the number of victims has now been scaled back to half the original number means that we now have a surplus of ritually charged flags. Rather than freighting the flags into space and jettisoning them into the heavens where they might ritualize our nation's release from the stubborn pursuit of body parts and dna molecules at Ground Zero, these flags were destined to return to earth, bearing with them the persistent dead weight of America's obdurate responsibility to physically account for each and every victim. We saw some of the same grim determination in the desperate attempt to recover the bodies buried under hundreds of feet of water off the coast of Nova Scotia, lost when Swissair Flight 111 plummeted into the sea. Why this mania to recover the physical remains of loved ones lost in catastrophe, particularly when what's left is apt to be unrecognizable if not grisly?

 Perhaps we are driven by the tantalizing possibilities offered by our own technologies. We seek the blood stains because we can actually make a positive identification with molecular evidence. We are a nation enthralled with forensics for whom Ground Zero offers a real-life stage equal to tv's new hit drama *Crime Scene Investigation*. Does it matter that funds earmarked to bring DNA testing to bear on the convictions of many of our nation's death-row inmates has been diverted to Ground Zero? Clearly, some lives—or deaths—count more than others, particularly when it comes to accountability at Ground Zero, where large insurance premium holders have more death capital than those who will receive government compensation alone. On a larger scale, looking beyond inmates and victims, Americans generally count more than the world's others. The value of the handful of American deaths occasioned by the bombing of Afghanistan—calculated as each was brought home for televised memorials—far outweighs Afghanistan's estimated four thousand civilian deaths who do not compute in the U.S. calculus of television coverage. These faceless, nameless nonvictims have the negative value comparable to a third world nation's IMF debt.

Ever since the Oklahoma City bombing, our media have harped on our nation's need to find "closure." In the case of the Murrah Federal Building, closure could only be obtained once we found, buried, and memorialized each and every victim; and then finalized our mourning with Timothy McVeigh's execution. The quest for closure became media fodder, filling the twenty-four-hour news networks and perpetuating our need to achieve—possibly document—what amounts to a collective psychic event based on a collective bookkeeping. The accountability of death puts mourning on a balance sheet where closure indicates an account paid. What about an unbalanced equation? Or possibly, an open account? What about the fiscal uncertainty that really defines our lives and typifies the exponential growth of capital as a system based on speculation, where bankruptcy is a fact of life? Fanatically craving closure, we attempt to bring accountability into our daily lives as futile counterbalance to a system that shreds accountability like an Enron balance sheet. What's lost in the desperate desire for closure as corrective to chaos is the possibility of imagining death as an open ending, as disappearance that absolves the living from possessive attachment.

In our unwillingness to simply let the dead disappear, we express a deep cultural antipathy for ambiguity. We are living in a time of obdurate literal mindedness that cannot tolerate anything that smacks of a symbolic disappearance. Like the insurance companies that detected false September 11 claims, we police death with the demand for proof.

Just as our dead must be accounted for, so too must Osama bin Laden be found "dead or alive." We find it intolerably frustrating that the object of our military manhunt eludes capture even while his video image keeps appearing on an upstart non-Western television station. In the same way that we excavate the rubble of the World Trade Center, sifting the debris for bloodstains and body parts, we search the caves of Tora Bora for Al Qaeda stragglers. A culture incapable of experiencing disappearance as cleansing release, a culture whose passion is reduced to the literal has become the epitome of the fundamentalism for which we condemn the Taliban.

The flags transported into space and conveyed back to earth are meant to be given to the families of the September 11 attack. Leaving aside the American hubris that assumes every victim's family will want an American flag, including the families of foreign nationals and those of the illegal immigrants thought to be in the World Trade Center's basements, the space flags bespeak an allegory for the twenty-first century, wherein religion merges with science and technology. Transported into space, the flags were literally brought closer to God. Have we devolved to the level of the child who imagines God in his heavenly throne among the clouds? Or do we imagine that the flags, like the space tourist Dennis Tito, were launched into the ultimate trip and meant to imbibe the essence of America's technological and scientific know-how as counterweight to the Russian know-how that Tito imbibed? By reason of their ritual journey, the space flags absolve contradiction. Consecrated, they return to earth bearing religious and technological benediction.

The distribution of the space flags to the victims' families commemorates the federalization of September 11. Employees of private enterprise have become with their deaths America's war heroes. Their transformation from private to public employees renders their families the beneficiaries of federal compensation. While precedent for federal compensation can be found in government payments to the victims of natural disasters such as floods, fires, and earthquakes, the federalization of the attacks of September 11 has the political benefit of nationalizing the event, which in turn provides a convenient rationale for America's undeclared war. With three thousand individuals who died for our country, who among us felt justified in taking a strong stand against the bombing of Afghanistan? Witness the contortions among the editors and writers of *The Nation,* our country's most widely distributed liberal newspaper, that promulgated the dubious category of a "just war." Moreover, with the government offering federal compensation, who among the victims' families will choose to forgo the sure and easy payment for the sake of launching a risky private suit? With its mass tort the government buys silence. It pays to eliminate the possibility of thousands of private suits that may not have garnered the claimants more money but would have uncovered possible areas of blame in the private sector.

Notwithstanding the secret CIA headquarters in the World Trade Center complex, the great majority of the victims died in the service of global finance capital. Like the thousands who lost their jobs and pensions because they staked their futures on Enron, the victims of the World Trade Center staked their futures on enterprises targeted because they are synonymous with our country's commitment to global capitalism. To raise a private suit is to demand that big business be deemed accountable.

Less grandiose than the space flags and more personal than the mailbox and car flags are the flags we sport on our T-shirts. Emblazoned across our chests, the flag becomes one with the rock bands and sports teams that also claim our allegiance and warrant a T-shirt's stamp of approval. The nation that condemns flag desecration shows no qualms over making the flag into a fashion statement. This is because the dictates of a society built on consumerism are supported by the Bill of Rights, where the individual's guarantee of freedom of speech has been extended to corporations as individual entities whose speech acts may include political contributions as well as T-shirt logos.

With flags on our shirts, we express the heartfelt desire to contribute our individual pledge to the collective endeavor, even while we simultaneously recognize that the American endeavor is to consume commodities and ensure their worldwide distribution. In the wake of September 11, many T-shirt ads emphasized that the shirt on sale was "Made in America." Would it matter if our flag T-shirts were screenprinted in Haitian sweatshops given the fact that many "official" Disney products come from such places, where they are sometimes made by children who are the age mates of the American children who wear Disney paraphernalia? For its triviality, the T-shirt flag concretizes the global circulation of the commodity. It is the mundane emblem for the welding of market capital to empire. Finally, all over the world we can all buy America even though the day is fast approaching when nothing will be made in America. No matter, all the world's citizens will be able to trade in our logos. Our friends and allies may find it "cool" to wear our flag, while our enemies will find it in the litter of their countries' war zones—stamped on the mine, bomb, and grenade fragments as indication that retribution is also made in America.

SLAVOJ ŽIŽEK

Welcome to the Desert of the Real!

The ultimate American paranoiac fantasy is that of an individual living in a small idyllic Californian city, a consumerist paradise, who suddenly starts to suspect that the world he lives in is a fake, a spectacle staged to convince him that he lives in a real world, while all the people around him are effectively actors and extras in a gigantic show. The most recent example of this is Peter Weir's *The Truman Show* (1998), with Jim Carrey playing the small-town clerk who gradually discovers the truth that he is the hero of a twenty-four-hour permanent TV show: his hometown is constructed on a gigantic studio set, with cameras following him around the clock. Among its predecessors, it is worth mentioning Philip Dick's *Time Out of Joint* (1959), in which a hero living a modest daily life in a small idyllic Californian city of the late 1950s gradually realizes that the whole town is a fake staged to keep him satisfied. The underlying experience of *Time Out of Joint* and of *The Truman Show* is that the late capitalist consumerist Californian paradise is, in its very hyper-reality, in a way *irreal*, substanceless, deprived of the material inertia.

So it is not only that Hollywood stages a semblance of real life deprived of the weight and inertia of materiality—in the late capitalist consumerist society, "real social life" itself somehow acquires the features of a staged fake, with our neighbors behaving in "real" life as stage actors and extras. Again, the ultimate truth of the capitalist utilitarian despiritualized universe is the dematerialization of the "real life" itself, its reversal into a spectral show. Among others, Christopher Isherwood gave expression to this unreality of the American daily life, exemplified in the motel room: "American motels are unreal! . . . they are deliberately designed to be unreal. . . . The Europeans hate us because we've retired to live inside our advertisements, like hermits going into caves to contemplate." Peter Sloterdijk's notion of the "sphere" is here literally realized, as the gigantic metal sphere that envelopes and isolates the entire city. Years ago, a series of science-fiction films like *Zardoz* or *Logan's Run* forecasted today's postmodern predicament by extending this fantasy to the community itself: the isolated group living an aseptic life in a secluded area longs for the experience of the real world of material decay.

The Wachowski brothers' hit *Matrix* (1999) brought this logic to its climax: the material reality we all experience and see around us is a virtual one, generated and coordinated by a gigantic megacomputer to which we are all attached; when the hero (played by Keanu Reeves) awakens into the "real reality," he sees a desolate landscape littered with burned ruins—what remained of Chicago after a global war. The resistance leader Morpheus utters the ironic greeting: "Welcome to the desert of the real." Was it not something of the similar order that took place in New York on September 11? Its citizens were introduced to the "desert of the real"—to us, corrupted by Hollywood, the landscape and the shots we saw of the collapsing towers could not but remind us of the most breathtaking scenes in the big catastrophe productions.

When we hear how the bombings were a totally unexpected shock, how the unimaginable Impossible happened, one should recall the other defining catastrophe from the beginning of the twentieth century, that of the *Titanic:* it was also a shock, but the space for it was already prepared in ideological fantasizing, since *Titanic* was the symbol of the might of the nineteenth-century industrial civilization. Does the same not hold for these bombings?

Not only were the media bombarding us all the time with the talk about the terrorist threat; this threat was also obviously libidinally invested—just recall the series of movies from *Escape from New York* to *Independence Day*. The unthinkable that happened was thus the object of fantasy: in a way, America got what it fantasized about, and this was the greatest surprise.

It is precisely now, when we are dealing with the raw Real of a catastrophe, that we should bear in mind the ideological and fantasmatic coordinates that determine its perception. If there is any symbolism in the collapse of the World Trade Center towers, it is not so much the old-fashioned notion of the "center of financial capitalism," but rather the notion that the towers stood for the center of the *virtual* capitalism, of financial speculations disconnected from the sphere of material production. The shattering impact of the bombings can be accounted for only against the background of the borderline that today separates the digitalized first world from the third world "desert of the Real." It is the awareness that we live in an insulated artificial universe which generates the notion that some ominous agent is threatening us all the time with total destruction.

Is, consequently, Osama bin Laden, the suspected mastermind behind the bombings, not the real-life counterpart of Ernst Stavro Blofeld, the master-criminal in most of the James Bond films, who was involved in the acts of global destruction? What one should recall here is that the only place in Hollywood films where we see the production process in all its intensity is when James Bond penetrates the master-criminal's secret domain and locates there the site of intense labor (distilling and packaging the drugs, constructing a rocket that will destroy New York . . .). When the master-criminal, after capturing Bond, usually takes him on a tour of his illegal factory, is this not the closest Hollywood comes to the socialist-realist proud presentation of the production in a factory? And the function of Bond's intervention, of course, is to explode in firecracks this site of production, allowing us to return to the daily semblance of our existence in a world with the "disappearing working class." Is it not that, in the exploding Twin Towers, this violence directed at the threatening Outside turned back at us?

The safe sphere in which Americans live is experienced as under threat from the Outside of terrorist attackers who are ruthlessly self-sacrificing *and* cowards, cunningly intelligent *and* primitive barbarians. Whenever we encounter such a purely evil Outside, we should gather the courage to endorse the Hegelian lesson: in this pure Outside, we should recognize the distilled version of our own essence. For the last five centuries, the (relative) prosperity and peace of the "civilized" West was bought by the export of ruthless violence and destruction into the "barbarian" Outside: the long story from the conquest of America to the slaughter in Congo. Cruel and indifferent as it may sound, we should also, now more than ever, bear in mind that the actual effect of these bombings is much more symbolic than real. The United States just got a taste of what goes on around the world on a daily basis, from Sarajevo to Groznyy, from Rwanda and Congo to

Sierra Leone. If one adds to the situation in New York snipers and gang rapes, one gets an idea about what Sarajevo was a decade ago.

It is when we watched on the TV screen the towers collapsing that it became possible to experience the falsity of the "reality TV shows": even if these shows are "for real," people still act in them—they simply play themselves. The standard disclaimer in a novel ("Characters in this text are a fiction. Any resemblance with real-life characters is purely contingent") holds also for the participants of the reality soaps: what we see there are fictional characters, even if they play themselves. Of course, the "return to the real" can be given different twists: rightist commentators like George Will immediately proclaimed the end of the American "holiday from history"—the impact of reality shattering the isolated tower of the liberal tolerant attitude and the Cultural Studies focus on textuality. Now, we are forced to strike back, to deal with real enemies in the real world . . . However, *whom* to strike? Whatever the response, it will never hit the *right* target, bringing us full satisfaction. The ridicule of America attacking Afghanistan cannot but strike the eye: if the greatest power in the world will destroy one of the poorest countries in which peasants barely survive on barren hills, will this not be the ultimate case of the impotent acting out?

There is a partial truth in the notion of the "clash of civilizations" attested here—witness the surprise of the average American: "How is it possible that these people have such a disregard for their own lives?" Does not this surprise reveal the rather sad fact that we, in the first world countries, find it more and more difficult even to imagine a public or universal Cause for which one would be ready to sacrifice one's life?

When, after the bombings, even the Taliban foreign minister said that he can "feel the pain" of the American children, did he not thereby confirm the hegemonic ideological role of this Bill Clinton trademark phrase? And the notion of America as a safe haven, of course, is also a fantasy: when a New Yorker commented on how, after the bombings, one can no longer walk safely on the city's streets, the irony of it was that, well before the bombings, the streets of New York were well-known for their dangers. If anything, the bombings gave rise to a new sense of solidarity, with the scenes of young African Americans helping an old Jewish gentleman to cross the street, scenes unimaginable before the attacks.

In the days immediately following the bombings, it is as if we dwell in the unique time between a traumatic event and its symbolic impact, like in those brief moments after we are deeply cut and before the full extent of the pain strikes us: it remains to be seen how the events will be symbolized, what their symbolic efficiency will be, what acts they will be evoked to justify. Even here, in these moments of utmost tension, this link is not automatic but contingent. There are already the first bad omens; the day after the bombing, I got a message from the editor of a journal in which a longer text of mine on Lenin was about to be published. The editor told me that they decided to postpone its publication. They considered it inopportune to publish a text on Lenin immediately after the attacks. Does this not point toward the ominous ideological rearticulations that will follow?

We don't yet know what consequences in economy, ideology, politics, war this event will have, but one thing is sure: the United States, which, till now, perceived itself as an island exempted from this kind of violence, witnessing this kind of thing only from the safe distance of the TV screen, is now directly involved. So the alternative is, Will Americans decide to fortify further their "sphere," or will they risk stepping out of it?

Either America will persist in, strengthen even, the attitude, "Why should this happen to us? Things like this don't happen *here*!"—leading to more aggression toward the threatening Outside, in short: to a paranoiac acting out—or America will finally risk stepping through the fantasmatic screen separating it from the Outside World, accepting its arrival into the Real world, making the long-overdue move from "Things like this should not happen *here*!" to "Things like this should not happen *anywhere*!" America's "holiday from history" was a fake: America's peace was bought by the catastrophes going on elsewhere. Therein resides the true lesson of the bombings.

PETER OCHS

September 11 and the Children of Abraham

"What shocked you about September 11?" I ask my students, and the question is still alive to them today, six months later (a long time in American memory!). Among their responses: "The shock of North American vulnerability, I didn't know *we* could be attacked"; "The brutality of the attacks, the fact that people driven by beliefs and ideals could act so cruelly"; "The shock simply of so many innocent lives lost and such destruction"; "The burst of awareness that what goes on in the rest of the world can go on here too, *and* that *our* actions may have such negative effects over *there*, and *their* actions such negative effects here"; "The shock that I don't now know what to do with my career. I hadn't counted on this; I thought all that mattered was what I wanted to study and what profession would be fulfilling. But what shall I do now? The rest of the world matters more than I realized"; "The shock that religion could matter so much, for good and for evil."

"And will this shock lead to lasting lessons or changes in the American character?" I ask for a show of hands: two-thirds of the students vote "no," one-third, "yes."

Is the American character profoundly changed by the events of September 11? Or was it a momentary opening—like the opening of the Red Sea for Ancient Israel—and now the waters have quickly closed over and very little has changed? Or was it a brief opening during which some significant numbers actually passed through, from a kind of bondage to a kind of freedom—as, for those few Israelites in the Exodus narrative, it was a moment of opportunity, to pass from physical bondage to that liberty that enabled them to stand at the foot of Mount Sinai and learn how to serve God instead of Pharaoh? Well, I don't know what September 11 meant for the United States. I don't know if it was a momentary interruption in the normal business of our economically driven patterns of social exchange and if the moment has already passed and what matters again are our individual salaries and family needs and a lingering irritation that we still have to think about military matters in foreign places. Of course, it might be unfair to think that, unless it is brought on, God forbid, by cataclysms far greater than the events of September 11, any significant societal change would have to be such a dramatic one to count as significant change. I don't know if, sometime later, we may look back and see that some necessarily small but significant transformation took place in certain social and religious institutions in the United States or the West—nor do I know if these will have been changes for the better or the worse.

I don't know all these things, but, for better or worse, I don't assume I need to understand things on a large scale in order to have something to say. To have something to say, as I understand it, is merely to find that some event has interrupted one's life in some way, that the interruption has itself stimulated some inner outpouring of words as if they were somehow going to fill the gap caused by the interruption, and then somebody else has asked to hear those words. So, yes the events of September 11 have interrupted some aspect of what I do and of what my community of thinking and worshipping does; and yes some words have by now arisen in me and my communities in the space of this interruption; and yes, Hauerwas has asked to hear those words, so I offer them. Here are four of these "words," or topics of response, each one linked as well to an image that evokes the topic for me.

1. An "Event" is what shocks me to turn to the *we* that guides me
in times of dislocation. The *we* names a community in history,
or a tradition, and, for me, this tradition goes back to the shock
of Sinai, of the Ye Shalls and Ye Shall Nots.

For me, normal, everyday times include moments of pain and confusion, because this is, after all, a time after the Garden of Eden and, except for the Sabbath, the time after the Garden is work time, six-days-of-the-week time, not-yet-the-end time when life shouldn't include such painful moments. But work time is also part of the divine plan and is also touched by its own measure of divine mercy. I locate this mercy in the fact that our everyday lives are serviced by social institutions that are usually capable, every day, of responding to and mending our everyday pains and confusions: families and small groups for love; hospitals for bodily wounds and illnesses; schools for confusions about how to understand the world; police for acts of violence; churches, synagogues, mosques, and ashrams for other levels of love.

But there are pains and confusions that, at a given time and place, even our service institutions cannot mend. I understand these to be symptoms of "Events," meaning interruptions in the social fabric of our everyday lives—big-time wounds—that cannot be mended without significant changes or reforms in our fundamental institutions. The symptoms of such Events cannot even be read properly by those who run our service institutions, since such symptoms would contradict, or remain invisible to, what these leaders or managers are trained to expect of the world. A mundane example is that illness you show your doctor, but he or she cannot see it, because it isn't in the medical books yet. To be sure, that illness may also bring with it more recognizable symptoms, and the doctor would be right to treat those. The problem is that treating them will not also remove their source, and they will return. A more dramatic example is September 11. I won't comment here on the horrible symptoms, or surface effects, that mark the events of that day—the deaths and injuries, the destruction, and also the terrorist crimes. The United States and other governments will respond to these symptoms, in kind, measure for measure, the way that doctor would respond to your surface conditions; this is what governments do. If September 11 is a symptom of an Event, and I think it is, then we who think and talk about such things must expect governments, as service institutions, to respond to the symptom itself, as they have been trained to do. I fear we would work in vain if we put all our energies into efforts to redirect the immediate actions of these governments: as if they, who are trained to maintain a given social structure, should be expected also to see the as-yet-invisible Event that we see and act accordingly. How would they act? Only as they already do! I fear it is only our task—we whose job it is to observe the not yet visible—to get cracking on our work of observation. What do we see? What hypotheses do we have to offer about how this society's service institutions must change if the society is to adjust to a new world it does not yet see but we must? How are those hypotheses to be brought to those who influence social leaders and managers so that the hypotheses can be tested through actual transformations of the policies that guide the service institutions?

Such questions already transform an *I* who is shocked by an Event into a *we* that responds to the shock. There appear to be three *we*'s implicit in these questions: the *we* who would offer hypotheses, the *we* who would test them, and the less visible *we* who would guide me in the first place to know how and when to join these other two. The first *we* refers, I believe, to communities of prognosticating thinkers, in all disciplines, but theologians are particularly suited to the task if they remember that they are servants of the invisible and not merely of extant institutions; here, Stanley Hauerwas is a model for us. The second *we* refers to the pragmatically minded among these thinkers, who have real-life connections with institutional leaders and who therefore can help mediate between the invisible and everyday practice. The third *we* is the one that I will talk about in the remaining pages of this essay. For me, this is the Jewish *we* that enables me, in moments of shock, not simply to be dumbfounded by symptoms that I do not understand but to locate guidelines for acting in the dark. My tradition is filled with memories of moments of darkness, of how Jewish prognosticators in the path have seen light in the darkness, and of how the God of history (or to whomever we refer the trials of history) has tested that light— was it light or an illusion of light? If it were not for the memories preserved by my tradition, I would have no basis for speaking at all right now. Through these memories, one might say, my ancestors suggest that we read the symptoms of September 11 in light of the historical images of *Chorban* ("destruction") and Exodus.

2. Chorban: the destruction of ancient Israel's temples.

Joining the Jewish *we*, I first associate the destruction of September 11 with the *Chorban*. This term traditionally refers to the "destruction" of either the First or Second Temples; I extend the term to name a cycle of horrible events in ancient and more recent Jewish memory. As recorded in the people Israel's scripture, or Torah, the northern ten tribes of the ancient Kingdom of Israel were destroyed in 731 B.C.E. by Assyria. Isaiah dubbed Assyria "rod of God's wrath," articulating what scholars have come to call the ancient "Deuteronomic theodicy," meaning the way that the prophetic school who wrote down the texts of Deuteronomy and Joshua-Kings explained why the God who had a Covenant with Israel would allow Israel to be destroyed. The explanation was, simply, reward and punishment, measure for measure: if Israel did what God wanted, its life would go well; if not, not. I read this to mean that if Israel lived well, its service institutions would always function as they are meant to function; if not, then Events would happen, interrupting the work of these institutions and leaving Israel with a choice: either read the signs of history and change your institutions accordingly, or else you will not live past this destruction. As prognosticator, Isaiah therefore told the Israelites of the two southern tribes, reform your institutions according to the explicit dictates of the revered Torah or we will all suffer the fate of the northern tribes.

According to the Torah, in 586 B.C.E. Babylonia conquered the two southern tribes, in the process destroying the temple in Jerusalem, the place through which Israel's priests kept Israel in touch with the God of Israel, expiating sins and preparing Israel thereby to reform her institutions. By the rivers of Babylon, Israel's exiles—Jeremiah and Ezekiel foremost among them—remembered the land and temple they had lost and reflected again on why God would let this happen. They understood the Deuteronomic theodicy to be inadequate this time: reward and punishment still apply to some events but not this one. In the words of Second Isaiah, Israel remained God's beloved servant, who was "wounded because of our sins . . . bearing the chastisement that made us whole."[1] Israel suffered, this time, as "Suffering Servant" suffering for humanity's sins, not its own. Israel returned under Persian rule, to build a second temple. In 70 C.E., Rome destroyed that temple, and during the years of war 70–135 C.E., Israel suffered the loss not only of its temple, but also of its land and the greater portion of its population. In those days and after, Israel's prognosticators were called "rabbis," or "rabbinic sages," authors of the books of Mishnah and Talmud that became the guidebooks of Jewish life in the Diaspora. The rabbis' voices were always multiple, dialogic, and so was their prognosis: Israel suffers partly or sometimes because of its sins, sometimes because of the sins of others, and sometimes, we just don't know—and we, too, the sages of Israel, can only shout up to God why? Have you forgotten Your Torah?

It's not that my tradition has taught me to read September 11 as if it were a *Chorban*, but that the tradition's responses to *Chorban* teach the

Jewish community today how in general to respond to what appear to be symptoms of an Event. Here are a few of the lessons:

· Events *do* happen, all social orders change, so do not be surprised if September 11 is a warning sign that some changes must come to our institutions if this society is going to survive.
· But Events are events *for* those who see them. Do not, therefore, worry about finding universal warrant or justification for the way you are led to read September 11 as an Event. Your reading must be tested, but, provided you have read well, the test will come in practice, not through endless theorizing.
· Until you have seen otherwise, you may assume that the Event is an event of oppression. Whether the society who suffers is an agent or victim of oppression, there is oppression somewhere of which September 11 is a symptom. The narratives of *Chorban* enable us to define "oppression" only with respect to its bitter fruit, or consequences; we must wait for another narrative, Exodus, to offer lessons about the sources of oppression. So, judged with respect to its bitter fruit, oppression is what renders a society's service institutions systemically dysfunctional. This means simply that these institutions fail to heal. Even without becoming direct instruments of violence, they simply fail to heal, and if they fail to heal, they render our workdays—that is, the days after the Garden of Eden—into days of hell and punishment rather than merely days of labor. In this way they subvert what we understand to be the divine plan for human life itself.
· When we, whose task it is at least to try to read signs of invisible things, see symptoms of oppression, we must turn our attention to them. *Our* labor must be to study these signs and the events that underlie them. This is the work of what we might call "prognostic reasoning," which should contribute to "reparative reasoning": the thinking that is aroused into life by the shock of any Event and that completes its life only once it has generated viable hypotheses about how some dimension of our societal structure must now change in order to help remove the oppressive conditions that underlie the Event. For us, the meaning of the theodicies of both Second and First Isaiah is that, as long as our society's members are among the victims of September 11, our social institutions need to change, whether or not they are direct sources of oppression. Even if some distant regime were, by itself, the source of our suffering, our suffering links us to that regime and to a responsibility for responding to its oppressiveness. In this case, we will most likely find ourselves to be both agents and victims of a complex array of oppressive practices. Reparative reasoning is not an individual affair but a task that calls on representatives of many different disciplines to work together as a com-

munity of reasoners—the kind of community our universities ought to nurture but rarely do.

3. Exodus: fleeing oppression.

Of what oppression is September 11 a symptom? Within Jewish tradition, the prototype for reasoning about this question is the narrative of Exodus. In a time of famine in their homeland, the Children of Israel settle in Egypt, beneficiaries of the protection and food supply of the king of Egypt, or Pharaoh. They stay for generations, until another Pharaoh takes power, one who "did not know them," and chooses to enslave them as forced laborers to help build his pyramid. After generations of enslavement, the Israelites' cries of suffering from the bondage "rose up to God. And God heard their cries and took notice." Tending his sheep on a mountain, Moses—an Israelite raised in the house of Pharaoh—turns aside to behold a burning bush. God's voice addresses him from out of the bush and enlists him as agent of Israel's redemption. Pharaoh is no god, but a human who has sinned against God by placing himself in God's stead; he is a mere human who cannot ultimately stand against those who serve God in his stead. Serving God alone, Moses leads the Children of Israel out of the land of oppression, through the parting Red Sea, to stand at Mount Sinai and receive the Torah of God, a covenant and constitution for their future lives in the Promised Land.

To read the signs of September 11 in light of a tradition of reading Exodus is to learn not to sit idly by the blood and suffering of one's people, even if it means sacrificing one's acquired social position (in Pharaoh's court? in the university? or government? or corporation?). It is to learn that to observe oppression is to become responsible for responding to it, and that the goal of this response is to remove the oppressed from the place or condition of oppression. The oppressor is a human who acts as a god, or the merely human adopted as infinite and absolute authority over human life. Here, Pharaoh is oppressor, as is his system of corvée labor, as are any of the institutions and individuals who serve as agents of Pharaoh and his system. According to this way of reading Exodus, we would expect September 11 to be a symptom of leaders, institutions, governments, or social-political systems that act, or are treated, as if they had infinite authority over human lives. According to the prototype of Exodus, oppression renders service institutions dysfunctional, because it removes God's merciful governance from the world after Eden, replacing the Creator's rule with the rule of something merely created.

In these terms, what entities or individuals in the world could fit this description and also exert any influence over the participants in September 11—including the terrorists and their victims? Only a community of inquirers could generate reasonable hypotheses, so I will attempt only to illustrate how we might reason toward such hypotheses.

We may suggest that, however corrupt and injurious the Western world's democracies may be, they do not appear to arrogate infinite authority to themselves. It may, however, be worth asking if any governments in the Middle East arrogate this authority to themselves. While no individual institutions in the West may serve as Pharaoh-like oppressors, it may, furthermore, be worth asking if any transnational systems of authority play this role. Is September 11, for example, a symptom of the lingering effects of Western colonialism in the recent past, as well as of Western economic and cultural imperialism? And what of the modern university's definition of "rationality" when it is adopted as an unquestioned criterion for judging what kind of discourse between societies is "good" or "meaningful" and what kind is "bad" or "meaningless"? Could a definition of rationality itself become oppressive, if it is applied in a way that excludes all other definitions? What, for example, if the definition of rationality that governs public discourse in Western universities and think tanks excludes what we called "reparative reasoning"? Or what, for that matter, of the role of sectarian religious thinking in certain Jewish, Muslim, and Christian institutions in the West and Middle East, from educational and religious institutions to national governments? What if sectarian religious thinking excludes the Western definition of rationality altogether as well as our model of reparative reasoning? What, furthermore, of the role of nationalism in both the West and Middle East: If nationalist models of regional governance preclude other models, would nationalism function as an oppressive model of authority? And what of global capitalism if adopted as an unrivaled practice of economic exchange in the West and Middle East: Would its unquestioned authority over rival forms of sub- or interregional economic practice warrant our calling it oppressive? According to the prototype of Exodus, we should label "oppressive" any institution or practice or model of practice that acquires infinite and unquestioned authority over human lives; God alone is God. But, if any of the institutions and practices mentioned above were deemed "oppressive," whom would we identify as their victims, and who would serve as Moses, agent of their liberation? In the case of individual, national regimes (for example, in the Middle East), we might label all their citizens as victims, and we might look within their populations for models of those who would serve as Moses. Who understands the workings of a given regime? Who understands how to address the regime as critic and its victims as agent of liberation? And who serves the Infinite One, alone? It would seem that a Moses, or a Moses-like group, would have to fill all these roles at once.

In the case of transnational practices, it seems we could not label any one people as victim, but rather all people who were governed by those practices, knowingly or not. To locate Moses(es), we might ask, Who understands the workings of a given practice? Who understands how to criticize those who practice it and how to guide its victims to alternative practices? And who serves the Infinite One, alone?

But how, finally, would Exodus remain a model for reparative reasoning when both the agents and victims of oppression are no longer limited to any one people? In response to such a question, the contemporary university still offers an Enlightenment model: because we are all agents and all victims of our tendency to oppression, we all need enlightenment, which means education in the method, power, and compassion of human reason. Two to three hundred years after its heyday, this remains a lovely ideal but one that has borne bitter fruit when put into practice. While the source of much goodwill in the university, this ideal is also a likely source of the modern West's oppressive imperialisms. For, who is to teach us all how to reason? The Enlightenment's assumption of a universal rationality has brought with it the presumption that certain, enlightened philosophers know precisely how we should all acquire it. Since this reasoning should enlighten everything we do, these philosophers have had to become sociologists, political theorists, and economists as well, fully prepared to tell us what forms of social, political, and economic life are most rational and therefore best for us all. Particularly when backed by strong and expansionist nation-states and market economies, this educational mission of the Enlightenment illustrates what we mean by cultural imperialism and cannot therefore serve as a means of liberation from the condition of imperialism or from the sorts of oppression that accompany it.

While I assume there should be other, viable proposals for liberating several peoples, at once, from these sorts of oppression, I have close experience with only one: the Children of Abraham Institute, a young movement that reenvisions the Exodus as a model for liberating Muslims and Christians, as well as Jews, from the dual oppressions of modern secular imperialism and religious sectarianism.

4. The Children of Abraham.

This time, there is no clear, scriptural prototype, but only a vaguely suggestive image: the Children of Abraham, Isaac and Ishmael, Jacob and Esau, competitors but also siblings and, all of them, inheritors of Abraham's covenant with the Creator of the World. "The Lord said to Abraham, 'Get out of your country, from your family, and from your father's house, to a land that I will show you. . . . I will bless you and make your name great. . . . and in you all the families of the earth shall be blessed.'"[2] This may be one of the epochs that tests Abraham's blessing. Will his children continue to fight with one another, or will they remember their common parentage and, by way of it, their shared place in God's blessing? At this point, I have to look in front of the scriptural text and ask if we cannot now see what could only be vaguely suggested in it. It is an image of not only one, but three peoples liberated in the Exodus: Jews, Christians, and Muslims, all three liberated from an epoch that seems to have been defined by multiple oppressions. On the one hand, there are the various, secular "-isms" of the modern West that have oppressed religious folks from all three traditions by defining their various faiths out of what counts as "rational" and thus worthy of a place in shaping the norms of the university, the nation-state, and the economy. On the other hand, there are the various sectarian movements within these religions themselves that have, in reacting against modern secularism, defined both the seculum and the other two scriptural traditions out of what counts as "blessed by God" and thus worthy of a place in shaping the "kingdom of God on earth."

If our three peoples can be led out from under both sorts of oppression, to what Promised Land would we be led? This question has recently led some religious Muslim, Jewish, and Christian scholars to form study circles in which texts of all three scriptural traditions are read together in a setting of both prayerful study and philosophic reflection: "scriptural reasoning," as the practice is named in one of these circles. The practice is at once faithful to the scriptural sources and disciplined in the intellectual pathways of an academy that has been liberated of its now-old, Enlightenment models and opened to the newer models of rationality that contribute as much to nuclear physics as they do to a rediscovery of the logics of scripture.

Could practices like this enable leaders of the three Abrahamic traditions to find common cause in their love of God and in their concern to end an epoch of multiple oppressions in the West? There are, of course, many reasons to say no: religion and nonreligion will remain opposing forces in the West, as will each religion against the others. But some Muslim, Christian, and Jewish scholars discover a reparative reasoning within each of their traditions that leads them to say yes: without sacrificing the integrity of their different modes of religious practice, they have found a way to study together, on occasion, and draw from each other's Scripture lessons. For them, *Chorban* and *Exodus* are images of *both* the Children of Israel's suffering and liberation *and* the suffering and liberation of *all* the Children of Abraham: Muslims and Christians, as well as Jews. The challenge—and perhaps our only hope—is to locate their Moseses and to discover how three Moseses would, together, lead their three peoples to a Promised Land we have not yet been shown.

NOTES

1   Isaiah 53.
2   Genesis 12.

JEAN BAUDRILLARD

L'Esprit du Terrorisme

We have had our share of world events from Diana's death to the World Cup, as well as violent and real events, from wars to genocide. We have not yet had any symbolic event of such magnitude that it is not only broadcast all over the world, but holds globalization itself in check— not one. Throughout the stagnation of the nineties, in the words of the Argentinean writer Macedonio Fernandez, events were on strike. Well, the strike is off. Events are back with such an ardor that we were even confronted with the World Trade Center attacks, by the absolute event, the "mother event," the pure event that concentrates in itself all the events that never took place.

These attacks turn not only the whole play of history and power relations topsy-turvy, but also the conditions of their analysis. Here one must take one's time. As long as events were stagnating, we had to anticipate them and stay ahead of the game. But when they suddenly drive forward with such thrust, we must slow down, without letting ourselves be buried under the morass of speeches and the warmongering cloud, and keep intact the unforgettable fulguration of images.

All the speeches and commentaries about September 11 betray the gigantic abreaction to the event itself and people's fascination with it. The moral condemnations, the national antiterrorism sacred union, are on par with the prodigious jubilation created by the desire to see the destruction of this global superpower, or more precisely, to watch it somehow destroy itself, commit a beautiful suicide. For it is this superpower that, through its unbearable power, is the secret cause of all the violence percolating all over the world, and consequently of the terrorist imagination, which unbeknownst to us, inhabits our psyche.

That we may have dreamed of that event, that everybody without exception, dreamed of it because no one cannot dream of the destruction

of a power that has become hegemonic to such a point, is unacceptable for Western moral consciousness. However, it is a fact that can be
measured against the pathetic violence shown by all the speeches and
discourses that want to erase the event.

We could even go so far as to say it is *they* who perpetrated the attack,
but it was *we* who wished it. If one does not take into account this fact
the event loses all its symbolic dimension and becomes a mere accident, a purely arbitrary act, the murderous phantasm of a few fanatics
whom it suffices to suppress. But we know better: hence, the whole
production of a delirious counterphobia to exorcize evil. Because evil
is everywhere, like an obscure object of desire. Without this deep complicity, the event would not have created such a big stir and in their
symbolic strategy, the terrorists knew without doubt that they could
count on this inadmissible complicity of evil.

It goes far beyond the hatred that the disinherited and the exploited
of the world feel for the global, hegemonic superpower—those who
happened to fall on the wrong side of world order. This invidious desire
also resides in the very hearts of those who share in the world order's
benefits. The allergy to any definitive order, to any ultimate power is
happily a universal reaction and the two World Trade Center towers
were the perfect embodiment of this definitive order precisely in their
twin nature.

No need for a death drive, or a destruction drive, nor even perverse
effects. It is that the logical and inexorable climb to power of power
itself exacerbates the will to destroy this power; and power itself is ac-
complice with its own destruction. When the two towers collapsed,
one had the impression that they were responding to the suicide of
the suicide-jets with their own suicide. We heard, "Even God cannot
declare war upon himself." Well, not true! The West, assuming God's
position (supine with divine omnipotence and absolute moral legitimacy) has become suicidal and declared war upon itself.

The innumerable catastrophe films bear testimony to this phantasm.
They conjure it up thanks to their power of images, while drowning
it in special effects. But the universal attraction they exert, equal in
that aspect to pornography, shows that the passage to the act is always
close. The system shows more of its velleity toward self-destruction,
the nearer it is to perfection or absolute power.

It is moreover very possible that the terrorists (no more than the experts) never forecast the Twin Towers collapse—that was, more than the strike on the Pentagon, the strongest symbolic shock. The symbolic collapse of a whole system happened through an invisible complicity, as if, by collapsing on their own, by committing suicide, the towers had played their part in the game, in order to crown the event.

In a way, it is the whole system that, through its internal fragility, gave assistance to the initial attack. The more the system concentrates itself globally, only constituting a single network, for instance, the more it becomes vulnerable at a single point. Already, a single Philippino hacker, with his laptop, was able to launch the I Love You virus and wreak havoc in networks all around the world. Here we see nineteen kamikazes who, thanks to the absolute weapon of death, multiplied by technological efficiency, have set in motion a global catastrophic process.

When the situation is thus monopolized by the world superpower, when one is confronted by this formidable condensation of all the functions of the technocratic machinery allied to the reign of the *pensée unique,* which other choice is left but the terrorist transference of the situation?[1] It is the system itself that has created the objective conditions for this brutal retaliation (*rétorsion*). By keeping for itself all the cards, it has forced the Other to change the rules of the game. And these new rules are more ferocious, because what is at stake is ferocious. To a system to whom the very excess of power poses an insoluble defiance, the terrorists answer through a definitive act whose exchange reaches the same impossibility. Terrorism is the act that makes restitution for an irreducible singularity at the heart of a generalized system of exchange. All the singularities (species, individuals, cultures) that have paid with their own death for the installation of a world circulation regulated by a single superpower avenge themselves today through this terrorist transference of the situation.

Terror against terror, there is no more ideology behind this. One is, from this point forward, far beyond ideology and politics. No ideology, no cause—not even the Islamic one—can explain the energy that feeds terror. It no longer aims at transforming the world. Like heresies in more ancient times, it aims at radicalizing the world through sacrifice, while the system aims at realizing the world by force.

Terrorism, like viruses, is everywhere. There is a world diffusion of terrorism that functions as the shadow of any system of domination, everywhere ready to awaken as a double agent. It inhabits the very heart of the culture that battles it. There is no longer any demarcation which allows us to discern it and the visible fracture (and the hatred) that oppose, all over the world, the exploited and underdeveloped to the West, secretly coincides with the fracture internal to the dominant system. The West can face up to any visible forms of antagonism. But the other with its viral structure, as if the whole system of domination secreted its own anti-apparatus, its own ferment of disappearance, against this form of almost automatic reversion of its own power, the system can do nothing. Terrorism is the shock wave of this silent phenomenon of reversion.

It is therefore a clash neither of civilizations nor of religions, and this goes far beyond Islam and America, upon which one attempts to focus the conflict in order to give oneself the illusion of a visible confrontation, and solution, by the use of force. It is more a question of a fundamental antagonism but one that designates through the specter of America (that may be the epicenter but not all, in and of itself, the incarnation of globalization) and through the specter of Islam (which itself is not the incarnation of terrorism), triumphant globalization grappling with itself. Along those lines, one could even speak about a world war—not the third, but the fourth and only, truly global one, since its stake is globalization itself. The first two world wars correspond to the classical image of war. The first one put an end to the supremacy of Europe and the colonial era. The second terminated Nazism. The third, that indeed took place, in the form of the cold war and dissuasion, defeated Communism. From one to the next, one always moved ever closer toward a single world order. Today, this single world order, having virtually reached its term, finds itself grappling with antagonistic forces diffused throughout the very heart of the global itself, present in all contemporary convulsions. It is a fractal, cellular war. It is a war of all singularities revolting like so many antibodies. This confrontation is so hard to grasp that, from time to time, it is necessary to salvage the very idea of war through spectacular staging (mise-en-scène), such as the Persian Gulf War or, now, the war in Afghanistan. But the fourth world war is elsewhere. It is what haunts all world order, all hegemonic domination. If Islam dominated the world, terrorism would rise against Islam. It is the very world itself that resists globalization.

Terrorism is immoral. The World Trade Center event, this symbolic defiance, is immoral and responds to a globalization that is itself, also immoral. Consequently we have no choice but to become, ourselves, immoral, and, if we want to understand something in this event, we have to see a little beyond Good and Evil. It is so rare that one is given the opportunity to access an event that defies not only morals but all other forms of interpretations, that one must try to have the intelligence of Evil. And this is where the crucial point resides: in the total misconception of Western philosophy, that of the Enlightenment as to the relationship between Good and Evil. We naively believe that the progress of Good, its climb to power in all areas (science, technique, democracy, rights of man) corresponds to a defeat of Evil. Nobody seems to have understood that Good and Evil climb to power at the same time and in the same move. The triumph of the one does not imply the vanquishing of the other; indeed it is quite the contrary. Evil is often metaphysically considered an accidental mishap; but this axiom, from which flow all the Manichean forms of struggle between Good and Evil, is illusory. Good does not reduce Evil, nor the inverse moreover. They are both inextricably bound and irreducible to each other. At the bottom, Good could only defeat Evil by renouncing its claim to be Good, because appropriating a global monopoly on power implicates it in a backlash of proportional violence.

In the traditional universe, there was still an equilibrium between Good and Evil according to a dialectical relationship that willy-nilly kept the moral universe's tension and balance in check (similar to the cold war, when the two world superpowers face-to-face guaranteed the balance of terror). There was no supremacy of one over the other. This equilibrium is broken the moment there is a total extrapolation of Good (a hegemony of the positive over any form of negativity, the exclusion of death, of any potentially adverse forms—the triumph of the values of Good in all areas). When this state is reached, equilibrium breaks down and it is as if Evil regains an invisible autonomy and expands exponentially.

All things being equal, it is a little bit like what is produced in the political sphere with the effacing of Communism and the global triumph of deregulated market forces. A phantasmatic enemy surges forward, permeating the whole planet, filtering through like a virus, emerging from all the interstices of power: Islam. Islam is only a moving front of the crystallization of this antagonism. This antagonism is everywhere and it is in each of us. Thus we have terror against terror—but asymmetrical terror. And it is this very asymmetry that leaves global power disarmed. Struggling with its own contradictions, globalization can only entrench itself in its own logic of power relations without being able to play on the field of symbolic defiance and death, about which it has no idea since it has erased death from its own culture.

Until now, this integrating superpower had widely succeeded in absorbing and reabsorbing all crisis and all negativity, creating in the same move a fundamentally agonizing situation, not only for the *damned of the earth* but also for its privileged ones ensconced in radical comfort. The event's fundamental difference is that the terrorists have stopped committing suicide for nothing, by efficiently and offensively putting their own death into play, according to a strategic intuition which very simply realized that the adversary is immensely fragile, that the system in its quasi-perfection is vulnerable to the least spark.

They succeeded in turning their own deaths into an absolute weapon against a system that lives off the exclusion of death, whose ideal is the dead zero (*zéro mort*). Any system at *dead zero* is a null-sum system, and all the means of dissuasion and destruction can do nothing against an enemy that has already turned its own death into counteroffensive weapon: "Who cares about American bombardments! Our men want to die as much as the Americans want to live!" Thence comes the disproportionate number of seven thousand dead inflicted in single blow to a dead zero system.[2]

Thus, here, everything is played out on death, not only because of the brutal irruption of death *live*, in real time, but because of the irruption of a "more than real" death: the symbolic and sacrificial death. This is the absolute event that does not tolerate any appeal.

Such is the spirit of terrorism.

Never attack the system in terms of the balance of power. That would be obeying the imaginary strategy (revolutionary) imposed by the system, which, in order to survive, ceaselessly brings those who battle it, on the terrain of reality which is forever its own. But move the struggle into the sphere of the symbolic, where the rule is that of defiance, reversion, and outbidding, such that death can only be responded to by an equal or superior death. The point is to defy the system by a sacrificial gift to which it can only answer with its own death and collapse.

The terrorist's hypothesis is that the system itself will commit suicide in response to multiple challenges posed in terms of death and suicide, for neither the system nor its power can escape the symbolic obligation. In this trap alone exists the only chance for their catastrophic scenario. In this vertiginous cycle of the impossible exchange of death, that of the terrorist is an infinitesimal point, but one that provokes a suction, a vacuum, a gigantic convection. Around this minute point, the whole system of reality and power, becomes denser, tetanizes itself, contracts and collapses in its own superefficiency.

The tactic of the terrorist model is to provoke an excess of reality and make the system collapse under the weight of that reality. The whole derisive dimension of the situation as well as the countermobilization of violence effectuated by the system power turn against the system itself, because terrorist acts both mirror exorbitantly the system's own violence and enact the symbolic violence that is forbidden to the system—that of its own death.

This is why all the visible and real power of the system cannot do much against the minute but symbolic death of a few individuals.

One must realize that a new terrorism is born, a new form of action, which plays the game and appropriates for itself the rules of the game in order to better perturb it. Not only do those people refuse to fight fair, since they bring their own death into play to which there is no possible response ("They are cowards"), they also appropriated for themselves the very weapons of the dominant power—money, stock market speculation, computer and aeronautic technologies, the specular dimensions and its media networks. They have assimilated all of these from modernity and globalization without deviating from their goal, which is to destroy them.

Adding insult to injury, they even used the daily banality of the American way of life as a mask: these people were two-faced. Sleeping in the suburbs, where they read and studied, with wife and kids, until one day they sprang into action, like time bombs. The faultless mastery of this clandestinity is as practically terrorist as the spectacular act of September 11, because it throws the cloak of suspicion on any individual. Isn't any inoffensive neighbor a potential terrorist? If they have passed unnoticed, then anyone (ourselves included) can be an unnoticed criminal (each airplane becomes suspect). And, at bottom, it is perhaps true. Perhaps it corresponds to an unconscious form of potential criminality, masked and carefully repressed, but always susceptible, if not to spring up, at least to vibrate secretly in time with the spectacle of Evil. Thus, the event ramifies itself in the little details, the source of a more subtle mental terrorism.

The radical difference is that the terrorists, while using the very weapons of the system itself, also have at their disposal a fatal weapon: their own death. If they had only turned the system's own weapons against itself, they would have been annihilated a long time ago. If they had only their own deaths to oppose it, they would have disappeared as quickly in a mere futile sacrifice. It is what terrorism has always done until now (for instance the Palestinian suicide bombings). This is why terrorism has been doomed to fail, until now.

The whole situation changes as soon as all available modern means are allied to the highly symbolic weapon of their own death. It multiplies the destructive potential ad infinitum. This multiplication of factors (which to us seem irreconcilable) gives the terrorists such superiority. The zero death strategy of a "clean" technological war misses the point of this transfiguration of "real" power by symbolic power.

The prodigious success of such a terrorist act poses a problem. In order to understand it, we must escape our Western point of view and try to go into the terrorists' minds and networks. Such an efficiency would presuppose on our behalf a maximum of cold rational calculation, rational brainstorming—the very rationality we find it so hard to imagine in others. And even if this was the case, there would have been, as with any rational organization or secret service, leaks and mistakes.

Hence, the secret of such a success is elsewhere. The difference is that, for the terrorists, it is not about a job contract, but a pact and sacrificial duty. Such an obligation is sheltered from all defection and corruption. The miracle is that it has been adapted to the globalization network, to the technological protocol, without losing the complicity between life and death. Contrary to the contract, a pact does not bind individuals (even their suicide does not equate with individual heroism). It is a collective sacrifice sealed by the exigencies of ideals. It is the conjugation of two apparatuses, that of operational structure and that of a symbolic pact, which has made possible an act of such disproportionate nature.

We no longer have any idea what a symbolic reckoning is, as in poker or potlatch: minimal stake for maximum results. It is exactly what the terrorists obtained in Manhattan, and it well illustrates chaos theory:

an initial shock provoking innumerable consequences, while the huge American military deployment (Desert Storm) only obtained derisive results—the hurricane, so to speak, ended up the battling of a butterfly's wings.

Suicidal terrorism is the terrorism of the have nots, but this is the terrorism of the rich. And this especially causes fear; they have become rich (and they have all the means) while wishing for our defeat. Of course, according to our value system, they cheat, since it's not fair play to put one's own death at stake. But they do not care, and the new rules of the game no longer belong to us.

We use everything possible to devaluate their act. We call them suicidal or martyrs. Only to add in the same breath that martyrdom is ineffective, that it has nothing to do with truth, and that it is even (quoting Nietzsche) "enemy number one" of the truth. Of course their death does not prove anything. But there is nothing to prove anyway, in a system where truth itself is unattainable. Or is it that we are the only ones to hold the truth? This highly moralistic argument reverses itself. If the voluntary martyrdom of the kamikazes does not prove anything, then the involuntary martyrdom of September 11 victims does not prove anything either. There is something unbecoming and obscene in turning martyrdom into a moral argument (it judges beforehand their suffering and death).

Likewise, it does not hold that these terrorists exchange their deaths against a place in paradise. Consequently, their act is not a "pure free-will act" and therefore not authentic. Their act would be "free" only if they did not believe in God, and if their death was without hope, as it is for us. However, Christian martyrs hoped for nothing else but this sublime equivalence. Therefore, here again, the terrorists do not fight fair, since they are entitled to the eternal life of which we can no longer even entertain the hope. Thus we mourn for our own lack of death, while the terrorists can turn death into a high-definition wager.

At the bottom, cause, proof, truth, reward, ends, and means are typical Western forms of accounting. We even evaluate death in terms of interest rates and quality-price relation. This economical reckoning is the calculation of the poor man, who no longer has the courage to put a price on it. What can happen, outside of war, which is itself but a conventional protective screen? One speaks of bioterrorism, of bacteriological war, or of nuclear terrorism, but all of this does not belong to the order of symbolic defiance, only to the order of the final solution: an annihilation without rhyme or reason, risk or glory.

It is a misunderstanding to see in the terrorist act a purely destructive logic. It seems to me that their own deaths cannot be separated from their act (it is precisely this connection that makes it a symbolic act) and it is not at all the impersonal elimination of the other. Everything resides in the defiance and the duel, in a dual, personal relation with the adverse power. Since it is the one that humiliates, it is the one that must be humiliated—and not simply exterminated. It must be made to lose face. This is never gained by mere force or by the suppression of the other. The other must be targeted and hurt in the full light of the adversarial struggle. In addition to the pact that binds terrorist to terrorist is some sort of a pact to duel with the adversary. It is therefore the contrary of the cowardice we accuse the terrorists of, and the opposite of what, for example, the Americans did during the Gulf War (and that they are doing in Afghanistan): invisible target/operational liquidation.

Of all these vicissitudes, we hold high the vision of the September 11 images. And we must hold on to the pregnancy of these images, and their fascination, since they constitute, like it or not, our primal scene. The images of New York, while they radicalize the world situation, have radicalized the relationship between image and reality. Amid the uninterrupted profusion of banal images and hyped events, the New York terrorist act has at once resuscitated images and events.

Terrorists have turned the system's weapons against it, and they have also exploited its real-time images and their instantaneous global diffusion. They appropriated them as well as stock exchange speculations, electronic information, and air traffic. The role of the image is highly ambiguous, for while it exalts the event, it also takes it hostage. The images play like an infinite multiplication, and at the same time they play like a diversion and neutralization (this had already happened for the events of May 1968 in France). This is what one always forgets when one speaks about the "dangers" of the media. The image consumes the event insofar as it absorbs the event and gives it to the consumer. Of course, the image gives the consumer an impact heretofore unimaginable, but as an event-image.

What, then, is a real event if everywhere the image, fiction, virtuality perfuse this very reality? In the present case, many believed (with a certain relief, perhaps) they saw the resurgence of the real, and of the violence of the real, within a universe pretending to be virtual: "There goes all your virtual stories! This is for real!" By the same token, many believed in a resurrection of history beyond its well-advertised end. So did reality actually overtake fiction? If it appears to have done so, it is only because reality absorbed the energy of fiction and itself became fiction. One could almost say that reality is jealous of fiction and real events are jealous of images . . . a sort of duel between them, to see who will be the most inconceivable.

The collapse of the Twin Towers is unimaginable, but that is not enough to make it a real event. A surplus of violence is not sufficient to make an opening onto reality, because reality is a principle and this principle has been lost. Reality and fiction have become a tangled mess. The fascination with the terrorist act is first and foremost the fascination for an image (the jubilatory and catastrophic consequences being themselves mostly imaginary).

In this case, therefore, the real is added to the images as a bonus of terror, an extra shiver. Not only is it terrifying, but it is also real. Rather than the violence of the real being there first, and the shiver of the image being added, the image comes first and the shiver of the real is added to it. It is something like one more fiction, a fiction going beyond fiction. J. J. Ballard (after Borges) spoke in this way about reinventing reality as the ultimate and most deadly fiction.

This terrorist violence is neither a reality backlash nor a history backlash. Not only is it terrifying, but what is more it is not "real," since it is worse than real in a certain way: it is symbolic. Violence in itself can be perfectly banal and inoffensive. Only symbolic violence can generate singularity. In the singularity of this event, in this Manhattan catastrophe film, the two elements of mass fascination of the twentieth century are fused to the highest degree: the white magic of cinema and the black magic of terrorism; the white light of the image and the black light of terrorism.

After the fact, one tries to impose a meaning, any meaning on the event, to find any interpretation of it, but there is none. One finds instead the radicality of the spectacle, the brutality of the spectacle, which alone is original and irreducible. The spectacle of terrorism imposes the terrorism of the spectacle. And against this immoral fascination (even if it unleashes a universal moral reaction) the political order is powerless. It is our own theater of cruelty; the only one left to us. It is an extraordinary one since it conjugates the acme of the spectacular with the acme of defiance. It is also the fulgurant micromodel of a kernel of real violence set in a maximized echo chamber (thus the purest possible form of the spectacular), and of a sacrificial model opposing the historic and politic model with the highest possible form of defiance.

The terrorists would be forgiven for any murder, if these murders had a meaning, if they could be interpreted as a historic form of violence—such is the moral axiom of "good violence." The terrorist would be forgiven for any kind of violence, if this violence was not broadcast by the media ("Terrorism would be nothing without the media.") But all this is illusory. There is no good use of the media: the media is part of the event itself, part of the terror, and its role plays in both directions.

The repressive act runs along the same unforeseeable spiral as the terrorist act: nobody knows when it is going to end and which reversals may occur. At the level of the image and information, it is not possible to distinguish between the spectacular and the symbolic, between the "crime" and its repression. And the uncontrollable chain of reversibility is the true victory of terrorism, a victory visible in the ramifications and subterranean infiltrations of the event—not only via direct economic, political, financial, and speculative recessions of the whole system, and the resulting moral and psychological recession that followed, but in the recession of the whole value system, the entire ideology of freedom, free trade, and so on, which is the pride of the Western world—everything it capitalizes on in order to exercise dominion all over the globe.

This repression has reached such a point that the idea of freedom, a new and recent idea, is already effacing itself in mores and minds, and free-market globalization is in the process of actualizing itself in an exactly inverse form: a globalized police state of total control, with a security terror. Deregulation is ending up in a maximum of constraints and restrictions equivalent to those typical of a fundamentalist society.

The decline of production, consumption, speculation, and growth (but not of course of corruption), everything happens as if the world system operated a strategic retreat, a harrowing revision of its values. It appears to be a defensive response to the impact of terrorism, but deep down, it is a response to more secretive injunctions. The forced regulation issues from absolute disorder, but such that the system imposes it upon itself, internalizing somehow its own defeat.

Another aspect of the terrorists' victory is that all the other forms of violence and destabilization of order play in its favor: information technology terrorism, biological terrorism, anthrax and rumor, everything is attributed to bin Laden. He could even claim to be the source of natural catastrophes. All the forms of disorganization and perverse circulation work to his profit. The very structure of the generalized global exchange plays in favor of the impossible exchange. It is like an "automatic writing" of terrorism nourished again by the involuntary terrorism of information—with all the panicked consequences that ensue. If, in this anthrax story, intoxication plays itself through instantaneous crystallization, like in a chemical solution where a mere molecule would be immersed, it is because the system reached a critical mass that renders it vulnerable to any form of aggression.

There are no solutions to this extreme situation, above all not even war, which only offers an "already been there" type of solution, with the same deluge of military forces, "spook information," useless carpet bombings, pathetic and hypocritical speeches, technological deployment, and intoxication campaigns. In short, like the Gulf War, any solution would be a nonevent, an event that did not really happen.

This, moreover, is its very raison d'être: to substitute a repetitive and déjà vu type of pseudo-event for a true and formidable event. The terrorist attack corresponds to the precession of the event over any of its interpretive models, while that of stupidly military and technological war corresponds inversely to a precession of the model over the event, therefore the factitious wager of a nonevent. War has become the prolongation of the absence of politics by other means.

Translated by Michel Valentin, University of Montana, Missoula

NOTES

1 "One way" manner of thinking.
2 The article was written a few days after September 11, which explains the numbers inaccuracy (translator's note).

DAVID JAMES DUNCAN

Our Good Fortune

On the last day of November 2001, a group of conservationists, writers, and thinkers gathered at the Boone and Crocket Club in Missoula, Montana, to discuss what, if anything, had changed in their lives in light of September 11, 2001, and the ensuing American military response. Three of those present were asked to speak before the gathering opened to discussion. These were David James Duncan's remarks.

The Wendell Berry and Brian Doyle quotations are used by permission. The complete Berry essay is included in this volume.

As I see it, we're all in a kiln, midway through a firing. We're all raw clay, as human beings have always been, but feeling more acutely, since September 11, the heat of transformation.

One thought I keep having: Thank God Americans are finally feeling *something.* The consumer coma that's been destroying so much of the world looked to me like it was going to last forever. I sense some consciousness where the coma used to be.

A question that haunts me: What are we being transformed into?

Another: Do we have any say in what we're being transformed into, or any power to guide the firing process?

Another: What is the best stance to take—what do we do with our bodies, minds, and spirits—while enduring the heat of the kiln?

A First Set of Thoughts. I tried to fly to New York two weeks ago, the same day 270 people died in a New York jet crash. JFK, my destination, closed as I was boarding in Missoula. I found a TV in the waiting area, saw burning buildings and closed airports, gave up, drove home, took a long nap. I was awakened by my travel agent, calling to say he'd booked me the last seat on an evening flight to LaGuardia, which had just re-opened. When I left again for the airport it was the first time in all my travels that my eleven-year-old daughter wept in fear and begged me not to go. Leaving for New York anyway was as close as I've come to any sort of war against terror. I called my daughter before dashing onto the plane; her courage had returned. The first skirmish had been won.

I'd never flown due east out of Missoula on a clear evening. The world below was so beautiful I felt as if I'd died and was seeing a here-after in the here. I saw my house, tiny beside Lolo Creek. The creek, then the Bitterroot, then Rock Creek, turned quicksilver in the late sunlight. The pilot had a voice like Mr. Rogers. I used his voice, and Jonathan Franzen's gruesomely funny new novel, to get across the con-tinent without fear but upped the ante to two red wines and prayer as we glided into New York. The night air was so clear, and Manhattan so lit up and beautiful, that I felt again as if I'd died and was landing in what E. L. Doctorow's last novel calls the city of God.

In God's city, sure enough, the twin towers had been removed.

But we landed safely. My luggage even made it. I caught a cab into the city, looked out the window.

E. L. Doctorow, *City of God:*

> Every scruffy, oversize, undersize, weird, fat, or bony or limping or muttering or foreign-looking, or green-haired punk-strutting, threaten-ing, crazy, angry, inconsolable person I see . . . is a New Yorker, which is to say as native to this diaspora as I am, and part of our great sputtering experiment in a universalist society proposing a world without nations where anyone can be anything and the ID is planetary.[1]

William Kittredge, *The Nature of Generosity:*

> I sauntered (à la Whitman) down Broadway toward Prince Street in Manhattan's SoHo district and was struck by happiness. The streets were crowded by people seeming to represent every racial mix and conti-nent and subcontinent, many of them speaking in tongues, as far as I could tell, sometimes singing in any one of a multitude of languages I couldn't place. So much humanity, with the old boy, myself, idling among them in the maze of ornate brickwork walls. . . . All the stories in the world surround us. We all have to deal with the run of metaphor loose near Broadway and Prince. It's possible to think of that as our good fortune.[2]

A Second Set of Thoughts. All the stories in the *world* surround us. Not just America's stories. The World Trade Center victims were international and consisted of many citizens born in Muslim countries as well as people born in the United States. My own current novel attempts, my lifelong friendships, and my inner life also connect directly to stories and people in parts of the world that some Americans now want to demonize in order to wage "guilt-free war." My son's middle name, for example, is Faredoon, after an ancient Persian king and a modern Maharashtra, India, hero and friend.

More examples: Two of my close friends for thirty years have been Carl and Judith Ernst. They were married on an Oregon farm I caretook in 1974. I caught, cooked, and fed them fresh trout on their wedding night. (Carl was apparently a bit jittery about his upcoming nuptials; he upchucked the trout.) He is now the mainstay of the Islamic Studies department at the University of North Carolina. He's fluent in six languages including Arabic and Persian, has become one of the West's leading scholars on Sufism, and has six brilliant books to his credit, yet remains a completely unpretentious man. It's nice for a monolingual peasant like me to recall that when I met Carl in the 70s he had an evening jones for a horrid beer called Brown Derby, which he'd quaff, then go, "Ahhhh! Tastes like a Brown Derby." He and Judy and their daughters lived for years in Pakistan, another year in India, and are now in Spain on a teaching sabbatical having to do, I think, with Andalusian Sufis. Carl and his Islamic Studies colleagues at UNC have received thousands of phone calls and e-mails from media people since September 11, begging for insight into the Islamic worldview before our ignorance kills us.

Another example: Jay Bonner. I met Jay in Palo Alto in 1973, via mutual friends we'd both hitchhiked to see at Stanford. We played a little Celtic music and Ping-Pong together and somehow parlayed that into friendship. While I moved on to mowing Oregon lawns and writing my first novel, Jay moved to London to attend the Royal College of Art. There he proved to be a genius at Islamic geometric design, tilework, and architecture, and also fell in love with a displaced Indian Parsi, Shireen Irani, with whom he now has a family in Sante Fe. In the late 80s Jay was hired to design six enormous outdoor domes for the vast pilgrimage center at Mecca—a project in some ways comparable, strange to say, to Michelangelo's Sistine Chapel. Jay's domes are gorgeous, and innovative, despite the strictures of tradition. I reckon I'm the only hick in Lolo, Montana, with a close friend whose work shields literally millions of Muslim pilgrims each year from the desert sun. Jay has many other Islamic projects to his credit, too—including, last year, a hospital I'd wager is the most beautiful in the world.

Because of Carl and Jay, their families, knowledge, lives, and their Muslim friends, I take it badly when I hear some media lordling such as CBS's Dan Rather, when asked by Larry King why the Muslim world hates America, say that it's because we're winners and they're losers, because some people are simply evil. On the contrary, Dan, *all the stories in the world surround us. And it's not only possible, it's a necessity, to think of this as our good fortune.*

A Third Set of Thoughts. The best response I've seen to the new war remains Wendell Berry's essay, written September 13, 2001, called "Thoughts in the Presence of Fear." It has since been reprinted in some two hundred publications and twenty languages, and I'm sure that many readers of this volume have seen it elsewhere. Since I've seen no clearer statement, I'm going to review some of it, for its profound sense of direction. The essay is a list of twenty-seven connected thoughts. These are just a few.

> I. The time will soon come when we will not be able to remember the horrors of September 11 without remembering also the unquestioning technological and economic optimism that ended on that day.
> II. This optimism rested on the proposition that we were living in a "new world order" and a "new economy" that would "grow" on and on, bringing a prosperity that would be "unprecedented."
> III. The dominant politicians, corporate officers, and investors who believed this proposition did not acknowledge that the prosperity was limited to a tiny percent of the world's people, and to an ever smaller number of people even in the United States; that it was founded upon the oppressive labor of poor people all over the world; and that its ecological costs increasingly threatened all life, including the lives of the supposedly prosperous.
> IV. The "developed nations" had given to the "free market" the status of a god, and were sacrificing to it their farmers, farmlands, and communities, their forests, wetlands, and prairies, their ecosystems and watersheds. They had accepted universal pollution and global warming as normal costs of doing business.

Skipping ahead—and condensing VII thru X in a manner that I hope won't horrify Mr. Berry:

> We did not anticipate anything like what has now happened. We did not foresee that all our innovations might be at once overridden by a kind of war that would . . . [trap us] in the webwork of communication and transport that was supposed to make us free. Nor did we foresee that the weaponry and war science we marketed and taught to the world would become available not just to recognized national governments . . . but also to dissident or fanatical groups and individuals—whose violence, though never worse than that of nations, is judged by the nations to be illegitimate. . . . We had accepted uncritically the belief that technology is only good . . . that it cannot serve our enemies . . . . We had accepted too the corollary belief that an economy . . . that is global in extent, technologically complex, and centralized is . . . protectable by "national defense."
>
> XI. We now have a clear, inescapable choice. . . . We can continue to promote a global economic system of unlimited "free trade" among corporations, held together by long and highly vulnerable lines of communication and supply, but now recognizing that such a system will have to be protected by a hugely expensive [global] police force . . . and that such a police force will be effective precisely to the extent that it oversways the freedom and privacy of the citizens of every nation.
>
> XII. Or we can promote a decentralized world economy which would have the aim of assuring to every nation and region a local self-sufficiency in life-supporting goods. This would not eliminate international trade, but it would tend toward a trade in surpluses after local needs had been met.
>
> [XIII–XV] One of the gravest dangers to us now, second only to further terrorist attacks . . . is that we will attempt to go on as before with the corporate problem of global "free trade," whatever the cost in freedom and civil rights, without self-questioning or self-criticism or public debate. . . . [T]he talk that we are hearing from politicians, bureaucrats, and commentators has so far tended to reduce the complex problems now facing us to issues of national unity, security, normality, and retaliation. National self-righteousness, like personal self-righteousness, is a mistake. It is misleading. It is a sign of weakness. . . . We are not innocent of making war against civilian populations.[3]

A Fourth Set of Thoughts. My first written response to September 11 is a brief essay, published on the same Orion website as Wendell's piece, called "a prayer for water & children."[4]

A portion of that essay:

In 1991, prior to Operation Desert Storm, the U.S. Defense Intelligence Agency researched what the effect would be of bombing the water storage systems and sewage treatment systems of Iraq until they were destroyed. An American journalist, Thomas Nagy, has investigated the DIA documents, which were declassified in 1995, and has written several articles about what he discovered. No major media or magazines have shown interest. I can see why: like the first whispers we once heard of the massacre at My Lai, they're too shameful to believe. The article I cite was in the September 2001 *Progressive*—a minor magazine, but editors of larger magazines were apparently unwilling to print the story. The documents quoted and paraphrased are all available online. Nagy's conclusions are his own but he's not pushy; he tells how to access the documents so we can draw our own conclusions.

The 1991 DIA documents—to my amazement as an activist water guardian—go into great technical detail about the sources and quality of Iraq's water; they note that Iraqi rivers contain biota and pollutants that, unless treated with chlorine, cause epidemic diseases like cholera, hepatitis, and typhoid. The documents note that chlorine had been embargoed by the sanctions and predict that if Iraq's water systems are destroyed it is poor Iraqis, especially children, who will be affected—not Saddam Hussein. Knowing this, our political and military leaders under the elder George Bush—in defiance of the Geneva Convention—systematically destroyed the water and sewage systems of Iraq anyway. The sanctions on chlorine and medicine remained in place, guaranteeing maximum loss of life.

The DIA documents continue. They mention epidemic outbreaks of acute diarrhea, dysentery, respiratory ailments, measles, diptheria, pertussis, meningitis, and other diseases, again and again causing problems —most notably death—for children. One document describes a refugee camp in which 80 percent of the population has come down with diarrhea, cholera, hepatitis B, measles, gastroenteritis. It reports that 80 percent of the resulting dead are children.

When, in the mid-90s, a team of Harvard doctors witnessed the epidemics and urged that sanctions barring medicine be lifted, our Defense Intelligence Agency responded by saying that the Iraqi regime was exaggerating the incidence of disease for political purposes. The sanctions and fouled water remained in place. They remain in place to this day. The United Nations—not some Iraqi propagandist, the UN—now reports that *five hundred thousand* Iraqi children age five and under have died as a result, and that five thousand more infants and children will continue to die each month until medicine and safe water are restored.

We all know children under five. How political are they? How pro-
or anti-Bush or -Saddam? How Islamic or Christian? Aren't they just
children? What is a terrorist? What is terror? Is there a greater terror
than watching your child die before your eyes? Even with the best medicine available, I've wrestled sheer terror, tending my feverish children
through the night when the thermometer hit 105. And when they've
entered convulsions, how well I remember the desperate cure: *cold clean
water*. I try to imagine tending my child with *no* medicine as 78 percent
of her body and 90 percent of her brain become water deliberately defiled by America's leaders. I try to imagine myself having nothing with
which to cool her but cloths dampened with ruined water. I try to imagine singing to her inert body, then putting away, forever, her abandoned
clothes, toys, shoes, as I try in the Name of the Compassionate, the Merciful, to forgive her killers. My mind balks. What is a terrorist but an
inflictor of pain and terror? How is this defiled water not a "weapon of
mass destruction"? Madeleine Albright and Colin Powell, in the interests of our "defense," again and again agree that the sanctions are working and that the cost is "worth it." Some 1.25 billion Muslims know this.
Some are insane with rage as a result. Now three thousand of us—three
week's worth of sanctioned-to-death children—have been denied life.
Americans are furious in turn. So bombs are falling, civil liberties vanishing, Arab-Israeli tensions are boiling, Pakistan is boiling, India is heat-
ing up, Pakistan and India have nukes. And five thousand more infants
and children will die this month for the crime of being born to mothers
who've done nothing but suffer under the rule of an Iraqi leader whom
the United States empowered in the first place.

"This is a war against evil," says George W. Bush, who in May 2000
gave $43 million to the Taliban knowing it buries women alive and then
in September 2001 posed beside newspaper headlines reading BUSH
GOES AFTER THE TERRORISTS' MONEY. If Bush is right, if this is truly
"a war against evil," then God help us. On the basis of simple love for
my own and all children, my own and all living waters, and my own and
all personal freedom, I believe the sanctions are child-killing insanity
that recklessly endanger us all. Only a servant of what Dr. Martin Luther
King called "the giant triplets of racism, extreme materialism, and militarism" could justify such a cost.

A Fifth Set of Thoughts. A fine friend, Portland writer Brian Doyle, two
days ago sent an essay that, though anything but scholarly, will be published in next month's *American Scholar*. I don't know if it's fair to call
Iraqi children and the Twin Tower victims direct cause and effect, but
it's certainly fair to call them Islamic and Western flesh, blood, and

innocence annihilated by ruthlessness. Here's a bit of Brian's essay, which is called "Leap":[6]

A couple leaped from the south tower, hand in hand. They reached for each other and their hands met and they jumped. Jennifer Brickhouse saw them falling, hand in hand.

Many people jumped. Perhaps hundreds. No one knows. They struck the pavement with such force that there was a pink mist in the air.

The mayor reported the mist.

A kindergarten boy who saw tiny people falling in flames told his teacher the birds were on fire. She ran with him on her shoulders out of the ashes.

Tiffany Keeling saw fireballs falling that she later realized were people. Jennifer Griffin saw people falling and wept as she told the story. Niko Winstral saw people free-falling backwards with their hands out for balance, as if parachuting. Joe Duncan on his roof on Duane Street looked up and saw people jumping. Henry Weintraub saw people "kicking as they flew out." John Carson saw six people "falling over themselves, falling, they were somersaulting." Steve Miller saw people jumping from a thousand feet in the air. Kirk Kjeldsen saw people flailing on the way down, people lining up and jumping, "too many people falling." Jane Tedder saw people leaping and the sight haunts her at night. Steve Tamas counted fourteen people jumping, then he stopped counting. Several onlookers were killed by people falling from the sky. A fireman was killed by a body falling from the sky. Stuart DeHann saw one woman's dress billowing as she fell, and he saw a shirtless man falling end over end, and he too saw the couple leap and fall hand in hand . . .

No one knows who they were: husband and wife, lovers, dear friends, colleagues, strangers thrown together at the window there at the lip of hell. Maybe they didn't even reach for each other consciously, maybe it was a reflex as they decided at the same time to take two running steps and jump out the shattered window. But John the Apostle wrote *love casteth out fear* and they did reach for each other, and leaped, and held on tight, falling endlessly into the smoking canyon, two hundred miles an hour, falling so far so fast they may have blacked out before they hit the pavement near Liberty Street so hard there was pink mist in the air . . . Jennifer Brickhouse saw them holding hands, and Stuart DeHann saw them holding hands, and I hold on to that.

A Final Set of Thoughts. "I went down to the river to pray, studyin' about the good ol' Way / An' who shall wear that starry crown, Lord, show me the way . . ."

Martin Luther King Jr., Riverside Church, New York City, 1967:

> A time comes when silence is betrayal. . . . Men do not easily assume the task of opposing their government's policy, especially in time of war. . . . We must speak with all the humility that is appropriate to our limited vision, but we must speak. For we are deeply in need of a new way beyond the darkness so close around us. . . . We are called upon to speak for the weak, for the voiceless, for the victims of our nation, for those it calls enemy, for no document from human hands can make these humans any less our brothers.

I hold on not only to the held hands of the leaping couple and to my Americanness but to the ideals of assassinated Americans like Dr. King and to the Islamic friends of lifelong American friends. I hold on to Gandhi's insistence even to the Hindus who murdered him that he was Muslim and Christian as well as Hindu. I hold on to the millions of pilgrims shaded by my friend Jay's domes; to the encounters my friend Carl has had with marvelous people at the tombs of Rumi, Hafiz, and others; to the poems of the same poets; and to my fair-skinned son's marvelous dark-skinned namesake, Faredoon. The landless people of Palestine, dying children of Iraq, puppet governments, fascist dictators, hideous trade practices, hideous foreign policy, and military coups the United States has facilitated, armed, and defended now endanger us so forthrightly it's making our leaders' denial-filled heads spin like tops—BUSH GOES AFTER THE TERRORISTS' MONEY.

"Problems cannot be solved," said Albert Einstein, "at the same level of consciousness that created them." I pray that a half-million dead infants and children, three thousand dead New Yorkers, and the spirit of Dr. King lift our consciousness to a new level. We are called upon to speak for the *weak*, for the *voiceless*, for the *victims* of our nation. One power I possess to win a war against evil and terrorism, and so defend those I love, is to refuse to inflict evil or terror myself. How many photos of dead firemen must we contemplate before we begin to truly honor them—by carrying water the way firemen, clouds, and rivers do, to anyone and everyone who'll die without it?

Jennifer Brickhouse and Stuart DeHann saw them holding hands as they fell. The kindergartner reported the flaming birds, the mayor the pink mist, the UN the half-million dead children. *All the stories in the world surround us.* We're in a kiln with India, Pakistan, Israel, Palestine, Iraq, Mobil, Shell, and Exxon. Even if we've no power to guide the firing, we possess the power to think infinitely more clearly and compassionately than Dan Rather, power to empathize, power to consume less and to consume more peacably. We have the power of our voices, power of prayer, power of our united stories.

It's still possible to think of this as our good fortune.

NOTES

1 E. L. Doctorow, *City of God* (New York: Random House, 2000), 11.
2 William Kittredge, *The Nature of Generosity* (New York: Knopf, 2000), 5–7.
3 Wendell Berry, "Thoughts in the Presence of Fear," published online at www.oriononline.org, September 13, 2001 (reprinted in this volume on pages 37–42).
4 David James Duncan, "a prayer for water & children," published online at www.oriononline.org, October 19, 2001.
5 Thomas Nagy, "The Secret Behind the Sanctions: How the U.S. Intentionally Destroyed Iraq's Water Supply," *The Progressive*, September 2001.
6 Brian Doyle, "Leap," *The American Scholar*, Winter 2002.

ANNE R. SLIFKIN

John Walker Lindh

In the aftermath of September 11 and the subsequent U.S. invasion of Afghanistan, John Walker Lindh, a twenty-year-old California man, was discovered at an Afghan prison at which Taliban soldiers were being held. Prisoners at this facility were involved in an uprising against their captors and had killed CIA agent Johnny Michael Spann. The media and the public were stunned to find an American among these captives and Walker Lindh gained instant notoriety as the "American Taliban." With this designation, a battle to influence the perceptions of the American public began: officials of the government and many in the media labeled Walker Lindh a traitor, while his family geared up for a counteroffensive calling him "a good boy who loves America."

Following Walker Lindh's capture, the American public has been fascinated by the very fact of his existence, by his background, and by his crimes. He is charged with conspiring to kill Americans, providing support to terrorist organizations, and using firearms during crimes of violence. As of this writing in early 2002, it is unclear whether evidence exists supporting these charges. It is also not clear whether he knew of or participated in the tragedy of September 11, the prison uprising, the death of Agent Spann, or any other killing. His main offense seems to have been to be in bed with the "bad guys." While in the world of public opinion this lifestyle and political choice may disgust or anger many, in the world of law, criminal charges should be based on an objective analysis of law and the Constitution. But, as we have watched Walker Lindh be apprehended and as we watch his unfolding involvement in the American judicial system we should consider whether the propaganda uses of this young man's plight are more important to the government than the question of what crimes he has committed.

What is this fascination with the "American Taliban" and in what form has this interest been manifested? The media and the Bush administration have worked to focus public attention on this story. With apparent lack of concern for constitutional issues such as the notion that an accused is presumed innocent until found guilty or that an accused has the right to a trial by a fair and impartial jury, Attorney General John Ashcroft and others in the administration have taken many opportunities to assure us of Walker Lindh's culpability. Likewise, the media has cooperated in giving high-priority coverage to this matter through both news programming and talk shows. Although it does not appear that Walker Lindh's actions or inactions made any difference to any lives other than those of himself and his family, this story has been given priority over other, more significant stories. For example, whether due to coincidence or plan, Walker Lindh's initial court appearance, which was well covered by the press, was conveniently scheduled by the government to occur on the same day as the opening of hearings on the collapse of Enron. Even after the court appearance was over, Enron coverage was again interrupted by the Attorney General giving a postcourt statement to again assert Walker Lindh's guilt. According to the *New York Times*, the major networks devoted "far more attention" to this court process than to the Enron hearings.[1]

The coverage of John Walker Lindh's story has been one of two contrasting extremes. On the one hand, we are presented with Walker Lindh as traitor, a vile young man whose conduct is seen as all the more despicable because he rejected the luxuries offered him by the affluence of his Marin County youth. On the other hand, we have been shown Walker Lindh as a misguided "innocent abroad" who, as barely more than a child, set out on a spiritual quest gone wrong, a young man who at most was a passive nonforce in the crimes for which he is charged.

Such contrasting portrayals of Walker Lindh incorporate within them the American tendency toward oversimplification. In this instance our media is doing so with respect to questions of patriotism and defining criminality in a white, upper-middle-class young man. Our quick willingness to define Walker Lindh as traitor reflects a not uncommon American perspective of patriotism that requires "true Americans" to believe in "America right or wrong" when foreign policy is in question. Walker Lindh as "misguided youth" reflects a long-standing differentiation made within the American judicial system and by societal perception when criminal behavior is suspected in affluent white as opposed to poor nonwhite young people.

It is somewhat dangerous to speculate before a trial as to what evidence will be presented before court and jury. But it is clear, even as we wait to hear the actual facts, that both Walker Lindh's family and the federal government have made numerous assertions as to the significance of this young man's actions. We are bombarded with the concept of Walker Lindh as traitor despite the fact that the government has chosen not to charge him with the crime of treason, probably because evidence cannot be collected to support such a charge. Nonetheless, rhetoric from the White House, attorney general's office, media, and interviews with members of the general public encourage the continuing belief among the majority of the American population that a traitor is what Walker Lindh really is.

To combat the perception of traitor, Frank Lindh, John's father, has put on his own public relations battle on behalf of his son. Lindh's theme is one that dovetails nicely into society's general response to upper-middle-class youth who find themselves caught in criminal activity. Frank Lindh describes his son as a "good boy"; "not really much more than a boy"; a "very sweet kid, very devout, very religious, [with a] sense of humor"; and an "outstanding student."[2] His son is a youth looking for spiritual fulfillment, who traveled to the Middle East and Central Asia in an all-consuming desire to understand Islam. This spiritual quest, Lindh would have us believe, has nothing to do with his son's patriotism as he proclaims, "John loves America."[3]

Unfortunately, Frank Lindh's assertions of his son's love of country are belied by Walker Lindh's own words. In an e-mail to his parents, Walker Lindh referred to President Bush as "your new president. I'm glad he's not mine." He has also expressed disdain for this country, wondering what good America has ever done for anyone. After being captured, Walker Lindh also expressed support for the September 11 attacks. In response to such statements Lindh argued, "I don't think his mind was working—I don't think he was thinking straight at the moment . . . after that kind of ordeal."[4] Regardless, it hardly appears that Walker Lindh "loves America." Yet, Lindh's rhetoric does serve to minimize the culpability of his son in a manner perhaps helpful at trial or in plea negotiations.

Minimizing the significance of "unacceptable" acts by affluent, white young people is not new in our society. The very public and longstanding "war on drugs" is a case in point. While thousands of young black men serve long sentences for often minor drug offenses, few middle- or upper-middle-class white youths are similarly imprisoned, despite clear evidence that illegal drug use is a bigger problem in white rather than nonwhite communities. Likewise, when affluent white young people are caught committing other crimes common to their age group, such as shoplifting and destruction of property, they rarely serve time. Instead, it is assumed these lawbreakers are "misguided," "confused," or "hanging out with the wrong crowd." It is further assumed that they will "grow out of" such criminal inclinations. Even the Bush girls, in Texas and Florida, have recently had their own difficulties complying with the law. But they are described as children who, on leaving home, cannot be fully controlled by their well-meaning parents, and like Lindh says of his son, are fundamentally "good" kids. Imprisonment is hardly a likely outcome for the Bush daughters, although poor nonwhite twenty-year-olds risk imprisonment for similar illegal use of drugs or alcohol or impersonating a doctor to obtain such a substance. This "good kid" defense is successfully made on behalf of many "misguided" white affluent youth each year. Thus, it makes sense to make it on behalf of Walker Lindh. At least Walker Lindh found himself charged with crimes as a result of an honest search for truth and meaning in life while youths taking drugs often do so in despair of the ability to find any meaning at all.

It is unlikely that most Americans will view Walker Lindh's situation with dispassion. Being caught as a part of a network that harbored Osama bin Laden will not be perceived by most in the same light as being caught with drugs, joyriding in a neighbor's car, or shoplifting at the local mall. As a result, many have trouble swallowing Lindh's defense of his son.

After Walker Lindh's arraignment on February 13, 2002, the family of CIA agent Spann, seemingly working in tandem with the government, spoke to the press. Gail Spann, Spann's mother, stated, "John Walker is a traitor because of the way he lived. It's so simple." Johnny Spann, Mike Spann's father, added, "Tell them, Americans will not tolerate traitors."[5]

Due to tragic circumstances, the Spanns are understandably emotionally involved in this arrest and trial in a way that fortunately is not true for most of us. But the fervor against Walker Lindh's actions, real and only perceived, is almost palpable among many. News journalists, speaking on panels or in discussions with other journalists, use the word "traitor." Countless television interviews with "ordinary Americans" parrot this sentiment. Feelings about Walker Lindh are so strong that Morrison and Foerster, the law firm where Walker Lindh's lawyer James Brosnahan is a partner, has decided that Brosnahan must represent Walker Lindh under his own name, and may not use the name of the firm. This decision, they say, is a result of many of the firm's employees' concerns for their safety.[6]

But, shouldn't we step back from outrage to ask whether the expression of unpopular sentiments is illegal or even "anti-American"? Should someone be so despised and dubbed a traitor for expressing his opinions? Should he be dubbed a traitor because of the way he lived? The First Amendment right to freedom of speech only has meaning if it applies to painful as well as bland speech. Since September 11 we have constantly heard about the importance of fighting for what America "stands for." We have been told, and seem to be telling ourselves through the media, that we should not give up the fight to preserve "our way of life." But if America doesn't "stand for" the First Amendment's guarantee of freedom of speech, if our "way of life" does not include the acceptance of diverse, and sometimes revolting, political speech, for what are we fighting?

Perhaps our "way of life" is being redefined from that of the values expressed in the Constitution to a definition more in line with corporate ideals. The disproportionate influence of large corporations on the definition of American society, politics, and way of life is nothing new. But at this time, while we focus on Al Qaeda and September 11, ironically the Enron collapse also has brought our focus to corporate ties to government. Evidence of Enron's successful buying of politicians, and thus, the U.S. government, is too blatant to ignore. And as Enron is exposed, George Bush, president of the world's oldest democracy, has taken a stand for protection of corporate privacy over the American public's right to know through his fight to prohibit access to information regarding his administration's contact with Enron. Is it too cynical to suggest that, from the perspective of the administration in Washington, "the American way of life," for which we are fighting, represents little more than some combination of unbridled capitalism coupled with cookouts and fireworks on the Fourth of July and a new interest in flying the flag? If such is true, then whether Walker Lindh has a right to free expression is of little consequence.

Government claims made against John Walker Lindh include an assertion that he knew of the September 11 plans several months ahead of time yet did nothing to warn our government of the terrorists' plans. Perhaps evidence will be presented at trial to support such claims. In the meantime, some degree of skepticism might be healthy. Isn't it unlikely that the Al Qaeda leadership would have shared such vital information with a Taliban soldier who was not in a leadership position? Isn't it even more unlikely that the Al Qaeda leadership would have shared this intelligence with an American youth? Would it have made any sense to risk divulging such sensitive information to someone who quite possibly still had ties to the United States and whose e-mails to his parents could have contained almost any information or thoughts? If Al Qaeda's secrets were as poorly guarded as this assertion seems to maintain, why was the United States' own intelligence network unable to gain similar information? Foreknowledge by Walker Lindh of September 11 seems unlikely. However, it is much easier to believe the government's assertion that Walker Lindh chose to remain with the Taliban even after hearing, after the fact, of September 11. But did this choice make Walker Lindh a criminal?

To view Walker Lindh's actions in context, we should better understand our government's own involvement in Afghanistan. America's involvement in Afghan wars and politics has been sporadic and inconsistent and, until September 11, our policy has not been anti-Taliban. In the late 1980s and early 1990s, as the Afghan Mujaheddin fought the Soviet Union for control of Afghanistan, we poured large sums of money and resources into this war for the fight against the Soviets. We supported Osama bin Laden, today Public Enemy Number One. He was one of the beneficiaries of our earlier largesse. In helping the Mujaheddin we helped destroy the Soviet Union. The Afghan war, which is often dubbed the Soviet's Vietnam, was in fact more devastating to the Soviet Union than Vietnam was to the United States. By supporting those opposed to the Soviets, we used Afghanistan as a major battlefield of the cold war, bringing on the end of Soviet control of Afghanistan. Soviet loss of the Afghan war is credited as being a significant factor in the collapse of the Soviet State. Thus, in aiding the Mujaheddin and bin Laden, we chose friends based on the expediency of gaining our cold war goals while setting up a situation that helped promote today's terrorism.

This is not to say that in supporting the Mujaheddin we made the Taliban inevitable. The war against the Soviets destroyed Afghanistan: infrastructure was bombed; landmines were spread over urban and rural landscapes; order in society was lost. But many Afghans believed that they could afford these losses because they were confident the powerful United States would supply them with resources after the war to clean up their environment and restore a sense of order. Instead, when the Soviet Union was pushed from Afghanistan, we packed our moneybags and lost interest in our cold war ally.

During the years between Soviet withdrawal and September 11, our foreign policy objectives in Afghanistan were unclear. Because we no longer provided economic or other aid we contributed to an Afghanistan mired in social turmoil. Tyranny by warlords, the Northern Alliance, and the Taliban became a part of the Afghan reality. Even to those entities, we did not have a consistent approach. And, despite its repression of women and disregard for fundamental rights, the Taliban was not our enemy. While our government was mainly silent on the issue of Afghanistan, some within the government and American industry believed Taliban rule would foster stability in Central Asia. Stability, among other things, would enhance the feasibility of building a long-desired oil pipeline through Afghanistan, a project seen as potentially profitable to some in the American energy industry. Taliban rule also was seen as having a potentially discouraging effect on Afghanistan's production of its opium crop. In fact, as recently as a few months before September 11, the U.S. government sent millions of dollars in foreign aid to the Taliban as an incentive to work toward drug eradication. Interestingly, this American foreign aid package was sent to Afghanistan at around the same time John Walker Lindh joined the Taliban army. And, despite John Ashcroft's assertion that Walker Lindh "chose to join the terrorists who wanted to kill Americans," in fact, Walker Lindh joined the Taliban, a recipient of U.S. aid, to fight the Northern Alliance.[7]

Thus, the Taliban to which Walker Lindh was attracted was a Taliban not at war with the United States, but a Taliban that was a recipient of U.S. aid, and a Taliban that succeeded in coming to power thanks, in part, to our government's support of the Mujaheddin and its subsequent failure to support the rebuilding of Afghanistan after Soviet withdrawal.

Looked at in this context, the concept of culpability becomes muddled. It is easier to scapegoat one person who has aligned himself with our new enemy than to take a critical look at cold war and post–cold war U.S. foreign policy initiatives and decisions. Yet to focus on the actions of John Walker Lindh, who, as far as we know, killed no one and had no impact on what Al Qaeda did or did not do, does not bring us closer to understanding our own country's contribution to instability in Afghanistan. Rather, it does the opposite, diverting our attention from important issues of American foreign policy to the interesting, but probably insignificant, choices of one young man.

John Walker Lindh is not the patriot portrayed by his father. He is probably also not a misguided youth. But probably, Walker Lindh is also not a traitor. If we believe that there is an America for which it is worth fighting, surely this America is a country of fair trials in which the Constitution and Bill of Rights is treasured. Surely the protections of our Constitution to give an accused a fair trial and to presume innocence of an accused should be guarded and celebrated. Surely this country worth fighting for also is a country in which speech, no matter how distasteful, is honored as a badge of freedom.

NOTES

1   Bill Carter, "TV's Interest in Arraignment of Taliban Fighter," *New York Times*, January 25, 2002; viewed online on January 25, 2002, at www.nytimes.com/2002/01/25/business/25MEDI.html.
2   *Larry King Live*, January 12, 2002.
3   Katherine Seelye, "American Charged As a Terrorist Makes First Court Appearance," *New York Times*, January 25, 2002; viewed online on January 25, 2002, at www.nytimes.com/2002/01/25/national/25WALK.html.
4   *Larry King Live*, January 12, 2002.
5   Larry Margasale, "Lindh Pleads Innocent, Denounced As Traitor by Slain Agent's Family," *Durham Herald-Sun*, February 14, 2002, A4.
6   "Firm Wants Distance from Lawyer," *New York Times*, February 1, 2002; viewed online on February 1, 2002, at www.nytimes.com/aponline/national/AP-American-Taliban-Lawyers.html.
7   Seelye, "American Charged."

STANLEY HAUERWAS

September 11, 2001

A Pacifist Response

I want to write honestly about September 11, 2001. But it is not easy. Even now, some months after that horrible event, I find it hard to know what can be said or, perhaps more difficult, what should be said. Even more difficult, I am not sure for what or how I should pray. I am a Christian. I am a Christian pacifist. Being Christian and being a pacifist are not two things for me. I would not be a pacifist if I were not a Christian, and I find it hard to understand how one can be a Christian without being a pacifist. But what does a pacifist have to say in the face of terror? Pray for peace? I have no use for sentimentality.

Indeed some have suggested pacifists have nothing to say in a time like the time after September 11, 2001. The editors of the magazine *First Things* assert that "those who in principle oppose the use of military force have no legitimate part in the discussion about how military force should be used."[1] They make this assertion because according to them the only form of pacifism that is defensible requires the disavowal by the pacifist of any political relevance. That is not the kind of pacifism I represent. I am a pacifist because I think nonviolence is the necessary condition for a politics not based on death. A politics that is not determined by the fear of death means no strong distinction can be drawn between politics and military force.

Yet I cannot deny that September 11, 2001, creates and requires a kind of silence. We desperately want to "explain" what happened. Explanation domesticates terror, making it part of "our" world. I believe attempts to explain must be resisted. Rather, we should learn to wait before what we know not, hoping to gain time and space sufficient to learn how to speak without lying. I should like to think pacifism names the habits and community necessary to gain the time and place that is an alternative to revenge. But I do not pretend that I know how that is accomplished.

Yet I do know that much that has been said since September 11, 2001, has been false. In the first hours and days following the fall of the towers, there was a stunned silence. President Bush flew from one safe haven to another, unsure what had or was still to happen. He was quite literally in the air. I wish he might have been able to maintain that posture, but he is the leader of the "free world." Something must be done. Something must be said. We must be in control. The silence must be shattered. He knew the American people must be comforted. Life must return to normal.

So he said, "We are at war." Magic words necessary to reclaim the everyday. War is such normalizing discourse. Americans know war. This is our Pearl Harbor. Life can return to normal. We are frightened, and ironically war makes us feel safe. The way to go on in the face of September 11, 2001, is to find someone to kill. Americans are, moreover, good at killing. We often fail to acknowledge how accomplished we are in the art of killing. Indeed we, the American people, have become masters of killing. In our battles, only the enemy has to die. Some in our military are embarrassed by our expertise in war making, but what can they do? They are but following orders.

So the silence created by destruction was soon shattered by the need for revenge—a revenge all the more unforgiving because we cannot forgive those who flew the planes for making us acknowledge our vulnerability. The flag that flew in mourning was soon transformed into a pride-filled thing; the bloodstained flag of victims transformed into the flag of the American indomitable spirit. We will prevail no matter how many people we must kill to rid ourselves of the knowledge Americans died as victims. Americans do not die as victims. They have to be heroes. So the stock trader who happened to work on the seventy-second floor becomes as heroic as the policemen and the firemen who were doing their jobs. No one who died on September 11, 2001, gets to die a meaningless death. That is why their deaths must be revenged.

I am a pacifist, so the American "we" cannot be my "me." But to be alienated from the American "we" is not easy. I am a neophyte pacifist. I never really wanted to be a pacifist. I had learned from Reinhold Niebuhr that if you desire justice you had better be ready to kill someone along the way. But then John Howard Yoder and his extraordinary book *The Politics of Jesus* came along. Yoder convinced me that if there is anything to this Christian "stuff," it must surely involve the conviction that the Son would rather die on the cross than for the world to be redeemed by violence. Moreover, the defeat of death through resurrection makes possible as well as necessary that Christians live nonviolently in a world of violence. Christian nonviolence is not a strategy to rid the world of violence, but rather the way Christians must live in a world of violence. In short, Christians are not nonviolent because we believe our nonviolence is a strategy to rid the world of war, but rather because faithful followers of Christ in a world of war cannot imagine being anything else than nonviolent.

But what does a pacifist have to say in the face of the terror September 11, 2001, names? I vaguely knew when I first declared I was a pacifist that there might be some serious consequences. To be nonviolent might even change my life. But I do not really think I understood what that change might entail until September 11. For example after I declared I was a pacifist, I quit singing the "Star-Spangled Banner." I will stand when it is sung, particularly at baseball games, but I do not sing. Not to sing the "Star-Spangled Banner" is a small thing that reminds me that my first loyalty is not to the United States but to God and God's church. I confess it never crossed my mind that such small acts might over the years make my response to September 11 quite different from that of the good people who sing "God Bless America"— so different that I am left in saddened silence.

That difference, moreover, haunts me. My father was a bricklayer and a good American. He worked hard all his life and hoped his work would not only support his family, but also make some contribution to our common life. He held a war-critical job in World War II, so he was never drafted. Only one of his five bricklaying brothers was in that war, but he was never exposed to combat. My family was never militarized, but as Texans they were good Americans. For most of my life I, too, was a good American, assuming that I owed much to the society that enabled me, the son of a bricklayer, to gain a Ph.D. at Yale—even if the Ph.D. was in theology.

Of course there was Vietnam. For many of us Vietnam was extended training necessary for the development of a more critical attitude toward the government of the United States. Yet most of us critical of the war in Vietnam did not think our opposition to that war made us less loyal Americans. Indeed the criticisms of the war were based on an appeal to the highest American ideals. Vietnam was a time of great tension, but the politics of the antiwar movement did not require those opposed to the war to think of themselves as fundamentally standing outside the American mainstream. Most critics of Vietnam (just as many that now criticize the war in Afghanistan) based their dissent on their adherence to American ideals that they felt the war was betraying. That but indicates why I feel so isolated even among the critics of the war in Afghanistan. I do not even share their allegiance to American ideals.

So I simply did not share the reaction of most Americans to the destruction of the World Trade Center. Of course I recoil from murder on such a scale, but I hope I remember that one murder is too many. That Americans have hurried to call what happened "war" strikes me as self-defeating. If this is war, then bin Laden has won. He thinks he is a warrior not a murderer. Just to the extent the language of war is used, he is honored. But in their hurry to call this war, Americans have no time for careful discriminations.

Where does that leave me? Does it mean, as an estranged friend recently wrote me, that I disdain all "natural loyalties" that bind us together as human beings, even submitting such loyalties to a harsh and unforgiving standard? Does it mean that I speak as a solitary individual, failing to acknowledge that our lives are interwoven with the lives of others, those who have gone before, those among whom we live, those with whom we identify, and those with whom we are in Christian communion? Do I refuse to acknowledge my life is made possible by the gifts of others? Do I forsake all forms of patriotism, failing to acknowledge that we as a people are better off because of the sacrifices that were made in World War II? To this I can only answer, "Yes." If you call patriotism "natural," I certainly do disavow that connection. Such a disavowal, I hope, does not mean I am inattentive to the gifts I have received from past and present neighbors.

In response to my friend I pointed out that because he, too, is a Christian I assumed he also disdained some "natural loyalties." After all he had his children baptized. The "natural love" between parents and children is surely reconfigured when children are baptized into the death and resurrection of Christ. Paul says:

Do you not know that all of us who have been baptized into Christ Jesus were baptized into his death? Therefore we have been buried with him by baptism into death, so that, just as Christ was raised from the dead by the glory of the Father, so we too might walk in the newness of life. For if we have been united with him in a death like his, we will certainly be united with him in a resurrection like his.[2]

Christians often tend to focus on being united with Christ in his resurrection, forgetting that we are also united with him in his death. What could that mean if it does not mean that Christians must be ready to die, indeed have their children die, rather than betray the Gospel? Any love not transformed by the love of God cannot help but be the source of the violence we perpetrate on one another in the name of justice. Such a love may appear harsh and dreadful from the perspective of the world, but Christians believe such a love is life-giving not life-denying.

Of course living a life of nonviolence may be harsh. Certainly you have to imagine, and perhaps even face, that you will have to watch the innocent suffer and even die for your convictions. But that is no different from those that claim they would fight a just war. After all, the just warrior is committed to avoiding any direct attack on noncombatants, which might well mean that more people will die because the just warrior refuses to do an evil that a good may come. For example, on just-war grounds the bombings of Hiroshima and Nagasaki were clearly murder. If you are serious about just war, you must be ready to say that it would be better that more people died on the beaches of Japan than to have committed one murder, much less the bombing of civilian populations.

This last observation may suggest that when all is said and done, a pacifist response to September 11, 2001, is just one more version of the anti-American sentiments expressed by what many consider to be the American Left. I say "what many consider" because it is very unclear if there is a Left left in America. Nowhere is that more apparent than in the support to the war on terrorism given by those who identify as the "Left." Yet much has been made of the injustice of American foreign policy that lends a kind of intelligibility to the hatred given form on September 11. I am no defender of American foreign policy, but the problem with such lines of criticism is that no matter how immoral what the American government may have done in the world, such immorality cannot explain or justify the attack on the World Trade Center.

American imperialism, often celebrated as the new globalism, is a frightening power. It is frightening not only because of the harm such power inflicts on the innocent, but because it is difficult to imagine alternatives. Pacifists are often challenged after an event like September 11 with the question, "Well, what alternative do you have to bombing Afghanistan?" Such a question assumes that pacifists must have an alternative foreign policy. My only response is I do not have a foreign policy. I have something better—a church constituted by people who would rather die than kill.

Indeed I fear that absent a countercommunity to challenge America, bin Laden has given Americans what they so desperately needed—a war without end. America is a country that lives off the moral capital of our wars. War names the time we send the youth to kill and die (maybe) in an effort to assure ourselves the lives we lead are worthy of such sacrifices. They kill and die to protect our "freedom." But what can freedom mean if the prime instance of the exercise of such freedom is to shop? The very fact that we can and do go to war is a moral necessity for a nation of consumers. War makes clear we must believe in something even if we are not sure what that something is, except that it has something to do with the "American way of life."

What a gift bin Laden has therefore given America. Americans were in despair because we won the cold war. Americans won by outspending the USSR, proving that we can waste more money on guns than they can or did. But what do Americans do after they have won a war? The war was necessary to give moral coherence. We had to cooperate with one another because we were at war. How can America make sense of what it means for us to be "a people" if we have no common enemy? We were in a dangerous funk having nothing better to do than entertain ourselves with the soap opera Bill Clinton was. Now we have something better to do. We can fight the war against terrorism.

The good thing, moreover, about the war on terrorism is it has no end, which makes it very doubtful that this war can be considered just. If a war is just, your enemy must know before the war begins what political purpose the war is to serve. In other words, they need to know from the beginning what the conditions are if they choose to surrender. So you cannot fight a just war if it is "a war to end all wars" (World

War I) or for "unconditional surrender" (World War II). But a "war on terrorism" is a war without limit. Americans want to wipe this enemy off the face of the earth. Moreover, America even gets to decide who counts and does not count as a terrorist.

Which means Americans get to have it any way they want it. Some that are captured, for example, are prisoners of war; some are detainees. No problem. When you are the biggest kid on the block, you can say whatever you want to say, even if what you say is nonsense. We all know the first casualty in war is truth. So the conservatives who have fought the war against "postmodernism" in the name of "objective truth," the same conservatives that now rule us, assume they can use language any way they please.

That Americans get to decide who is and who is not a terrorist means that this is not only a war without clear purpose, but also a war without end. From now on we can be in a perpetual state of war. America is always at her best when she is on permanent war footing. Moreover, when our country is at war, it has no space to worry about the extraordinary inequities that constitute our society, no time to worry about poverty or those parts of the world that are ravaged by hunger and genocide. Everything—civil liberties, due process, the protection of the law—must be subordinated to the one great moral enterprise of winning the unending war against terrorism.

At the heart of the American desire to wage endless war is the American fear of death. The American love of high-tech medicine is but the other side of the war against terrorism. Americans are determined to be safe, to be able to get out of this life alive. On September 11, Americans were confronted with their worst fear—a people ready to die as an expression of their profound moral commitments. Some speculate such people must have chosen death because they were desperate or, at least, they were so desperate that death was preferable to life. Yet their willingness to die stands in stark contrast to a politics that asks of its members in response to September 11 to shop.

Ian Buruma and Avishai Margalit observe in their article "Occidentalism" that lack of heroism is the hallmark of a bourgeois ethos.[3] Heroes court death. The bourgeois is addicted to personal safety. They concede that much in an affluent, market-driven society is mediocre, "but when contempt for bourgeois creature comforts becomes contempt for life itself you know the West is under attack." According to Buruma and Margalit, the West (which they point out is not just the geographical West) should oppose the full force of calculating anti-bourgeois heroism, of which Al Qaeda is but one representative, through the means we know best—cutting off their money supply. Of course, Buruma and Margalit do not tell us how that can be done, given the need for oil to sustain the bourgeois society they favor.

Christians are not called to be heroes or shoppers. We are called to be holy. We do not think holiness is an individual achievement, but rather a set of practices to sustain a people who refuse to have their lives determined by the fear and denial of death. We believe by so living we offer our non-Christian brothers and sisters an alternative to all politics based on the denial of death. Christians are acutely aware that we seldom are faithful to the gifts God has given us, but we hope the confession of our sins is a sign of hope in a world without hope. This means pacifists do have a response to September 11, 2001. Our response is to continue living in a manner that witnesses to our belief that the world was not changed on September 11, 2001. The world was changed during the celebration of Passover in A.D. 33.

Mark and Louise Zwick, founders of the Houston Catholic Worker House of Hospitality, embody the life made possible by the death and resurrection of Jesus. They know, moreover, that Christian nonviolence cannot and must not be understood as a position that is no more than being "against violence." If pacifism is no more than "not violence," it betrays the form of life to which Christians believe they have been called by Christ. Drawing on Nicholas Berdyaev, the Zwicks rightly observe that "the split between the Gospel and our culture is the drama of our times," but they also remind us that "one does not free persons by detaching them from the bonds that paralyze them: one frees persons by attaching them to their destiny." Christian nonviolence is but another name for the friendship we believe God has made possible and constitutes the alternative to the violence that grips our lives.

I began by noting that I am not sure for what I should pray. But prayer often is a form of silence. The following prayer I hope does not drown out silence. I wrote the prayer as a devotion to begin a Duke Divinity School general meeting. I was able to write the prayer because of a short article I had just read in the *Houston Catholic Worker* by Jean Vanier.[4] Vanier is the founder of the L'arche movement—a movement that believes God has saved us by giving us the good work of living with and learning to be friends with those the world calls retarded. I end with this prayer because it is all I have to give.

> Great God of surprise, our lives continue to be haunted by the specter of September 11, 2001. Life must go on and we go on keeping on—even meeting again as the Divinity School Council. Is this what Barth meant in 1933 when he said we must go on "as though nothing has happened"? To go on as though nothing has happened can sound like a counsel of despair, of helplessness, of hopelessness. We want to act, to do something to reclaim the way things were. Which, I guess, is but a reminder that one of the reasons we are so shocked, so violated, by September 11 is the challenge presented to our prideful presumption that we are in control, that we are going to get out of life alive. To go on "as though nothing has happened" surely requires us to acknowledge you are God and we are not. It is hard to remember that Jesus did not come to make us safe, but rather he came to make us disciples, citizens of your new age, a kingdom of surprise. That we live in the end times is surely the basis for our conviction that you have given us all the time we need to respond to September 11 with "small acts of beauty and tenderness," which Jean Vanier tells us, if done with humility and confidence "will bring unity to the world and break the chain of violence." So we pray give us humility that we may remember that the work we do today, the work we do every day, is false and pretentious if it fails to serve those who day in and day out are your small gestures of beauty and tenderness.

POSTSCRIPT *A Sermon a Year Later*

Micah 4: 1–5
Ephesians 2: 13–18
Matthew 5: 43–48

September 11, 2001, a day of terror. September 11, 2001, "a day of infamy," for those who remember Pearl Harbor. September 11, 2001, a day when I remember where I was and what I was doing, not unlike when I heard that Kennedy had been shot. September 11, 2001, a day that changed the world for those who long to live in a world without change. September 11, 2001, a day in which Americans discovered senseless violence can be quite effective, particularly because it is senseless. September 11, 2001, a day when Christians, long accommodated to the sentimentalities of American culture, discovered they had nothing of use to say.

A year later we find we are still wrapped in silence—a silence that could be redemptive if it were an expression of patient sadness. But such a silence is hard. The images are too strong. We try to resist, to forget, but such forgetting seems too much like a betrayal of those who died. We remember the beautiful arc the second plane made before erupting into the brilliant fireball that burned away any hope that all might not be lost. The terror those in the upper floors must have felt knowing they were doomed. Bodies, desperate bodies, choosing to float briefly on air rather than be trapped and incinerated. It was as if the whole world were caught in slow motion as the great towers imploded, leaving barren sky. New York, New York, no longer a wonderful town. We divert our gaze, not wanting to be reminded what is missing.

An apocalyptic moment Christians in America cannot ignore. Surely something like how we felt as we survived the days after September 11, 2001, is how the followers of Jesus felt after the crucifixion. Pure terror. The one on whom all hope was placed, the one we gave up all to follow, the one we had hoped was the one to redeem Israel, dead. It is not even clear who killed him or why he was killed. Another meaningless death against the blackness of a meaningless cosmos. Best to face the fact that it is kill or be killed. In such a world meaning is determined by those with the largest swords. They are the ones who will write the histories making it possible for us to know what "really happened."

Thank God, for the time being we are on the winning side. We get to call the violently secured order that makes our lives possible—peace. Only terrorists refuse to accept the peace our order names. The only way, moreover, to deal with terrorists is vengeance. Justice demands vengeance. We cannot let the innocent die meaningless deaths. They were not victims. No American gets to die a victim. Sacrificially they died that we might live. They are freedom's martyrs. Lives made more significant by how they died than could have ever been imagined by how they lived. Their deaths will not be in vain.

But wait—some say He has been raised from the dead. He appeared to the disciples showing them his nail-marked hands and feet. He even ate a broiled fish. He ascended to heaven and they worshiped him. Worshiped him? You can only worship God. Yet it says clearly, Luke

24: 52, they worshiped him. What are we to make of that? We confess we are not quite sure. We have been at it for two thousand years and we are still "not quite sure." We often think we must find some way to explain the meaning of his death. We call such efforts "atonement theories." But the scripture makes clear we do not get to vindicate Christ. We do not need to avenge his death. His ascension to the Father is the only vindication needed.

In his book *He Came Preaching Peace*, John Howard Yoder observes that in the New Testament the death of Christ is sometimes described as a sacrifice, sometimes as a ransom—descriptions we normally assume name our reconciliation with God over the barrier of our sins. But Yoder observes the barrier between people, a barrier as real as the wall of masonry in Jerusalem that separated the outer court for Gentiles from the temple proper, is not made up of anybody's sins. Rather,

> the barrier is the historical fact of separate stories. It is not a barrier of guilt, but of culture and communication. It is not a barrier between each person and God but between one group and another. It is not the case that inner or personal peace comes first, with the hope that once the inward condition is set right then the restored person will do some social good. In this text it is the other way around. Two estranged *histories* are made into one. Two hostile *communities* are reconciled.[5]

Note the breaking of this barrier is not something we must try to do. The breaking has been done. What was hidden from the ages is now revealed. We live in a new time. We live in an apocalyptic time. So it is only now that the rulers and authorities, the principalities and powers, can learn through the church what the rich variety of God's wisdom has always been (Ephesians 3: 10–11). God has judged between the peoples, God has beat the swords of the nations into plowshares. God has abolished war. We need no longer to learn of war.

But who is the "we" that no longer learns of war? Why is it those who were taught by the One raised that we must love our enemies? How can we possibly be told to love enemies—enemies who think nothing of wanton murder? A good question, but one those who live in the new age inaugurated by Christ need not ask. We know it is possible to love our enemies. Otherwise why would Christ in the Sermon on the Mount ask that we so love? Are we to make Christ a liar? If we do not think it possible to love our enemies then we should plainly say Jesus is not the messiah. But Jesus is the messiah, not dead but alive, indeed present to us in this meal of the New Age.

So we find ourselves living in the aftermath of two apocalyptic events. Those events produce two people with two quite different stories. The one fears and worships death as their only lord; the other fears and worships the Lord of death. The people of the September 11 apocalypse, the people who worship death, do not believe that God has removed the barrier between Jew and Gentile. The people of the September 11 apocalypse do not believe that Jesus has been raised from death. So these people of the September 11 apocalypse are determined to have vengeance. They are determined to make their world safe, no matter what cost others must bare to insure their safety. The people of the September 11 apocalypse rage against death, believing through the memory of their accomplishments they do not have to die.

Jesus people are also an apocalyptic people. They are so because they worship the Lord of death. Like the people of the September 11 apocalypse, the Jesus people are also a storied people. But they do not think they get to make their story up. Their story, moreover, is certainly not a story of their accomplishments. It is a story of their sinful unfaithfulness. It is the story of their living as if the work God accomplished in Christ is somehow not sufficient for our salvation. It is the story of the impatience of the Jesus people desperate to convince ourselves and those outside the church that our God exists and on the whole is a pretty good guy. It is the story of our unwillingness to acknowledge to ourselves and others that we live in a dangerous world, a world of death, made all the more dangerous by our unbridled desire for safety.

If that is the story of the Jesus people, why, we must ask, would anyone want to be part of that story? The world is terrible enough. Why cannot we recognize that when all is said and done, we are pretty much the same, so let's just try to get along? Tempted though they may be by that story, the Jesus people know that cannot be their story. It cannot be their story, because their story is not really about them. The story that makes the Jesus people a storied people is the story of God and God's unfailing love of us. How extraordinary. How wonderful. It really is not all about "us." It is about God. A God not rendered powerless by events like September 11, 2001, but the God that has made his church, the Jesus people, the alternative to those that would rule the world in the name of putting right the terror of September 11, 2001.

But are we Jesus people? We think we might like to be Jesus people, but we know we are those storied by September 11, 2001. We may not want "to kill the bastards," but the images and the feelings we felt that day cannot be denied. I am not suggesting that we simply try harder to be Jesus people. Such trying I fear too often only increases our narcissism, underwriting the presumption it is all about us. Perhaps a beginning is to recognize that we are an apocalyptic people, a new age people, who have been given all we need not to be captured by the powers fueled by our fear of death. Such a people do not need to try to be better, but rather only to receive the gifts we have been given.

Gifts as simple as bread and wine made by the Spirit, the body and blood of the One whose sacrifice is the end of all sacrifice. At this table we find God's justice. We deserve death, but God refuses our refusal, making us His storied people, His Jesus people, so that the world may know there is an alternative to terror. That alternative, at once terrible and wonderful, is us. Here at this table God lifts us up so that we become for the world the end of all sacrifices. How extraordinary. How frightening. How wonderful. Amen.

NOTES

1   "In a Time of War," *First Things* (December 2001).
2   Romans 6:3–5.
3   *New York Review of Books*, January 17, 2002, 4–7.
4   "L'arche Founder Responds to Violence," *Houston Catholic Worker*, November 16, 2001.
5   John Howard Yoder, *He Came Preaching Peace* (Eugene, Or.: Wipf and Stock Publishers, 1996), 111–12.

SRINIVAS ARAVAMUDAN

Ground Zero; or, The Implosion

of Church and State

At this very moment in the United States, the category of religion is being invoked largely within a trilateralism of Judaeo-Christian-Islamic responses in their broadest sense. These religious fields can address each other, despite their huge differences, because they make available a large set of common dispositions and attitudes. The core belief in the Pentateuch is shared among them. Even if they have been involved in continuing historical blood feuds and various jockeyings for superiority, practitioners of these religions share an atavistic sense of knowing (and also misrecognizing) each other. Such mutual knowledge may be traced through the very history of the evolution of these religions from an original Jewish monotheism — or to be more precise, monolatry, as the Jewish Bible frequently acknowledges the existence of other, albeit false gods. From the followers of Jesus Christ, a messianic Jew, came a Christianity that embraced many aspects of its Jewish origins even as it invented the cancer of antisemitism. Against the background of local tribal polytheism in Arabia arose an Islam that acknowledged Jewish and Christian precursors as prophets, even as it promulgated a new form of radical iconoclasm and monotheism.

These three traditions share at least five -isms. First, textualism. Judaeo-Christian-Muslim (religious) practitioners are *ehel-e-kitab*, or people of the book, as this idea is expressed elegantly in Arabic. There are central religious texts — the Jewish Bible, the Gospels, and the Qur'an — that variously enshrine, override, and reiterate religious fundamentals. Second, doctrinalism. Judaeo-Christian-Muslim believers foreground the necessity to construct consistent doctrine through a hermeneutic relation between texts and readers. Of course, there is a rich panoply of clashing and differing doctrines that has developed, but it is worth considering the history of universalization that these doctrines have undergone, which is what makes them visible unto each other. Third, moralism. While doctrinalism synthesizes the ontology and the cosmology and makes for a universe of consistent meanings, moralism reanchors those meanings in individual subjects, who are then exhorted to act according to specific ethical imperatives. The Ten Commandments form a crude cribsheet. Fourth, congregationalism. All these religions function by giving great but not necessarily exclusive importance to communitarian forms of worship, sacrament, and ritual. Thus we find constituted severally the Children of Abraham; the flock of Christ, the shepherd; and the *umma*, or the *qom*, whose members acknowledge Muhammad as Allah's last and most important prophet. Of course, there are privatized or nonparticipatory forms of belief and practice at work in all three traditions, but the core of each asserts communitarian sharing. Fifth, supremacism. The Judeo-Christian-Muslim religions avow universal applicability, special pleading, chosen people, providentialism, or implicit superiority in relation to nonpractitioners—maybe partly in relation to each other, but especially when framed against a host of paganisms, polytheisms, animisms, syncretisms, New Ageisms, atheisms, and various other belief-practices. By singling out such points, I am not making the claim that these religious traditions are inherently regressive; all three have been put to multiple political and progressive uses as well as oppressive ones. However, these five aspects, if not critically disengaged from a nation-form that inexorably justifies and legitimates the state-form, will be in danger of becoming complicit with all the actions of the state-form as it gears itself for war against its conveniently defined enemy.

While I am not suggesting that the United States is a theocracy, it is worth exploring the nature of state-tolerated secularism in this country at moments of state-defined national crisis. I am not a scholar of the separation of church and state, which has a rich legal and ecclesiastical history in many parts of the world. There are as many histories of church and state—or, I should say, there are as many histories of the successful or unsuccessful separation of transcendentalist foundationalism from temporal power—as there are modern states. Given this diversity, one of the key features that distinguishes the United States sociologically from many of its Western European allies is the overwhelming belief in the divine here, according to some surveys as much as 80 to 90 percent. Similar surveys find that many Western European countries, despite their rich religious history, are composed of a citizenry whose majority—sometimes up to 70 to 80 percent—are atheistic or agnostic by most conventional criteria. Of course, we have always been taught that, despite the country's overwhelming religiosity, the government of the United States is secular and does not favor any particular religious group over another. Religious freedom and the freedom to worship are enshrined in the First Amendment. It has also been suggested that the absence of an official state religion in the United States can be traced to the particular experiences of the dissenting Protestant groups who dominated the first Anglo-European colonies. In many instances fleeing religious oppression, early colonists crafted practices of religious toleration and sectarian equity among each other. Once this freedom was constitutionalized (largely with various Christian sects in mind), Jewish, Mormon, and eventually Muslim, Sikh, Buddhist, Hindu, and other practitioners could worship, congregate, and proselytize.

There is, however, a fundamental set of problems and disagreements regarding the First Amendment. A proliferation of religious groupings means the increased possibility of tensions among them. It also raises concerns regarding the abuse of the First Amendment by one group, or an individual indulging in hate speech against other individuals or groups. The protection afforded to groups under the Fourteenth Amendment has, with a few exceptions, been legally far less effectively enforced than First Amendment protection. This bias has been supported by libertarian organizations such as the ACLU that frequently defend right-wing intolerance as a matter of principle. It is clear that in terms of its actual consequences the First Amendment means for the vast majority of the country's citizenry a freedom *to* worship as one chooses, more so than a freedom *from* worship itself. This freedom, while formally equalitarian and individualist, obviously acquires lesser or greater strength at moments of crisis when civil liberties are cut back.

Nevertheless, Free Speech, or First Amendment Tolerance, is the manner in which religious and even self-expressive freedom has been conceptualized in the United States: as a passive tolerance of others that derives from the fundamentally religious desires of early (and, I would say, seventeenth-century European) experiences. The "founding" Christian nonconformists generated a heroic narrative of exceptionalism and providentialism that forms part of the doctrinal structure of Protestant Christianity—but, of course, this narrative continues to billow around us as a secularized national patriotic ideology. Clearly, this ideology did not just come from nowhere, even if it does not overtly claim its religious and historical roots. Just for contrast's sake, we should remind ourselves of other more active forms of secularism. The antireligious republicanism of the French Revolution, for instance, sought to extirpate the domination through its vast lands and monasteries of the Catholic Church; at the same time, this ideology sought to create a citizenry who were utterly modern. The same went for the relentlessly secular form of modernization that Kemal Ataturk introduced in Turkey, forcing traditional Muslim dress like the fez and the headscarf out of the public sphere. I'm not suggesting that these other forms of secularism are better—they have, for instance, contributed to the fierce intolerance by the French state of Muslim children who wanted to wear headscarves and the backlash movement of Islamic fundamentalism in Turkey that can argue it has been victimized by the suppression of religious freedoms. What I want to establish through these comparisons is that the fundamental attributes of U.S. nationalism have always derived from the moral doctrines of a nation of passive religious freedoms, formed and nurtured against the narrative of past religious trauma and persecution and conveniently kept alive and renewed by the state when in pursuit of militarist agendas. Hence, tolerance of religious pluralism rather than a critique of the perniciousness of religious ideology characterizes the relationship between religion and the state in the United States.

In this respect, many of the early narratives of the Puritans who are captured by Indians and then return to the Christian fold are remarkable documentary resources. Mary Rowlandson's captivity-and-redemption narrative of 1682, for example, is one such text. Witness important recognitions in the preface of the limits of Rowlandson's ideology: "It is no new thing for Gods precious ones to drink as deep as others, of the Cup of common Calamity."[1] The "self" recognizes that it is chosen by God but is also equal with unchosen others in suffering calamity.

Nonetheless, the national self, the self that has been subject to persecution by others, suffers a setback, then returns and revindicates itself in triumph. It is an activity that takes place at different moments for each generation, and one that can be revalidated through mechanisms such as war. During times of war, the entire world receives an un-equivocal message: "If you're not with us, you're against us." I'm led back to the analogy of the Puritans among the Indians, with respect to the war that is to be conducted against the apparently ubiquitous but also highly elusive terrorists. Their seeming lack of a state, their shadowy appearances and disappearances, their inherent evil and un-regenerateness, and their moral turpitude are in Manichean contrast with the fundamental goodness and deliverance from evil that sup-posedly represents the United States and its government, which, along with a credulous and pliant media, has less memory—less than even the unfortunate Ronald Reagan right now—of its violent and punitive military actions on a global stage.

Jerry Falwell and Pat Robertson's rhetoric revealed some of the more interesting interpretations—at least from a pathological point of view —of tribulation as a national catastrophe, brought on not just by evil adversaries but the godless life and sexual deviance of Americans them-selves. Clearly, the right-wing commentators were echoing views that many in the current administration might privately share, but they were shut up immediately for the simple reason that they were not "staying on message." The religious right reveals a tendency, shared with earlier religious nationalists, to convert contingent events into causes for a sermon on national sinfulness; this is famously known as the American jeremiad, studied brilliantly by Sacvan Bercovitch.[2] God punishes the Americans for their fall from grace but saves them if and when they turn back to their moral natures. But the White House reined in the attack dogs, and instead the president argued in his Sep-tember 14, 2001, speech that "freedom and fear, justice and cruelty have always been at war. And God is not neutral between them. May God grant us wisdom and may he watch over the United States of America." Of course, God is clearly on the side of the largest batallions. Or is He, in these times when the newest military theories consider the un-leashing of new forms of "asymmetrical" warfare? It is undoubtedly a strange God who will sanction cruel and fearful means of combining U.S. national interests with his presumptive divine plan for the uni-verse. Is it not remarkable that political leaders can suggest that God watches over the United States in its campaign for justice and against cruelty, and no one thinks to object on behalf of the 95 percent of humanity who are not U.S. citizens?

There is a deep structuring role played by Puritan religion during this national crisis that suggests a historical return of the not-so-very repressed. In his speech to the nation, Bush asked the citizenry to continue praying, even as he suggested that the nation's grief had successfully been converted to anger. According to him, "prayer has comforted us in sorrow and will strengthen us for the journey ahead." There was no better indication than with this comment that religious feelings were being instrumentalized and marshalled by the state in its campaign. Congregationalism is hijacked by leading it to nationalism and warmongering. Protofascist unity must be demonstrated, and not just in terms of the lopsided votes in the House and the Senate to give the militarists a blank check for war, but also in terms of an invocation of God, and country, and the American flag, and a contentless freedom at every turn. The media have to provide amplification. This derivation of a shadowy justification from a cellular network of congregationalist practitioners perhaps does resemble the very thing it seeks to destroy, the Al Qaeda. Appeals to congregationalism slide uncritically from a "we" that is empathetically formed in relation to those who have been injured—actually a spectatorial "we" formed through media participation—to one that aggrandizes itself into a national "we," and then deliberates and speaks about the past, present, and future actions of the state in terms of that very "we." This kind of sliding is especially visible at moments of crisis, when the public sphere shrinks and is almost entirely replaced by the media. The media, in turn, take up the role of representing the nation to itself and make the state into a pure and unmediated agent of the general will, which is why even the legislature (representative of the people) simply echoes the will of the administration (indeed, monarch). I am surprised at how unsurprising it has become for so many in the United States to think so un-self-consciously from the standpoint of the state. The "we" is a daisy chain that goes all the way to the top, to the Wee Willie Winkie who scowled and nudged through the speech of retaliation against a still unidentified enemy in the immediate aftermath of September 11.

When it comes to the question of supremacism, the initial use of the term "crusade" was no random choice of phrase, even if it was airbrushed out of the vocabulary when its historical allusion became inconvenient. Ultimately, it is supremacism that determines the contentless freedom of the United States and its client states when an alliance among them is deliberately equated with the civilized world.

However, there is considerable sophistication as well in the political attempt to separate the undefined terrorists from the larger body of Islam. There has been an important tokenist embrace of U.S. Muslims, as evidenced by the unprecedented summoning of a Muslim cleric to commence the overwhelmingly Christian memorial services held September 14, 2001 at the National Cathedral—even though these services anyway featured a military choir singing "Onward Christian Soldiers" to an assembly of the entire current political leadership and such past leaders as Bush Sr., Carter, Clinton, and Gore. Meanwhile, the new media are unworking textualism and national political accountability through hyperbolic and hypertextual use of images, citation, and jump cuts. Osama has been elevated to the diabolical status of "the evil one," a stand-in for Satan himself. Should we give the president points for inadvertent humor in his resurrection of the "Great Satan" vocabulary, trademarked by Ayatollah Khomeini and skillfully used against the United States? A crusade updated for the times, perhaps?

My last point regards the supremacist logic that expresses itself in the barely veiled religious code given to the ensuing war, conveniently titled, at one point, Operation Infinite Justice. This blatant religious appeal was already being scaled back—later into Enduring Freedom—after it was critiqued by both Protestant and Muslim clerics as sinfully prideful and as an arrogant and religious-sounding cloak for secular military action. Defense Secretary Donald Rumsfeld tersely acknowledged that the code name for the operation was under review. But the manner of naming does not surprise me. Couldn't a finite justice treat the horrendous acts that took place on September 11 as the result of a vast international criminal conspiracy? These acts could very easily be prosecuted through existing laws and international treaties involving extradition, or even through an international tribunal that would sift through the evidence rather than take the CNN-CIA version of the world—or the combination of media enactment and conspiracy theory—as truth. As Bush said, "Whether we bring our enemies to justice or bring justice to our enemies, justice will be done."[3] I'm sure CNN would love to give us a front-row seat for this morality play for the next few years.

The same man was pondering, a few days earlier, the heavy cost of his equation of justice with retaliatory violence: in his own words, "We cannot use a $2 million cruise missile to take out a $10 tent." Perhaps no other comment has revealed the rhetoric of civilization as effectively for what it is. If we dissolve the euphemism, after all, we realize that the cruise missile would not be seeking the tent so much as seeking to destroy those huddled under it. Bemoaning the fact that Afghanistan has no high-value targets, can this president and his civilization afford the cost of going after its valueless and nomadic other in a war without end? While Oklahoma City bomber Timothy McVeigh and the 1993 World Trade Center bombers were dealt with adequately as criminal conspirators without the United States necessarily having to attack anywhere, the September 11 episode threatens us with doctrinalist retaliation by a rogue state that is likely to kill many innocent civilians directly or indirectly in its pursuit of political hegemony and remasculinization. In conclusion, if the United States stood for the supposedly civilized superiority of the rule of law rather than the random acts of politically inspired violence deemed terrorism, it would not be embarking on a military operation once ironically named Operation Infinite Justice. Retaliation reproduces the very thing it seeks to combat.

Indeed, we should ventriloquize and satirize this unelected but appointed president, who has cautioned his audiences famously not to "misunderestimate" him.

> Make no mistake. Florida is not one of the states "harboring terrorists" that are to be attacked, even if several terrorists trained at its flight schools. Nor will it be Saudi Arabia, whose citizens were fifteen of the nineteen hijackers, nor Pakistan, who nurtured the Taliban as its favored client. Make no mistake: Florida is run by our brother, and it is therefore for us rather than against us. Our brother delivered us from evil— I mean, the African American vote. Our father's appointees, who art in heaven—or rather, the Supremest Court of all—delivered us from the lawsuits, from the minor inconvenience of not winning the national popular vote, and from having to concede the election had there been a state-wide recount. We have already delivered the tax cut. We can now proceed full-speed from the Muslim offense toward the missile defense. We will also please the oil barons by redrawing the map of the Middle East over the next few years. Our oil stocks should do well. The defense industry will soon be laughing all the way to the bank. The end of the cold war had them worried, but now we know that its new replacement will be far better, and we will call it endless war with bait-and-switch enemies. So, please make no mistake: Florida delivered us. Therefore, pray for us. We will have to make a few sacrifices. Just as

we arbitrarily detain those driving while black, our new safety procedures will identify those who are flying while Muslim. We can reorient the economy toward advanced surveillance technologies involving computer-assisted, laser-guided racial profiling and FBI file matching of suspects, using a large number of measurements such as pupil size, ear shape, facial bone angles, and skin tone. We may have to use secret evidence to detain, deport, and despatch suspected terrorists, but we do this with your safety in mind. There is no need to worry. Hug your children. The state of the union is strong, and the nation is behind us. Even though the evil one has declared war against US, God, we know, is with US.

NOTES

1 Anonymous preface to *The Sovereignty and Goodness of God, Together with the Faithfulness of His Promises Displayed,* by Mary Rowlandson (Cambridge, Mass.: Samuel Green, 1682).

2 Sacvan Bercovitch, *The American Jeremiad* (Madison: University of Wisconsin Press, 1978).

3 September 20, 2001.

DONALD E. PEASE

Afterword

From Virgin Land to Ground Zero

The essays gathered in *Dissent from the Homeland* acknowledge a major reorganization of the regulatory fictions through which the state exercises governmental rule. This afterword constitutes an attempt to elucidate the master fiction the Bush administration has invoked to legitimate the "war on terrorism." Each of the key words in its title (*Virgin Land* and *Ground Zero*) refers to a governing metaphor that has anchored U.S. publics to quite different state formations. They are freighted with metaphorical significance and performative force. The narrative organized around the Virgin Land metaphor associated U.S. publics with the national security state and entailed the collective wish to disavow the historical fact of U.S. forcible resettlement of indigenous peoples from their homelands. The narrative accompanying *Ground Zero* has linked the people traumatized by the events that took place on September 11 with a homeland security state, which emerged with a loss of belief in the inviolability of the native land. I attempt to sketch the genealogy of these narrative formations and briefly examine the political and cultural implications of the shift in dominant narratives from a secured innocent nation to a wounded, insecure emergency state.

Both narratives involve the state's proffering the exercise of governmental rule elsewhere in exchange for its public agreeing to an abridgment of civil liberties. The Virgin Land narrative was strengthened when the Marshall Plan in Europe and the global rivalry with the USSR required a model of U.S. history that would justify the exercise of governance across the first and third worlds. The belief that it constituted a deterrence to the putative imperialism of the Soviet Union allowed the U.S. people to attribute responsibility for the state's extension of its own imperial powers to the national enemy rather than the national security state.

The Virgin Land metaphor was originally devised to fulfill Europe's wish to start life afresh by relinquishing history for the secular dream of constructing a New Eden. The belief that the new world was discovered and settled by the Europeans who had emigrated there resulted from the coupling of a shared fantasy with historical amnesia. The metaphor gratified European emigrants' need to believe that the continental expanse of the territory that would become the United States was initially an unpopulated space; identification of the landscape as Virgin Land turned it into a blank page, understood to be the ideal surface onto which to inscribe the history of U.S. Manifest Destiny. The narrative placed the movement of the national people across the continent in opposition to the savagery attributed to the wilderness as well as the native people, who figured as indistinguishable from the wilderness. Later, the same narrative fostered an understanding of the campaign of Indian Removal as nature's beneficent choice of the Anglo-American settlers over the native inhabitants for its cultivation.

Overall *Virgin Land* enabled the American people to replace the fact that the land was already settled by a vast native population with the belief that it was unoccupied. And the substitution of this belief for historical actuality enabled Americans to disavow the resettlement and extermination of entire populations. However, the belief as well as the disavowal were also linked to the historical fact that since the War of 1812 U.S. civilian populations had not been subject to foreign attack. The nation's sense of inviolability associated the belief in a virgin land with the desire that U.S. soil remain forever unviolated by foreign aggression. But the fact of U.S. invulnerability suggests that the Other against which the belief in Virgin Land was directed had reference neither to a national enemy nor to the nation's shameful history. When conjoined with the belief that the violation of a native people's homeland took place on foreign soil rather than Virgin Land, the composite named what determined the United States' uniqueness.

But the events that took place at Ground Zero actualized both of the scenarios the belief in Virgin Land had been designed to ward off. At Ground Zero, U.S. Virgin Land had not merely been violated by foreign invaders; this violation assumed the form of the forcible dislocation of a population, a phenomenon the metaphor of Virgin Land had formerly occluded. The buildings erected to symbolize the U.S. rise to world dominance were turned into horrific spectacles of the violent removal of occupants from their site of residence.

The transformation of Virgin Land into Ground Zero brought into sight an inhuman terrain, which the national imaginary had been constructed to conceal. While the term *Ground Zero* was chosen to evoke the unimaginable nature of the events that took place on September 11, 2001, the state's association of the events with the demand for the securing of the "homeland" had an uncanny effect. For when it displaced the metaphor of the Virgin Land, the term *homeland* rendered the devastation precipitated at Ground Zero at once utterly unexpected yet weirdly recollective.

After they were figured in relation to the Homeland Security Act, the unprecedented events of September 11 seemed familiar because they recalled the suppressed knowledge of the United States' origins in the devastation of a native people's homeland. They also appeared familiar, as the signifier *Ground Zero* attests, because the unimaginable sight of the crumbling Twin Towers recovered memories of the firebombings of civilian populations over Dresden and Tokyo, as well as the unspeakable aftereffects of the atomic fallout on the inhabitants of Hiroshima and Nagasaki.

The events of September 11 brought to light the Other to the self-representation of the United States. *Ground Zero* evoked the specter of the nation-founding violence out of whose exclusion the fantasy of the Virgin Land had been organized. With the loss of the fantasy, the violence it covered over swallowed up the entire field of visibility. At Ground Zero the fantasy of radical innocence upon which the nation was founded encountered the violence it had formerly concealed.

The catastrophic events of September 11 precipitated a "reality" that society could neither comprehend nor master. By transporting them to symbolic grounds, the national mythology lessened the events' traumatizing power and performed the social function of providing an imaginary response to a disaster that could not otherwise be assimilated to the preexisting order of things.

The state's reply to September 11 supplanted it with a symbolic drama that was partly autonomous of the events that called it forth. In his September 20, 2001, address to the nation, President Bush rendered the primary integers in the nation's narrative of what happened on September 11 into terms that authorized his state of emergency:

> On September 11, enemies of freedom committed an act of war against our country. Americans have known wars, but for the past 136 years they have been wars on foreign soil, except for one Sunday in 1941. Americans have known the casualties of war, but not at the center of a great city on a peaceful morning. . . . Americans have known surprise attacks, but never before on thousands of civilians. . . . All of us this was brought upon us in a single day, and night fell on a different world. . . . I will not forget the wound to our country and those who inflicted it. . . . Our grief has turned to anger and anger to resolution. Whether we bring our enemies to justice or bring justice to our enemies, justice will be done.

In times of national emergency, the state exploits the public's reluctance to surrender its beliefs to critical scrutiny and elevates mythology into a ruling imperative. Mythology solicits belief through the generalization of the logic of fetishism. U.S. citizens may have known very well that the historical record would not warrant the belief that the colonists who emigrated to America discovered a virgin land, but they nevertheless found it expedient to embrace that belief over the historical record. They found it so because the belief that America was a virgin land fostered the complementary belief in the radical innocence of the American people.

When George Bush cited the historically accurate fact that with the exception of "one Sunday in 1941" the United States had not "for the last 136 years" been subject to foreign invasion, he linked the public's belief in the myth of a virgin land with the historical record. But when he did so, Bush did not supply the U.S. public with historical grounds for the collective belief in a virgin land. As we have seen, the myth that America was a virgin land endowed the fact that U.S. soil had almost never been subject to foreign violation with a moral rationale: the Virgin Land was inviolate because the American people were innocent.

In describing the surprise attack as a "wound to our country," Bush interpreted this violation on mythological and historical registers. The wound was directed against the Virgin Land as well as against citizens' mythic perception of their radical innocence. The state of emergency Bush established at Ground Zero was endowed with the responsibility to defend the homeland because the foreign violation of "our" Virgin Land had alienated the national people from their imaginary way of inhabiting the nation. But the violation of the land's "virginity" required the state to bring the event that the public had formerly disavowed—the forcible dispossession of an entire national people from their homeland—into spectacular visibility.

After depicting the citizenry as having been alienated from the mythology productive of their imaginary relation to the state, Bush linked a generalized sense of alienation with the vulnerability of the "homeland," which thereafter became the target of the security apparatus. *Homeland* refers to a country of origin or native land, the region in which one's home is located. The metaphor of the homeland fostered the collective representation of a vulnerable citizenry that had become internally estranged from its "country of origin" and dependent upon the protection of the state. While the homeland was associated with the geographical dimensions of the nation-state, its security required the state to extend its policing authority to the dimension of the globe.

When the signifier *homeland* was substituted for *Virgin Land*, the national security state was supplanted by the emergency state. Whereas *Virgin Land* enforced the disavowal of the state's destruction of the indigenous population's homelands, Ground Zero inspired the emergency state to produce the spectacle of the destruction of a native people's homeland as if it were a compensation for the loss of the land's "virginity." Indeed the state's interpolation of the public to the enjoyment of its spectacular construction of a devastated Afghani homeland would appear to have become the precondition for the emergence of the new political settlement.

The invasion of Afghanistan (after "our grief . . . turned to anger") resulted in the production of an unsecured homeland, as if that spectacle were itself the realization of the U.S. public's collectively repressed desire (for the forced depopulation of a homeland). When U.S. Special Forces carried out Operation Infinite Justice in the Afghani wilderness, the emergency state publicly displayed the violent separation of a native people from their homeland that the Virgin Land narrative had been structured to hide. With the invasion of Afghanistan, the figurative meanings associated with *Virgin Land* were demetaphorized into the actuality of the state's violence.

The state's spectacular violation of the rights of its "enemies" was thereby made to coincide with the emergency state's radical abridgment of domestic civil rights. The putative insecurity of the homeland's civilian population and the threat of terrorist attack were coconstituting aspects of the homeland security state. The state's representation of a vulnerable civilian population in need of protection was fashioned in opposition to the detainees and the captured Al Qaeda and Taliban, who were subjected to the power of the state yet lacked the protection of their rights or liberties. This new settlement invited the public to sacrifice its civil liberties in exchange for the enjoyment of the spectacle of the violation of these terrorists' rights.

The fact that the spectacle of the "justice" we brought to our enemies took place on Guantánamo Bay requires some brief explanation. Bush anticipated the use of this space as the staging ground for the state's violation of the Geneva Conventions by alluding, with the phrase "except for one Sunday in 1941," to the sole foreign attack on the United States since the War of 1812. But this attack did not exactly take place on U.S. soil: On December 7, 1941, Hawaii was not a state, and Pearl Harbor was officially designated, like Guantánamo Bay, Cuba, an unincorporated territory.

The exceptional nature of the attacks that took place on this unintegrated territory supplied the state with a metaphoric precedent for its choice to produce in a comparable space its own exceptions to the rules of law and war. The Justice Department referred to Guantánamo Bay's exceptional status as an unincorporated territorial possession of the United States to justify its contention that as a "foreign territory" it lay outside the jurisdiction of any United States court. It was this foreign status of Guantánamo Bay, its exemption from the juridical reach of any state or nation, that enabled the emergency state to demonstrate its monopoly over the exception to the rules of law there.

But the act of transferring these "enemies" to Guantánamo itself brought about the magical transformation in the condition of the persons interned there. By rendering them at once stateless and countryless, transporting them to Guantánamo Bay set the internees beyond the pale of humanity. The very same gesture that placed them outside the condition of territorial belonging provided the mytho-logic for the deprivation of their human rights. They were interned on Guantánamo Bay because they lacked the protection of human rights, and they lacked human rights because they were displaced onto Guantánamo Bay. The transfer of these unlawful combatants from Afghanistan to Guantánamo Bay rendered what was undecidable in Bush's musing over whether "we bring our enemies to justice or bring justice to our enemies" juridically practicable.

On Guantánamo Bay the state made certain individuals exceptions to the laws that protected the due process rights of citizens, and exceptions as well to the Geneva Conventions that endowed prisoners of war with the right to refuse to respond to interrogation. Stripped of the rights of citizens *and* prisoners of war, these persons were reduced to the status of unprotected *bios,* bare flesh. As the embodiments of animated flesh whose lives the state could terminate according to decisions that were outside juridical regulation, these unlawful combatants were invoked by the state to justify its self-determined exception to the rule of law. The emergency state arrogated to itself the power to operate beyond the jurisdiction of the laws regulating the world of nations by producing individuals whom it could hold without due process and whom it could kill without being accused of murder.

The detention camps erected in Guantánamo Bay by the Halliburton Company occupied a realm outside the law in which the emergency state's practices were naturalized by a mythology that rendered them exempt from critical scrutiny. The mythological structures that accompanied the state's fashioning of exceptions to legal categories triggered a recursive operation that reinforced the state's exercise of the power to fashion exceptions to its own rules. The public entered this realm of "legalized illegality" when it was bound as a witness to the denial of existing juridical categories and the basic dignities of legal process to those interred at Guantánamo Bay. The people ratified the power of the state to declare itself an exception to its own rule by participating visually in the construction of exceptions to the human condition.

The emergency state invoked the terrorists' recourse to unlawful combat as the pretext for its violation of the laws regulating due process and the rules regulating the conduct of war. The state violated its own rules, that is to say, in the name of protecting those rules against a force that was said to operate according to different rules. In order to protect the rule of law as such from this alien legality, the state declared itself the occupant of a position that was not subject to the rules it must protect. As Attorney General John Ashcroft explained, in order to protect the entirety of the law against attack, the state transgressed its own laws. All concerns of ethics, human rights, due process, constitutional hierarchies, and the division of governmental power were subordinated to this urgent eschatological mission.

The vacuum opened up by the vanishing of objective reality into the singularity of Ground Zero was thereby filled in by the mythologized reality in which the emergency state erected its version of realpolitik and the forcible detention of unlawful combatants made complementary sense. With its undisclosed abductions of persons within U.S. territorial homeland, the Bush administration shifted its war on terrorism from the Afghani desert to the bodies of those it suspected of domestic terrorism. Ignoring the time-consuming details of due process, the state condensed the juridical-penal process into the moment of abduction, collapsing accusation, judgment, and punishment. The terrorist may have supplied its official rationale, but the detainee was in fact the cause *and* effect of the state of emergency. The state, having victimized these detainees through the removal of all of their legal rights, magically transformed itself into the potential target of its victims when it constructed them as the unlawful enemies of the state.

The state of emergency, not subject to the rules of law that it enforces, inhabits a realm that is quite literally beyond good and evil. After September 11, civil rights groups estimated that more than eleven hundred terrorist suspects disappeared into a juridical maze where they were denied lawyers, beaten by guards and fellow inmates, subjected to sensory deprivation, and forced to take lie detector tests. Because current immigration laws permit indefinite detainment, no criminal charges were required to warrant the abductees' internment. Their guilt could not be proven, so this "transfer" of detainees to Camp X-Ray is a euphemism for extrajudicial measures.

The detainees' disappearance into a complex of juridical unaccountability and Guantánamo did not impose a mythology on the public so much as it encouraged it to agree to the abridgment of civil liberties in exchange for the spectacle of persons utterly stripped of all rights and liberties and rendered subject to the full power of the law. Afghanistan and Guantánamo Bay did not constitute contradictions but exceptions to the national mythopoesis. The public in its role as audience for these operations implicitly endorsed this rite of passage through the acceptance of a discourse of legalized illegality, crystallized in phrases like "enemy combatants" and "material witness" and "persons of interest."

The burden of these remarks is to explain the intertext that supplies with its regulatory powers George Bush's phrase, "All of us this was brought upon us in a single day, and night fell on a different world." In tracking the radical shift in the governing frames of reference as the transition from Virgin Land to Ground Zero, I also indicate how the nodal points that coordinate governing representations are themselves subject to change. In losing the covering myth of the Virgin Land, U.S. publics were deprived of the alibi of radical innocence. Establishing the prerogatives of the emergency state at Ground Zero, Bush has conscripted the traumatic power of the events that took place there to offer preemptive strikes as compensation for the loss. The Bush administration would supplant the loss of the belief that underwrote U.S. exceptionalism with the arrogation of the power to occupy the position of the exception to the laws of the World of Nations. But insofar as the emergency state's exceptions to the rules of law and war are themselves instantiations of force that lack the grounding support of regulation, they resemble the traumatic events upon which they depend for their power to rule. As such, these exceptions will maintain their power to rule only as long as U.S. publics remain captivated by the spectacles of violence the state has erected at the site of Ground Zero. When the emergency state is itself exposed as the cause of the traumas it purports to oppose, its exceptions will be laid bare as criminal violations of a terrorizing state. At that time (alas, only at that time) the emergency state will itself disappear into the singularity of the Ground Zero out of which it emerged.

Contributors

SRINIVAS ARAVAMUDAN is an associate professor of English at Duke University. He is the author of *Tropicopolitans: Colonialism and Agency, 1688–1804* (1999) and *Guru English: South Asian Religion in Cosmopolitan Contexts* (forthcoming, 2004).

JEAN BAUDRILLARD is a professor emeritus at the University of Paris. He is a professor of philosophy of culture and media criticism at the European Graduate School in Saas-Fee, Switzerland, where he teaches an intensive summer seminar. He is the author of numerous articles and books, including *System of Objects, Consumer Society, Critique of the Political Economy of the Sign, The Mirror of Production, Symbolic Exchange and Death, On Seduction, Simulacra and Simulation, Fatal Strategies, America, The Transparency of Evil,* and *Cool Memories.*

MICHAEL J. BAXTER, a Catholic priest and member of the Congregation of the Holy Cross, is an assistant professor of theology at the University of Notre Dame. He has published articles in the *DePaul Law Review, Pro Ecclesia, Communio, The Thomist,* and other journals. During the fall of 1984, he cofounded Andre House, a house of hospitality serving the poor and homeless of downtown Phoenix, where he lived and worked until the fall of 1988. He is national secretary for the Catholic Peace Fellowship, an organization dedicated to supporting Catholics and others who conscientiously object to participation in war. He is currently writing a book on Catholic social ethics in the United States, tentatively entitled *Seeking the Other City.*

ROBERT N. BELLAH is Elliott Professor of Sociology Emeritus at the University of California at Berkeley. He was educated at Harvard University, receiving the B.A. in 1950 and the Ph.D. in 1955. His publications include *Tokugawa Religion, Beyond Belief, The Broken Covenant,* and *The New Religious Consciousness.* In 1985 he published *Habits of the Heart: Individualism and Commitment in American Life,* written in collaboration with Richard Madsen, William Sullivan, Ann Swidler, and Steven Tipton. In 1991 the same five authors published *The Good Society*. In 2000 Bellah was awarded the National Humanities Medal by President Clinton.

DANIEL BERRIGAN is a Catholic priest, social activist, and poet who has written more than fifty books, including *The Trial of the Catonsville Nine* (1970), *Wisdom: The Feminine Face of God* (2002), *And the Risen Bread: Selected Poems 1957-1997*, and *Uncommon Prayer* (1978), as well as numerous films.

WENDELL BERRY is a conservationist, farmer, essayist, novelist, and poet. He has worked a farm in Henry County, Kentucky, since 1965. He is a former professor of English at the University of Kentucky and a past fellow of both the Guggenheim Foundation and the Rockefeller Foundation. He has received numerous awards for his work, including an award from the National Institute and Academy of Arts and Letters in 1971, and most recently, the T. S. Eliot Award. He has written more than thirty books, including *Home Economics, The Unsettling of America: Culture and Agriculture, The Gift of Good Land, Another Turn of the Crank, Recollected Essays: 1965-1980, Sex, Economy, Freedom, and Community*, and *Meeting the Expectations of the Land*, edited with Wes Jackson and Bruce Colman.

VINCENT J. CORNELL is the director of the King Fahd Center for Middle East and Islamic Studies at the University of Arkansas. He has devoted more than twenty years to the study of Sufism in Morocco and Islamic Spain. His book *Realm of the Saint: Power and Authority in Moroccan Sufism* (1998) is widely regarded as a scholarly breakthrough. He is currently engaged in a study of Islam and the philosophy of liberalism.

DAVID JAMES DUNCAN is a father, fly fisher, water and conservation activist, occasional teacher, and author of *The River Why, The Brothers K, River Teeth*, and *My Story as Told by Water*, which was nominated for a National Book Award and won the 2001 Western States Book Award in nonfiction.

STANLEY M. HAUERWAS is Gilbert T. Rowe Professor of Theological Ethics at Duke Divinity School. His books include *Truthfulness and Tragedy: Further Investigations in Christian Ethics* (1977), *The Peaceable Kingdom: A Primer in Christian Ethics* (1983), *Resident Aliens: Life in the Christian Colony*, with Will Willimon (1989), *The Truth about God: The Ten Commandments in Christian Life*, with Will Willimon (1999), *With the Grain of the Universe: The Church's Witness and Natural Theology* (2001), and *The Hauerwas Reader*, edited by John Berkman and Michael Cartwright.

FREDRIC R. JAMESON is William A. Lane Jr. Professor of Comparative Literature, a professor of Romance studies (French), and chair of the Literature Program at Duke University. His most recent books include *Postmodernism, or, The Cultural Logic of Late Capitalism* (1991), which won the MLA Lowell Award, *Seeds of Time* (1994), *Brecht and Method* (1998), *The Cultural*

Turn (1998), and *A Singular Modernity* (2002). His most frequently taught courses cover modernism, third world literature and cinema, Marx and Freud, Jean-Paul Sartre, the modern French novel and cinema, and the Frankfurt School. He serves on the editorial advisory board for the *South Atlantic Quarterly.*

FRANK LENTRICCHIA is Katherine Everett Gilbert Professor of Literature at Duke University. His most recent novel, *Lucchesi and The Whale,* was published in 2001. His critical books include *After the New Criticism, Ariel and the Police,* and *Modernist Quartet.* He has recently written a book with Jody McAuliffe entitled *Crimes of Art and Terror* (2003).

CATHERINE LUTZ is a professor of anthropology at the University of North Carolina at Chapel Hill and an activist. She is the author of *Homefront: A Military City and the American Twentieth Century* and *Unnatural Emotions: Everyday Sentiments on a Micronesian Atoll and Their Challenge to Western Theory.* She is coauthor of *Reading National Geographic* and of the forthcoming *If This Is Democracy: Public Interests and Private Politics in a Neoliberal Age.* She has also produced *Micronesia As Strategic Colony: The Impact of U.S. Policy on Micronesian Health and Culture* for Cultural Survival and *Making Soldiers in the Public Schools: An Analysis of the Army JROTC Curriculum,* with Lesley Bartlett, for the American Friends Service Committee.

JODY MCAULIFFE is an associate professor of the Practice of Theater Studies and Slavic Languages and Literatures at Duke University, and a member of the Society of Stage Directors and Choreographers. Her fiction has appeared in *Southwest Review* and *Literary Imagination,* and her criticism includes *Plays, Movies, and Critics* (1993). She has recently written a book with Frank Lentricchia entitled *Crimes of Art and Terror* (2003).

JOHN MILBANK is Frances Myers Ball Professor of Philosophical Theology at the University of Virginia. He was previously a Reader in Philosophical Theology at the University of Cambridge and a Fellow of Peterhouse. He is the author of, among other works, *Theology and Social Theory: Beyond Secular Reason; The Word Made Strange: Theology, Language, Culture; Truth in Aquinas* (with Catherine Pickstock); and a book of poems, *The Mercurial Wood.* Together with Catherine Pickstock and Graham Ward he is a coeditor of *Radical Orthodoxy: A New Theology,* and of Routledge's *Radical Orthodoxy* series. His most recent book, *Being Reconciled: Ontology and Pardon,* was published in 2002. He is an Anglo-Catholic and a Socialist.

PETER OCHS is Edgar Bronfman Professor of Modern Judaic Studies at the University of Virginia. He shares in the work of several societies dedicated to the three Children of Abraham. He cofounded the Society for (Jewish) Textual Reasoning, and the Society for Scriptural Reasoning (a society for Jewish-Muslim-Christian theological study). He is coeditor, with Stanley Hauerwas, of the series *Radical Traditions: (Jewish, Christian, and Muslim) Theology in a Postcritical Key*, and he participates in the Jewish-Christian-Muslim dialogues of the Shalom Hartman Institute in Jerusalem. Among his recent titles are (as coeditor) *Christianity in Jewish Terms* and *Reviewing the Covenant* and (as author) *Peirce, Pragmatism, and the Logic of Scripture*.

DONALD E. PEASE is Avalon Foundation Chair of the Humanities at Dartmouth College. The author of *Visionary Compacts: American Renaissance Writing in Cultural Context* and the editor of eight volumes including *The American Renaissance Reconsidered, Cultures of U.S. Imperialism* (with Amy Kaplan), *Revisionist Interventions into the American Canon, Postnational Narratives*, and *Futures of American Studies* (2002), Pease is general editor for the book series *New Americanists*, published by Duke University Press; founding director of the Summer Institute for American Studies at Dartmouth; and head of Dartmouth's Liberal Studies Program. In the Hilary term of 2001, Pease served as Drue Heinz Professor of American Literature at Oxford.

ANNE R. SLIFKIN is a civil litigation lawyer, mediator, and arbiter practicing in Raleigh, North Carolina. She serves on both the mediation and arbitration panels of the Duke University Private Adjudication Center. She publishes regularly in legal periodicals and has lectured at legal meetings, the National Institute of Trial Advocacy, and the law schools of the University of North Carolina, Chapel Hill, and Duke University.

ROWAN WILLIAMS, the Archbishop of Canterbury, has written a number of books on the history of theology and spirituality and published collections of articles and sermons, as well as a book of poems in 1994. He has been involved in various commissions on theology and theological education, the Dearing Working Party on Church Schools, and he chaired the group that produced the report "Wales: A Moral Society?" in 1996. He published *On Christian Theology* in 2000 and *Writing in the Dust: After September 11* in 2002.

SUSAN WILLIS is an associate professor in the Literature Program and English at Duke University. She teaches courses in minority writing and popular culture. She is the author of *Specifying: Black Women Writing the American Experience* and *A Primer for Daily Life*. She is coauthor of *Inside the Mouse: Work and Play at Disney World*. Her work aims at revealing the contradictions of capitalism in everyday life and discovering the utopian content in culture.

SLAVOJ ŽIŽEK is a professor at the Institute of Sociology, University of Ljubljana. His most recent books are *The Fragile Absolute, or Why the Christian Legacy Is Worth Fighting For; The Art of the Ridiculous Sublime: On David Lynch's Lost Highway; Contingency, Hegemony, Universality: Contemporary Dialogues on the Left;* and *Enjoy Your Symptom! Jacques Lacan in Hollywood and Out*.

Index

Library of Congress Cataloging-in-Publication Data

Dissent from the homeland : essays after September 11 /
edited by Stanley Hauerwas and Frank Lentricchia.

p. cm.

ISBN 0-8223-3231-0 (cloth : alk. paper) —

ISBN 0-8223-3221-3 (pbk. : alk. paper)

1. United States—Politics and government—2001-   2. United
States—Foreign relations—1989-   3. September 11 Terrorist
Attacks, 2001—Causes.   4. September 11 Terrorist Attacks,
2001—Influence.   5. Dissenters—United States.   6. Religion
and politics—United States.   7. National characteristics,
American.   8. National security—United States.   9. Terrorism—
Philosophy.   10. War on Terrorism, 2001-   I. Hauerwas,
Stanley, 1940-   II. Lentricchia, Frank.

E903.D47   2003

973.931—dc21   2003006486